THE NEW LEFT
Legacy and Continuity

THE NEW LEFT
Legacy and Continuity

Dimitrios Roussopoulos, editor

BLACK
ROSE
BOOKS

Montreal/New York/London

Black Rose Books No. KK354

National Library of Canada Cataloguing in Publication Data

The New Left : legacy and continuity / Dimitrios Roussopoulos, editor

Includes bibliographical references.

13 digit ISBN 978-1-55164-299-4 : 10 digit ISBN: 1-55164-299-9 (bound)
13 digit ISBN 978-1-55164-298-7 : 10 digit ISBN: 1-55164-298-0 (pbk.)

1. Right and left (Political science)--History--20th century. 2. New Left.
3. Social movements. I. Roussopoulos, Dimitrios I., 1936- .

HN17.5N482 2007   320.53   C2007-901915-3

BLACK ROSE BOOKS

C.P. 1258	2250 Military Road	99 Wallis Road
Succ. Place du Parc	Tonawanda, NY	London, E9 5LN
Montréal, H2X 4A7	14150	England
Canada	USA	UK

To order books:

In Canada: (phone) 1-800-565-9523 (fax) 1-800-221-9985
email: utpbooks@utpress.utoronto.ca

In the United States: (phone) 1-800-283-3572 (fax) 1-651-917-6406

In the UK & Europe: (phone) 44 (0)20 8986-4854 (fax) 44 (0)20 8533-5821
email: order@centralbooks.com

Our Web Site address: http://www.blackrosebooks.net

A publication of the Institute of Policy Alternatives of Montréal (IPAM)

Printed in Canada

CONTENTS

INTRODUCTION

by *Dimitrios Roussopoulos*

This anthology is meant to focus and colour the emergence of the New Left during the latter half of the 20th century and into that of our own. In doing so it will analyze the legacy of the New Left of the 1960s and the continuity that exists between the past and today, two different generations.

The Left is in crisis, perhaps the deepest in its history. This fact is generally acknowledged. The collapse of Marxism-Leninism as a practiced ideology, the spinning into narrower circles of social democracy because of it's attempts to better manage market-capitalism, the marginalization of the anti-authoritarian Left and the inability of the libertarian Left to break-out of a self-imposed ghetto of merchandizing propaganda, these are all marks of a profound malaise.

Nevertheless a renewal of some sort is in process, it is therefore appropriate to examine its evolution, with a special interest as to what has been learnt from the past. How a new world movement arose? What is its driving social forces, its agenda, and its rallying focus?

On June 5, 1993, I organised and chaired a roundtable during the Learned Societies Conference at Carleton University, Ottawa, an academic meeting held annually where left-wing academics often come together. The theme of the roundtable was "The Legacy of the New Left." The purpose was to review what the *heritage* of that turbulent decade of the 1960s was for us, but not necessarily to critically analyse history.

Dimitrios Roussopoulos is a political economist who has written many articles and books on social and politico-economic issues. He is a leading urban activist working toward democratic and ecological cities. He is the author and/or editor of many books including The Public Place, Dissidence: Essays Against the Mainstream, *and most recently,* Participatory Democracy: Democratizing Democracy.

The meeting place was packed with interested people, with many outside the room unable to enter. The panelists included Andrea Levy and Anthony Hyde, whose presentations are included in this book, as well as Joan Newman-Kuyek, a community organiser and veteran of the New Left period, Clayton Ruby, a Toronto lawyer who was also a 60s activist, and Bill Hartzog, a Montreal lawyer who fled the U.S. during the Vietnam war while active with the Students for a Democratic Society.

The New Left [with first letters upper case] designates an inclusive politics including analyses and propositions derived from or inspiring the various movements and bearing a specific reference to social, political and cultural change. The expression is usually used in a specifically political language. The word movement [either singular or plural, with a lower case 'm'] designates a particular section of the Movement which developed around a specific theme or during a particular period. For example the "civil-rights movement," "free speech movement," "anti-war movement," and the "women's liberation movement," etc.

Movement [singular, with an upper case 'M'] included, in North America, the major organisations of the New Left such as the Student Non-Violent Coordinating Committee, the Student for a Democratic Society, the Student Union for Peace Action, but also signified a programme for radical change, actions and attitudes which developed over a decade, including not only political and social aspects, but psychological and cultural ones as well.

The greatest contribution of the New Left of the 1960s was its determination to build a culture of popular participation by everyday women and men at every level of daily life, including work and society at large. We know that people do not learn the importance of democratic power in a political vacuum. The development of a vigilant citizenry requires public involvement in building and sustaining democratic political organisations and communities. Political consciousness which is key to genuine democracy, as well as moral wisdom and compassion cannot be cultivated in the silence of mediation or in therapeutic personal growth workshops.

The revolutions in Central and Eastern Europe, and the former Soviet Union forced a rethinking of democratic strategies as the recent major political changes and experiments going on now in Brazil, Argentina, Chile, Bolivia and Venezuela. The legacy of the New Left is more relevant than ever with its critique of the corporate liberalism and in recent decades of the drive by transnational corporations to dominate a world economy based of market capitalism. Contemporary history is a mixture of dangers ranging from ecocide to the wholesale economic exploitation of the majority of humanity. The goal of furthering political democracy alongside economic democracy remains a solid outline for a radical programme for fundamental change, and this seems to be popping up in many regions.

One thing seems also certain. The instinct of the young radicals who framed the political debate of the 1960s in terms of a community-centred democratic political theory laid the basis for the new political discourse that guides radical democratic experimentation among the new generation. The discourse of democracy has won over all others and it now remains for us to deepen its meaning and fulfill its promise just as the New Left began doing some three decades ago.

The essays by Andrea Levy and Anthony Hyde begin an examination of this legacy in its fullness. Reaching back to 1968, that seminal year in the history of the New Left especially in France, we have the reflections of some of the key actors of the famous general strike: Danny Cohn-Bendit, Jacques Sauvageot and Alain Geismar. Making the links between the uprising in Paris and that of New York's Columbia University, Jacques Martin offers readers a useful comparative analysis. To round off this part of the examination there is a report of what happened to some of the key actors of the 1960s in the USA. Mark Rudd of Columbia University SDS and Weathermen fame adds a perceptive essay on the death of the first SDS, and Katherina Haris offers us an overview of the decade drawing lessons from the legacy. Greg Calvert, a national SDS general secretary offers us a deeper understanding of the origins and basis of participatory democracy and finally Tom Hayden who wrote the first draft of the *Port Huron Statement* also discusses the legacy but brings us into the present and reveals the relevance of participatory democracy today.

The essence of participatory democracy that inspired the best of the New Left has spread in the succeeding decades to many corners of our globe. Whether it is the political and social ecologists, or the students and workers of Beijing, the notion that grassroots democracy can create a common political vision for a world-wide politics has gained adherents in societies from the First World to the Fourth.

The new movements that arose around and following the battle of Seattle in 1999 dramatically kick started the new anti-globalisation or more accurately the new anti-capitalist international movement. Natasha Kapoor, who as a new generation on the ground activist, makes the connection between legacy and continuity. Like so many others she sees great hope around the organisation of the World Social Forum which has brought thousands of activists together, in major international gatherings but also regional meetings on all continents. The alternative movements to the current economic and political forces driving the world economy have become better organised through improved communication and networking on a planetary scale. The World Social Forum (WSF) is the cutting edge gathering but much goes on around this new international also.

The first WSF meeting was in January 2001 in Porto Alegre, Brazil, where some 5000 people gathered. The second in 2003 was held in the same city where 12,000 official delegates from 125 countries attended. There were 60,000 attendees, 652 workshops and 27 plenary roundtables. The fourth WSF was held in Mumbai, India in January 2004, many more than the 75,000 expected attended. The fifth WSF 2005 in Porto Alegre had 155,000 registered participants. The seventh WSF in Nairobi, Kenya in January 2007 drew 66,000 registered attendees and 1,400 participating organisations from 110 countries. This form of intense international organisation did not exist in the 1960s. The WSF has annual meetings to coordinate world campaigns, share and refine organizing programmes, and to inform each other about movements from around the world and the pressing issues of the day. It has tended to meet in January as an alternative to the World Economic Forum meetings in Davos, Switzerland, were the corporate elite meet with their political attaches. The first ever U.S. Social Forum will be held in Atlanta in July, although there have been several local social forums held to date. There have been social forums in Toronto and other cities, but the first province-wide social forum will take place in Quebec, August 2007. To be sure the WSF has been criticized, particularly by communist and socialist political parties.

Finally as a veteran of the 1960s and still an engaged activist today, I bring together the various threads into a tentative ending to this collection. What I find outstanding is that there is an impressive understanding of the political inter-play between the local, regional and transnational issues at the heart of the new project for social and political change as reflected in the World Social Forum notwithstanding its many problems and challenges. The understanding of this inter-play has significant strategic implications, and consequently makes the city and the municipality a priority political arena not only re-connecting the link between community-building and citizenship but it also grounds participatory democracy as was attempted by the previous New Left generation. In a number of cities and regions a regeneration of activism is taking place. Critical literature on the sixties continues to be written and published in part because a new generation is interested in knowing more.

During June 2007 a major international conference on the 1960s will be held at Queen's University in Canada. Its programme reads like that of an academic conclave. Titled the "New World Coming, the sixties and the shaping of global consciousness" the conference is bringing together many scholars and intellectuals who have studied the decade but who appear to also be looking for answers relevant for today (www.queeensu.ca/history/News/NewWorldComing.htm).

The Students for a Democratic Society has been re-born in the USA and is on the rise with a militancy and maturity and has brought together the new generation with many of the seasoned veterans of the past. It has a SDSwiki Project which is open to its members and is designed as a place where information, work on collective documents, shared lessons learned in grassroots movements, photos, radio and video feeds can be shared. Actions undertaken recently include the barricade and occupation of Chevron's international offices in the Bay Area with reports on the Youtube. The SDS web-site (http://www.studentsforademocraticsociety.org/) covers a long list of activism throughout 2007. SDS is engaged in a lot of anti-war actions, including arrests on Wall Street. The second SDS National Convention will take place July 27-31, 2007 at Wayne State University in Detroit.

A sister organisation to SDS is the Movement for a Democratic Society founded in August 2006, with SDS founder Al Haber as co-president with Penelope Rosemont. On the Board of MDS are Mark Rudd, Paul Buhle, Jeff Jones, Carl Davidson, Stanley Aronowitz, Angela Davis, Barbara Ehrenreich, Bernadine Dohrn, Tom Hayden and Howard Zinn amongst others (http://mds-inc.antiauthoritarian.net/).

The greatest contribution of the New Left of the 1960s was its determination to build a culture and politics of popular participation at every level of society, a participation that directly involved women and men in improving their quality of life by addressing daily problems. A radical conception of democracy, inspired the movements for civil rights, for world peace and human solidarity, and it evolved in the following decade as a large movement for gender and sexual equality. It framed the social and political debate, in terms of community-centered democratic theory, that continues to guide, and inspire, well into the 21st century.

As the contributors to this anthology revisit the sixties to identify its ongoing impact on North American politics and culture, it becomes evident how this legacy has blended with, and influenced today's world-wide social movements, in particular, the anti-globalisation movement, and the 'Right to the City' movement: the successes and failures of civil society organisations as they struggle for a voice at various levels of decision-making are examined, as are the new movements of the urban disenfranchised.

Apart from evoking memories of the past peace and freedom struggles from those who worked on the social movements of the 1960s, this book also includes a number of essays from a rising generation of intellectuals, too young to have experienced the 1960s firsthand, their perspective enables them to offer fresh insights.

Dimitrios Roussopoulos
May 2007

—LEGACY—

PROGENY AND PROGRESS?
Reflections On The Legacy Of The New Left

by Andrea Levy

Many if not most assessments of the legacy of the New Left bear the stamp of reminiscence; evocations of struggles past, and sometimes hopes present, reflections on errors committed and regretted. Having made history, a generation which produced more than its fair share of academics settled down to write it, and, at a remove of twenty or thirty years, examine its relevance for our time. There is often a muted *mea culpa* in these semi-autobiographical musings, a self-flagellatory tone that immediately relieves the reader of any suspicions of romanticism or nostalgia about a bygone age and a lost youth. Self-reflection and self-doubt were part of the psychological hallmark of the New Left at its best—although as Michael Lerner has observed in a measured celebration of the 60s in America and its bequest, these traits if exaggerated can and did cross the border into the self-destructive.[1]

As someone born at the tail end of the baby-boom who came of political age in the sobered and sobering decade of the eighties, I am very much aware of the extent to which my own history is intimately intertwined with the legacy of the New Left, even as I grew up in a household of the unreconstructed Old Left.[2] The 'new politics' I participated and continue to participate in, my freedom as a woman to pursue avenues once largely the preserve of men, the ease with which I was able to concentrate on studies in radical social theory at the university, my growing doubts as a teenager about the legitimacy or usefulness of the dogmatic—in both organizational form and substantive content—politics of the Bolshevik Left, all these form part of my personal endowment from the sixties.

Andrea Levy, PhD, is a writer, editor, and translator who has published articles in books and journals on the New Left, the ecology movement, the peace movement, and the ideas of André Gorz. She is currently working on Faith in Faithlessness: An Anthology of Atheism, *(Black Rose Books: November 2007). This essay was first published in 1994 in* Our Generation, *Vol. 24, No. 2.*

These comments are intended to suggest the obvious: that any assessment of the legacy of the New Left for subsequent decades and generations is highly conditioned by the prism through which the light of the past is refracted; much depends, that is, on whether the historical significance of the New Left is judged exclusively or only partially in terms of the goals it set for itself and upon the current relation of the individual analyst to those goals.

Setting aside the hysterical diatribes of the death of culture critics like Allan Bloom in America and the more sophisticated culturalist right in Western Europe, there is, predictably, no consensus even on the broad left-liberal spectrum with respect to the overall historical impact of the New Left within specific national contexts, let alone more globally. Judged purely on its own terms, the New Left, insofar as it aimed at nothing less than the total transformation of society, was a total failure, but I think this is an extremely narrow way of posing the problem. Hence while there is a germ of truth in Régis Debray's very cynical conclusions (limited by him to the French context but potentially generalizable) that through the inscrutable cunning of history the events of 1968 served to assist the bourgeoisie to effect a much needed modernization, bringing the political and social order into harmony with the imperatives of an advanced capitalist economy, it does not exhaust the story.[3]

Nor does another pessimistic reading of the New Left as having helped to delegitimate the welfare State contributing to the crisis of social democracy and paving the way for the triumph of the New Right.[4] We should not ignore the capacity of the existing system to absorb and neutralize dissent—epitomized in our decade in the commercialized "60s revival" in North America. But nor should we neglect the movements' successes, such as the American New Left's contribution to ending the war in Vietnam—a central issue for the New Left internationally—although such successes may indeed have contributed to the relative decline of radical left politics in subsequent decades.

What I propose to examine in this essay are what I consider to be some of the significant resonances but also reversals of the New Left's legacy for Left theory and practice in the last quarter century.

I should state at the outset that by New Left I am primarily referring to the libertarian early New Left—the New Left of the Port Huron Statement and the anti- War movement in the U.S., of the March 22nd Committee in France, the Extra-parliamentary Opposition in Germany and so on, that is to say very broadly the New Left before the onset of an international pattern of fragmentation into dogmatic rigidly structured Marxist-Leninist, Trotskyist, Maoist and terrorist sects in the later

60s. I acknowledge that I am creating here a kind of ideal type, for the common enough division of the New Left globally into an early heroic phase and a later destructive one does not stand up entirely to historical scrutiny. Many conflicting tendencies coexisted throughout the sixties even within individual New Left formations. In the case of France, to be sure, such convenient periodization is impossible to sustain as the groupuscules operated alongside the more libertarian currents, and the central theme of autogestion led an active life after the defeat of May. And as Maurice Isserman suggests of the New Left in America, thinking in terms of a "process of accretion" is a more accurate way to understand the evolution of the decade than the idea of successive mutations.[5] Furthermore, drawing on material from The United States, France, and Germany to make some general statements about the legacy of the New Left obviates the possibility of any adequate treatment of national specificities. Sweeping generalizations are unavoidable in an essay of this length and kind and they should be taken for what they are: abstraction at the high cost of rigor and the suppression of particularities which are the stuff of historical research. At the same time, the New Left movements in North America and Western Europe undeniably partook of a common ethos, and at the level of the admittedly imprecise category of "vision" shared in more than they differed.

Whatever their inevitable limitations, both internal and external, the student movements in their varied manifestations engaged in a relentless and profound questioning of the prevailing social order and the dominant worldview, by which route many of their ranks arrived at an incisive critique of the social system as a whole, a deeper understanding of what appeared superficially as discrete social problems. Within their own preserve—the university—they rejected what they perceived as stultifying curricula and the flawed pretensions of value-free scholarship; they questioned the implications of specialization and the professional careers for which their education destined them; they challenged the system of examinations which they saw as encouraging regurgitation rather than measuring learning and which they understood to function as a means of selection and segregation. Beyond the university, and with the recognition that the problems of the university express in part the contradictions of the larger society, the New Left students rejected as fraudulent political systems which are cloaked in the vestments of democracy but preclude genuine participation in decision-making; they rejected as dehumanizing and unresponsive bureaucratic systems of administration which operate according to standard procedure without regard for varied and changing individual needs; they rejected as exploitive and alienating advanced capitalist economic and social systems which perpetuate class divisions, servitude and work devoid of stimulation and gratification, which engender and profit from undevelopment overseas, which allocate resources irrationally without regard for vital human needs, and which produce weapons of mass destruction and commodities for mass stupefaction; and they rejected as manipulative communications systems employed to indoctrinate and distract, rather than inform and educate, rendering dissent difficult and alternatives chimerical.

The students put forward no blueprint for changing the world they repudiated, believing that only collective human action and creation could engender new contents and new forms.

However, they were inspired by a vision of human emancipation which surpassed that of national parties and unions of the Left whose conception of social change had grown significantly circumscribed by the reigning economism in theory and practice. The radical students resurrected and affirmed utopian thinking. Not themselves prisoners of material deprivation, they fashioned and articulated a vision of systemic transformation that embodied social and cultural change without which the restructuring of the economic order central to the theory of the traditional Left was seen to yield little but another authoritarian system where quantity still took precedence over quality. As the 29th thesis of the "Appeal from the Sorbonne" affirmed, "The bourgeois revolution was judicial; the proletarian revolution was economic. Ours will be social and cultural so that man can become himself."

There is fairly wide agreement in the literature that while the New Left failed to produce a social or political revolution it did indeed auger in a cultural revolution which has had a transformative affect on, for example, attitudes to family, sexuality and work. Again there are many variants of this analysis. My own not isolated perspective is that through its persistent social criticism and dissenting actions, the New Left helped to sensitize hundreds of thousands of young people to the issues of racism, imperialism and militarism, and media manipulation; to the barrenness of societies wholly devoted to consumerism in turn rendered possible by the reproduction of meaningless and dehumanized work, to the limits of formal democracy and the need for more substantive forms of democratic participation and to the duty to question authority, among other questions which have lost little of their pertinence in our time. It can be demonstrated that this critical spirit has continued to resonate albeit less palpably in the last two decades, especially among the constituencies of the new social movements which I will discuss below.

Another related point that tends toward consensus is that the New Left irrevocably reconfigured the boundaries of the political. It developed a critique of advanced capitalism which went far beyond the bread and butter issues of the Old Left tradition. As Stuart Hall remarks in his reflections in 1989 on the New Left in England and describing the first issue published in 1960 of the *New Left Review*:

> ...we spoke of racial oppression, housing, property deterioration and short-sighted urban planning alongside the more traditional themes of poverty and unemployment; we spoke of young Blacks on the street while youth clubs were closed, working mothers without creches and children without playgrounds, as equally central to any modern conception of the 'degradations' of modern capitalism.[6]

From the insistence on culture as a constitutive element of social reality, through the stress on the quality of everyday life to the feminist revelation that the personal is political, the New Left permanently transformed our conception of the political and of the nature and limits of political work.

The legacy of the New Left cannot be discussed without some consideration of developments in the academy given both that the New Left was itself a university-based movement and that following the sixties there occurred a migration of many New Left activists and sympathizers into the universities in North America and Western Europe. It may appear puzzling then that it is here that the New Left legacy is arguably least in evidence. All has been relatively quiet on the Western university front in the last two decades. The most notable disruption of university life was the French student protest of 1986, notable most perhaps for its self-conscious repudiation of the powerful imagination that defined the Zeitgeist of May '68. Its rather uninspired slogan was 1986 is not 1968.

The cause of the protest was the introduction of the Devaquet bill, named for the minister of education under Jacques Chirac's government. The bill was designed to introduce tougher entrance standards, higher tuition fees and to reduce the role of students in university government, among other things. The student protests which resulted in clashes with the police and the death of one student succeeded in forcing the eventual withdrawal of the bill and Devaquet's resignation. With that the movement expired. The students hardly sought to extend the issue they had raised to a discussion of the larger society, and the government, by its rapid accommodation of immediate demands, undoubtedly haunted by the spectre of 68, was shrewd enough to avoid repeating the mistakes of the de Gaulle regime.[7]

In Germany, university life was given colour by the Sponti (Spontaneist) movement which spread through West German universities in the mid to late 1970s, gaining representation on and sometimes control of student govern-ments.[8] The Spontis were associated with the Alternative movement which sought through the creation of a wide variety of community projects to develop al-ternative lifestyles at a remove from the dominant culture. In Frankfurt, the Spontis were led by Daniel Cohn-Bendit, the de facto leader of the March 22nd movement in France in May 1968. Although in theory the movement drew on the tradition of classical anarchism, in its rejection of political organization and protest, its accent on withdrawal from the existing society, and its preoccupation with spontaneity and personal feelings, it was seen by some observers to reflect the pessimism of the post-1968 generation. But it is also true that the Spontis and the Alternative scene formed part of the breeding ground for a new ecological consciousness.

In the United States, there was an active anti-apartheid movement which gave rise to protest in many universities over the issue of divestment. But again they tended to confine themselves to the issue at hand. Arrests were generally a polite affair—the American police operating on campus had learned the lessons of the 60s better than their French counterparts. This serves to illustrate by negative example the important—some observers would say singular—role of intransi-gence and repression in galvanizing student protest in the 60s.

But there is another more significant reason why the students of the post-1960s period have been more quiescent than their predecessors and that is new pressures arising from the economic contraction which set in globally, espe-cially after the oil crisis of 1973. Faced with stiffer competition for jobs inside and outside the universities, students are widely reported to have dug in to their books, working harder in pursuit of the degrees which constituted the entrance tickets to the new middle class.

Writing in 1987, former SDS President Todd Gitlin now a professor of sociol-ogy at Berkeley, remarked wistfully, "My generation numbers teachers more activist (for the moment) than their students..."[9] This may be true but it requires qualifica-tion; for one of the consequences of the migration into the academy of 60s radi-cals—and again the pattern is not unique to the U.S.[10]—has been seen as a progressive process of depoliticization of the Left intellectual community, even as it has been attacked by conservatives for bringing radical chaos to reign in academia. This is essentially the thesis of Russell Jacoby's The Last Intellectuals, one of the most readable and relevant studies dealing with this question in the American context. In this book Jacoby laments the near extinction of what C.Wright Mills, one of the leading New Left theorists called the public intellectual—writers and critics independent of institutional affiliation who wrote for an educated lay public. Today's intellectuals, Jacoby charges, write for one another in professional journals. It seems all the more remarkable that the absent generation of public intellectuals Jacoby tracks is the generation of the New Left. But it does not defy explanation.

It results among other things from the imperatives of professionalization which promote conformity and specialization. Of course, as Jacoby concedes, the positive dimension of the academicization of radical thought consists in the production of an enormous body of radical, feminist, and neo-Marxist scholarship. However, as any voyage through the pages of academic journals reveals, this scholarship has grown increasingly technicalized, specialized, self-referenial and largely inaccessible to the uninitiated. Complementing Jacoby's argument, Rachel Bowlby notes that:

> ...the institutionalization of women's studies and of feminist perspectives in the humanities generally has meant a continued expansion through the 70s of academic approaches to feminist questions—coupled, however, with a progressive loss of directly political impetus common to other movements of the sixties.[11]

There is another factor in this depoliticization of radical scholarship which is worth mentioning. In a climate of post-modern moral relativism, the idea—expressed by C.Wright Mills in the 50s and repeated in our decade by one of the few remaining public intellectuals Noam Chomsky—that the intellectual should be the moral conscience of society tends to be regarded as at best quaint and at worst terroristic.

Michel Foucault, luminary of the French intellectual community in the 1970s and 80s, has been called by one knowledgeable commentator, "the figure most responsible for breaking with the totalizing ambition of intellectuals."[12] Although his importance should be duly acknowledged Foucault's conception of the intellectual which has had wide echoes is arguably quietistic. For one thing Foucault describes the role of what he calls the specific intellectual as:

> ...not to shape others' political will; it is through the analyses he carries out in his own field, to question over and over again what is postulated as self-evident, to disturb people's mental habits, the way they do and think things, to dissipate what is familiar and accepted, to reexamine rules and institutions...to participate in the formation of a political will.[13]

On balance, this seems like an ambitious and interesting project, but even if we refrain from questioning its wholly negative function, we ought to ask whose mental habits Foucault is considering; for his own work, however brilliant and insightful, is written in hermetic language imitated—sometimes to the point of caricature by current work in the post-structuralist and deconstructionist tradition—which cannot but remain entirely obscure to an audience outside the academy. Foucault equates and reduces political activism to critical analysis. And in the end he admits that for him intellectual work is related to "...aestheticism, meaning transforming yourself."[14]

What does this have to do with the New Left? For the answer we have to turn very briefly to the advent of post-structuralism in France, which was born of the defeat of May 68, abandoned many of the basic premises of the New Left for a Nietzsche-inspired repudiation of Enlightenment, and crossed the ocean to settle in comfortably in the North American academy.[15] In Germany too, Nietzsche was rediscovered by disillusioned New Leftists who undertook a critique of rationalism often shading off into a celebration of irrationalism, subjectivity and the body.[16]

The filiation of post-structuralism with the New Left as a relation of defeat has oft been noted. As Terry Eagleton puts it:

> Post-structuralism was a product of that blend of euphoria and disillusionment, liberation and dissipation, carnival and catastrophe, which was 1968. Unable to break the structures of state power, post-structuralists found it possible instead to subvert the structures of language... The student movement was flushed off the streets and driven underground into discourse.[17]

He goes on to assert that post-structuralism's enemies became "coherent belief systems of any kind."

In this worldview, any attempt to understand or act upon society as a whole is inherently totalitarian. It rejects not only any effort to conceptualize a normative totality—what a new social whole would look like—it finds equally inimical any notion of an analytical totality—the idea that the component parts of society are integrally related and may not be understood in isolation from the whole. While the normative totality leads to the suppression of difference in a false harmony, the analytical totality can be nothing more than a grand narrative, a fiction with no possible truth-value.

To quote an adherent of deconstruction:

...there is no objective reference point, separate from culture and politics, available to distinguish truth from ideology, fact from opinion, or representation from interpretation. And thus philosophy, science, economics, literary criticism, and the other "intellectual" disciplines can be interpreted according to the same process that has been traditionally reserved for literature and art—they too can be read merely as "texts" organizing the thick texture of the world according to its own metaphors. They enjoy no privileged *vis à vis* the "merely" aesthetic or subjective because they too are simply languages, simply ways of carving up what seems similar and what seems different in the world.[18]

And a little further on he asserts, "the point is that there is no grand organizing theory or principle with which to justify our social choices as neutral or apolitical, as the product of reason or truth rather than of passion or ideology."[19]

How, in face of this sort of epistemological nihilism, how we are to ground a choice between fascism and democracy on the basis of anything other than personal inclination is obscure to me. With the Enlightenment call, in the name of reason, to extirpate myth and superstition viewed one-sidedly as part and parcel of a white western male legacy of oppression, the creation of myth is legitimated as the only possible positive scholarly or political project—one story is as good as another. As Barbara Ehrenreich stated in an interview, "what are we left with if we abolish a knowable universe, if we say there is nothing in the universe but human points of view, human narratives? Then there is nothing but our Selves... This is Solipsism, a dead end."[20]

With reason in unqualified disrepute (for many of the detractors of Western Rationality offer none of the nuances of the Frankfurt School's attempt to distinguish between instrumental and substantive reason) we are served recourse to feelings as the only philosophically tenable form of political discourse. But a politics based on an appeal to feelings is an invitation to demagoguery not debate.

The post-structuralist critique specifically of totality, although it has certain merits, is carried to extremes and often resembles in all essentials Karl Popper's assault on what he idiosyncratically referred to as historicism. As such, if it is undraped of the patina of radicalism in which it is wrapped, it seems quite compatible with the conclusions if not the approach of liberal pluralism. The distance between the post-structuralist negation of social theory (which has many other distressing political implications that have been illuminated in a host of excellent critiques) and the New Left vision is unbridgeable.

For one of the chief distinguishing features of the New Left was its concern with grasping the whole, naming the system, seeing the interrelations among the apparently disparate phenomena it confronted, and I daresay, seeing the historical process as, if not wholly rational, at least intelligible and subject to rational analysis. Post-structuralism reflects and celebrates the fragmentation of knowledge and social reality and buttresses in theory the fragmentation of the Left itself into disconnected, single issue groups. If this sounds like an exaggeration, allow me to return to Foucault again and to his assessment of the beneficial bequest of May 68:

> When we look back at this episode in French history, we will see in it the growth of a new kind of left thought which...has completely transformed the horizons of the contemporary Left movement. We might well imagine this particular Left culture as being allergic to any party organization, incapable of finding its real expression in anything but *groupuscules* and individualities.[21]

What for Foucault is a legacy of hope, is for others, including myself, a prophesy of and recipe for ineffectualness and marginality. It remains to be seen whether he will have the last word on the heritage of the New Left.

There is a not uncoincidental convergence between the post-structuralist critique of universalism, the emphasis on otherness and difference, the contemptuous view of 'western rationality' and what have been aptly dubbed identity politics —although the politics of identity fails to assimilate the implications of post-structuralism for any stable identity, halting the infinite play of differences at a selected group identity which usually tacitly invokes some form of biological essentialism or irreducible difference.[22]

It is one counterpart in practice of the rejection in philosophy of universalizing social theory, which grows out of the defeat of the New Left's agenda for far-reaching social change as well as out of a critique of Marxism and revulsion for the regimes of actually existing socialism, including those idealized by the New Left in the 60s. But its origins can be traced more precisely within a given national context. There has been much discussion in the mainstream media in North America in recent years on this subject. Here I will focus on developments in the United States where this form of politics has found its most vocal expression, although there are parallels to be found elsewhere.[23] I should state at the outset that the entire issue of identity politics and its concomitant, political correctness, has been dismissed by much of the current Left in America as a non-issue and a conspiracy of the Right to discredit Left politics. While I agree completely that the Right has attempted in the most disingenuous fashion to make political hay of these questions, I do not believe this disposes of a substantive issue with serious consequences for the future of Left politics. I will argue that although both defenders, practitioners and conservative detractors of identity politics are united in their conception of it as a movement of the Left, there are serious doubts that can be raised about its relation to anything recognizable as left politics.

Identity politics has been defined in various ways but broadly it signifies a politics of particularism, the politics of belonging to a specific oppressed group which has been victimized or excluded from the dominant system of power and representation. As a political practice it involves struggles over language, over access to institutions and representation within them, over symbolic representation, over cultural subsidies, and so on.

In its manifestation in the U.S., this politics has its roots in the Civil Rights and Black Power movements, in the New Left, and to a lesser extent in the ethnic revival that swept America in the late 60s and early 70s putting an end to the theretofore widely accepted assimilationist ideal of the melting pot.

Identity politics is very much a child of the New Left, but it is regarded as a wayward child by some former new left activists, such as former SDS President Todd Gitlin and feminist writer Ellen Willis, who are among its most comprehending but penetrating critics.[24] There are diverging analyses of the roots of identity politics within the New Left, one of the most persuasive being that of Ellen Willis, who argues that its appeal rests in an initially radical and liberating insight shared by the New Left and ultimately traceable to Marxism that domination is a structural problem. The class struggle paradigm, she argues, was transposed onto racial and gender politics. Ilene Philipson takes a different approach to the origins of identity politics, situating their genesis in the 60s quest for the authentic self in reaction to the grey conformity of 50s America. However, she complements Willis' analysis in her argument that the appeal of identity politics for many, especially students, lies in the ability to translate fears of personal failure and a sense of alienation into political terms in a culture of individual competition which ascribes failure to individual inadequacy.[25] She stops short here of the more liberal charge which is not entirely without merit that valuable as the basic insight is it poses the danger of acting as a solvent of all notions of personal responsibility. But she does suggest that rooting the problem of alienation in structural discrimination on the basis of gender and race obscures the recognition that in a competitive capitalist society feelings of alienation are almost universal.

Another point made by many critical commentators on the subject is that with the breakup of the New Left the politics of group identity provided a desired sense of community. To take an applicable phrase from Michael Rustin somewhat out of context, "The erosion of collective life and moral solidarity in this atomizing society appears to have affected the left as much as more traditional associations such as churches and families."[26] This is significant for the appeal of identity politics far beyond a left constituency in the current context in many advanced capitalist societies of increasing social isolation and the transformation of family structures, although in fairness the same argument has been made about the appeal of the New Left to young people in the 60s.[27] The essential question, however, is for what political ends identity crisis is mobilized.

I would argue as well that identity politics is very much a product of the unresolved problem of agency in the New Left. With the justifiable abandonment of the Old Left notion of the working class as the sole and preordained revolutionary agent, rather than attempting to theorize a more pluralistic understanding of the agency of social change, a variety of substitutes for the starring role were seized upon. Every oppressed group was potentially the revolutionary subject and could stake a prior moral and political claim accordingly. Two decades later, identity politics threatens to replace the old labour metaphysic with a new race-gender-sexual orientation metaphysic.

In Todd Gitlin's analysis identity politics is partly the fruit of the New Left's inadequate development of a universalist politics. He maintains that the attempt by SDS to base a new universalism on the rather vague notion of participatory democracy was bound to fail ("Freedom as an endless meeting was only alluring to those who had the time and taste to go to meetings endlessly.")[28] and that what kept the movement temporarily from dissolving as it did in the late 60s into the divisions of gender, race, and sexual orientation was the unifying power of the anti-war protest. He argues furthermore that the cohort that entered the universities as junior faculty in the 70s and 80s had cut its teeth on this later politics of difference the goals of which could be implemented far more easily in the universities than in society at large.

Like Russell Jacoby in his balance sheet of the academicization of Marxism and other left theory, Left critics of identity politics do not deny the important contributions that the focus on difference has made, including the extension of scholarship into new domains and a new sensitivity to and respect for diversity in the academy, in government and in law. Where all the left critics of identity politics tend to agree is that whatever the radical insights which gave rise to it and however salutary and necessary the assertion of hitherto submerged and silenced voices has been, the pendulum has swung too far and the radical thrust has been transmuted through the filter of identity politics into its opposite. Ultimately the politics of identity can have very conservative implications. Indeed, in a trenchant essay published recently in *Harper's* David Rieff argues that multiculturalism American-style, far from being subversive, is an expression of the ethos of capitalism in its latest global phase, where international firms are profitably celebrating difference with the growth of niche marketing, among other phenomena.[29]

As a program, the logical outcome of notions of radical and irreconcilable difference is a politics of separatism rather than commonality. Moreover, a politics of identity can draw people away from a critical understanding of the operations of the social system taken as a whole. For it usually entails affirming rights to inclusion in the existing system of social relations without challenging the functions and structures of that system.

As Gitlin argues:

> A good deal of the Cultural Left felt its way, even if half-jokingly, toward a weak unity based not so much on a universalist premise or ideal but rather on a common enemy—that notorious White Male. Beneath this, they had become willy-nilly pluralists, a fact frequently disguised by the rhetoric of revolution hanging over from the late sixties.[30]

This is well illustrated by the recent controversy over the Clinton administration's decision to allow professed homosexuals into the military. The gay community and its allies on what passes for the left rallied to what may be a legitimate civil rights issue, and although the support was by no means monolithic within the gay community (testifying again to the limits of a politics tied to a single identity), the focus of attention was not on the American military as a reactionary institution bent on the maintenance of arms production and export and deeply implicated in the long history of domestic and foreign repression, an institution which has often been dedicated to exterminating, let alone excluding the Other and an institution, it should be added, relentlessly attacked by the New Left during the war in Vietnam and by the peace movement in the 70s and 80s. By the standards implicit in this claim to inclusion, the Vietnam War for which purposes the military welcomed into its fold and sent to their deaths vast numbers of black youths can be seen as a leap forward in affirmative action. It is ironic, moreover, that not a few of those called-up to serve in Vietnam posed as homosexuals to avoid the draft.

The same kind of charge can be raised about the debate over the canon. The point isn't to argue that the canon can't afford a multicultural facelift. What is astonishing is that while this intense controversy waged on American campuses, absorbing the energies of many progressives, very little was said about a very basic problem of the university system as it exists in America, and which was again a major issue of the New Left, which saw the universities not only as class preserve but as designed to train a new class of technicians and managers for advanced capitalism. The point is that the issue of the canon central to the politics of identity hardly spoke to a much more direct and consequential form of exclusion than that of syllabi over-representing dead white males, namely that educational opportunities are directly proportional to income, tuition fees have been rising, and the only people likely to be entering the universities are members of a fairly elite economic group. The clamour for diversity in faculty members and reading lists ignored a more fundamental issue of the exclusivity of the student body in all its gender and racial diversity which could not be resolved without a real transformation of the educational system. American society as it exists can accommodate multicultural curricula with much less difficulty—albeit with much wailing and gnashing of teeth from the cultural conservatives—than it can accept lowering or abolishing tuition fees and creating family and social environments conducive to learning. And as David Caute, among others, have observed, university administrators also learned a few lessons from the sixties.[31] As Todd Gitlin says bluntly of academic proponents of identity politics who have cultivated a vested professional interest in Otherness, "The specialists in difference may do their best to deny the fact that for a quarter of a century, they have been fighting over the English department while the Right held the White House as its private fiefdom."[32]

There are many other problems with identity politics, not least of which is the substitution of rational argument with the attempt to morally validate one's position through identification with an oppressed group, and morally discredit any position which does not take its lead from the prevailing opinion of that group, resulting in the degradation of the substance of public debate.

This phenomenon is, for Ellen Willis, the essence of identity politics.[33] Here again, the influence of post-structuralism can be discerned; for rational argument itself has been cast as an indissociable part of the oppressive legacy of Enlightenment and viewed as the preserve of the Western White Male. That this idea, which is usually advanced with all the well-honed weapons of the purportedly western white male armoury, actually has racist and sexist implications has not been lost on some critical spirits. In a debate published by *Z Magazine* Noam Chomsky comments:

> ...the entire idea of "white male science" reminds me, I'm afraid, of "Jewish physics." ...I rather doubt that the non-white , non-male students, friends and colleagues with whom I work would be much impressed with the doctrine that their thinking and understanding differ from "white male science" because of their "culture or gender and race." I suspect that "surprise" would not be quite the proper word for their reaction.[34]

Identity politics represents not only the balkanization of the remnants of the left but also the abandonment of a larger vision or project of social transformation; taken to its logical extremes, the elevation of difference as the sole thing which defines us renders the very idea of commonly held values on which such a vision can only be based not only theoretically dubious but nefariously homogenizing. We appear to be on the verge of forgetting—admittedly in light of some compelling historical reasons outlined in the critique of Enlightenment universalism—what the New Left sought to demonstrate, that commonality does not need imply the obliteration of diversity, that the opposite pole of difference does not have to be sameness but rather solidarity.

Also, as Ellen Willis argues, we are all possessed of multiple identities and it was precisely against any notion of a fixed and immutable identity that the New Left struggled. Identity politics by contrast singles out one element of our identity and elevates it to the determining element—a form of vulgar culturalism as it were—at the expense or ignorance of other elements with competing claims of allegiance.

In sum then, identity politics is in many respects a travesty of the legacy of the New Left, for with their preeminence in the progressive political arena, the urgent insights of the 60s about the mendacity of American society's claims to equality and the imperative for the hitherto silenced to recover a voice have been divorced from another equally central set of assumptions about the common substratum of humanity in which we all partake and our ability to conceive a common good which cuts across racial, gender and—yes—occasionally even class lines.

The legacy of the New Left then lives in the Academy, if it lives at all, only in a very ambiguous form. For a more animate legacy we have to look beyond the terrain of the university proper and there, it is widely agreed, the strongest claim to the New Left succession lies with the so-called New Social Movements, and partic-

ularly the early feminist movement, the peace movement and the ecology movement. I qualify the term 'new' because there is a fairly intense debate among
students of these movements over whether they can be said in any meaningful
way to be new, a debate which I needn't enter for my present purposes.[35] The new
social movements or new politics proliferated in the early 1970s and gained momentum in the 80s throughout Western Europe and North America around a variety of issues such as women's liberation, the arms race, nuclear power, racism
and municipal democracy.

Of course there are very significant variations in national patterns: they have
been relatively weaker in France partly due to the incorporation, and often subsequent evisceration, of many of the social movement issues into mainstream party
agendas. This cooptation process happened only in the late 1980s in West Germany where the social movement phenomenon exhibited the greatest strength.[36]
They have been a relatively weaker force also in the United States for a variety of
reasons including the constraints of the two-party system (which for example
placed constraints on Jesse Jackson's attempt to forge a rainbow coalition) and a
faster pace of professionalization of issues.[37]

It is arguable that the new social movements have already become the
proper of historical study because their 'moment' has receded, partly as a result of
increasing institutionalization.

What I would like to explore briefly is the ways in which the New Left shaped
the concerns of these movements, but particularly the Green movement, by taking
up a number of themes. I want to show both the positive continuities with the New
Left and the inheritance of some of the unresolved problems of the New Left. Before doing this, however, I should note two things: the New Left paved the way for
the new movements, set a substantial part of the agenda and provided some of
the informal political and intellectual leadership but it did not supply all the troops.
It is important, lest the continuities be exaggerated, to point out that very many activists and sympathizers of the New Left—and this is true in the United States, in
France and in Germany—either abandoned political activity altogether with the decline of the New Left, often going on to successful careers in business and the pro-
fessions (a phenomenon reflected in the very production as well as the content of
the popular film *The Big Chill* and the television series Thirty-Something in the U.S.), or
underwent a depoliticization through a turning inward in the form of religious and
spiritual quests—"encounter culture" to borrow Todd Gitlin's phrase, or in some
instances embraced the New Right, such as David Horowitz in the U.S. and the

New Philosophers in France, or integrated themselves with varying degrees of ease and with variable endurance into the existing mass parties of the left—the Democratic Party in the States (even Abbie Hoffman worked for Jesse Jackson's rainbow coalition and Tom Hayden is of course the atavar of this trend), the revamped Parti Socialiste in France (Michel Rocard was, after all, a *soixante-huitard* of sorts), and the SPD in West Germany (between 1968 and 1974 the membership of the youth wing of the SPD more than doubled).[38] And it should also be recalled that the women's movement, which of all the new social movements has had the greatest impact in terms of cultural, political and social reform, had what we could call a negative origin in the New Left, as feminist consciousness grew partly in reaction to the male chauvinism manifest in the student movements and perceived as a contradiction of basic New Left principles. On the other hand, it is also true that the demographic profile of supporters and members of the New Social Movements is very similar to an imagined grown up generation of the sixties: urban, young, highly educated, white collar and professional. So it can be safely assumed that there is some direct continuity between the students who participated in or were influenced by the New Left and supporters, sympathizers and, where applicable, electorates of the new politics.

My focus in this section will be on the German Greens, as it has been argued with justice that these are the "true heirs" of both the German New Left specifically and the New Left as an international movement.[39] The claim of succession can be extended to encompass the streams of political ecology in France, social ecology in the United States and radical—although not deep—ecology currents elsewhere. Most obvious is the continuity in leading personalities and theorists—Daniel Cohn-Bendit in Germany, André Gorz in France, and Murray Bookchin in the U.S., to name only a few of the better known figures. Nor should the wide influence of these thinkers in the radical green movements and parties be underestimated.

In the French journal *Écologie Politique* for example, Jean-Paul Deléage refers to Gorz as perhaps the greatest inspiration among the theorists who inform the worldview of les Verts.[40]

Furthermore, many radical Greens self-consciously understand themselves as heirs of the New Left and positively evaluate this heritage. Greens in France, Germany and the United States have all explicitly drawn the links between the New Left and their own preoccupations. For example, a statement of principles issued by radical Greens in Vermont and New Hampshire declares (with a hint of national pride):

> The Greens' notions of participatory democracy, social responsibility, ecology, and non-violence—which became the "four pillars" of the West German Greens—were first made into household words by the New Left Movements in the 60s in America. To the extent that Green politics fulfils its potential it can be said to be a coming of age of the New Left.[41]

The same text points to another reason why the Greens arguably have a stronger claim than other movements to the heritage of the New Left: the attempt to understand issues in a holistic way, a point I discussed earlier in relation to the political implications of post-structuralism.

Maintaining that single issue and single constituency movements have gone as far as they can go, the statement cited above calls for "a holistic movement that connects issues and constituencies around a shared conception of the common good."[42] Thus, Green parties in North America and Europe take up the idea which the American SDS actually used as one of its slogans that "the issues are interrelated."

The Greens have a more encompassing structural or systemic critique of contemporary society, in contrast with the post-structuralist eschewal of totalizing analyses.

It arises from an admixture of the old and new Left emphasis on the dialectical interrelations of parts in an overarching social system with its insistence on the need for structural analysis and change and the basic premises of the ecological worldview. The very notion of an eco-system whose parts are mutually interactive and dependent is holistic. Responding to an attack on Green holism from a Popperian perspective, the French political ecologist Jean-Paul Deléage put the same idea slightly differently. The term ecosphere, he explains, designates a network of relations of interdependence which includes human beings.[43] He maintains that the ecological model is not holist but monist—that is, it seeks to establish the unity of the living world. Of course, holism is not intrinsically radical. The notion of society as an organic totality can and has served to justify and entrench existing hierarchical social divisions.[44] But when imbued with left libertarian values, a holistic perspective points towards the insufficiency of piecemeal reform. At the same time, as Carl Boggs points out, the German Green understanding of totality departs from the (orthodox) Marxist notion inasmuch as it does not subscribe to the idea of primary and secondary contradictions: "...the struggle for a liberated society cannot be reduced to changes in any one aspect of the totality (e.g., the economy), any particular set of institutions, any single constituency or agency.[45]

Another distinguishing characteristic linking the greens to the New Left (and marking their distance from the post-structuralist denunciation of grand social projects) is the affirmation of the utopian spirit. For radical Greens espouse a vision of far-reaching social transformation on a global scale which would involve nothing less than the redefinition of relations between human beings and between man and nature. They envision the creation of a more harmonious and just social order in which the nation-State would give way to regional economic communities linked with one another in a supranational association, in which the imbalance between North and South would be redressed, in which gender equality would prevail and social inequalities diminish, and in which people would engage in meaningful socially useful and environmentally sound work while having greater leisure time at their disposal. That the Greens tend to be somewhat vague on the means of achieving these goals is not the issue here (and in fact they do advance many concrete proposals, although these frequently take the form of moral exhortation.[46] The point is that in giving new life to the utopian spirit the Greens provide both a critical mirror with which to examine the present and an orientation for progressive political action.

On the other hand, I don't want to exaggerate the distance of the Green movement from some of the contemporary intellectual currents that I referred to earlier in this essay, for there are obvious points of overlap. Green movements and parties are clearly a mixed bag ideologically. *Die Grünen*, for example, encompass a variety of currents—realists and fundamentalists, eco-socialists and eco-libertarians and feminists—which have coexisted often in a state of mutual disagreement and mistrust. In the United States, where there is no Green party at the national level, there have been deep divisions among, for example, Left Greens and deep ecologists. And there are significant tendencies within the green movement, such as the *fundis* in Germany (whose most renowned representative was former DDR citizen and socialist theorist Rudolph Bahro) whose critique of modernity converges at many points with that of much post-structuralist philosophy—as, for instance, the abandonment, in face of ecological disaster, of all notions of progress, and the dogmatic rejection of science and technology per se as inherently destructive because imbued with the logic of domination (which carries beyond the point of usefulness the New Left insight that technology is not neutral in either its design or its deployment). In a probing and not unsympathetic treatment of the German Greens, Hans-Georg Betz views the Greens (as well as the new German Right) as in some exemplifying what he understands as the politics of post-modernism—to summarize rather brutally, an assault on the "project of modernity" which comprised a belief in the emancipatory possibilities of reason and knowledge and gave rise to various "grand narratives" or totalizing accounts of the historical process such as Positivism and Marxism.[47] But he grants that it is primarily advanced capitalism that the Greens condemn, rather than the project of modernity in toto. Moreover, some of the elements of Green politics which Betz characterizes as quintessentially postmodern were central to the New Left, such as the vision of self-determined unalienated work (which, far from a post-modern idea, has been an integral part of the utopian dimension of socialist politics from Charles Fourier forward). Hence, while the Greens may indeed reflect in some ways the so-called post-modern turn, I would argue that they do not for the most part share in either the liberal or nihilist implications of much post-modern thought. On the contrary, at many points they take up and develop the basic preoccupations of the New Left.

As I have already suggested the themes that connect the Greens, and particularly the German Greens, with the heritage of the New Left are multiple, and I can do no more justice to some of them than enumeration: the critique of consumer society, of the waste of non-renewable resources and the rejection of the possibility or desirability of limitless economic growth—a critique of productivism initiated by the New Left in opposition to the dominant liberal and socialist assumptions. Jean-Paul Deléage takes this opposition to production for its own sake as the foundation of a new humanist ethic—an ethic of responsibility for the conditions of human existence.[48] Another point I want to make which applies to the new social movements more broadly is about ends and means, about the different conception of the process of social change implicit in and espoused by the new politics. While some students of the New Left, such as Daniel Singer and George Katsiaficas, have argued that upheavals of the sixties put revolution back on the agenda of the advanced capitalist countries, it is clear that the New Left bequeathed an understanding of social revolution as a long-term, more diffuse process than the conception of revolution prevalent even among New Left activists, who inclined through much of the sixties towards an image of a cataclysmic moment in which the world would be turned upside down. It was a somewhat paradoxical combination of the decentralist, anti-statist, non-violent values of the New Left and the failure of its increasingly telescopic revolutionary aims that extinguished the apocalyptic vision of social transformation which has been a quintessential part of the revolutionary socialist tradition from the time of the French Revolution. (Whether it has been stricken from the historical record indefinitely is an interesting question for speculation.) Perhaps the first significant expression of the demise of this tradition in Europe was German SDS leader Rudi Dutschke's declaration in 1968 that, "A revolutionary dialectic of the correct transitions must regard the 'long march through the institutions' as a practical and critical action in all social spheres."[49] This set the stage for a more gradualist view of radical social change, although some of the new social movements which embraced it remained until very recently outside and suspicious of the institutions, a point to which I will return.

Although one of its most severe failings was the romanticization of the revolutions and revolutionary leaders of the Third World, it was one of the New Left's greatest virtues that it expressed a serious concern with the inequities of the North-South divide and with the enduring problem of imperialism. The exploitation of the developing world by the affluent nations of the West takes a variety of different forms in our time, but we need only look to the Mexican *maquiladoras* and to the destruction of the Brazilian rainforest under the guidance of the IMF to remind us that this is an ongoing and critical problem with devastating ecological as well as social consequences. Here again this consciousness endured in the international peace movement, which sought to expose the consequences of arms exports to and militarism in the third world, and in third world solidarity movements which have had genuine if limited impact on national and international policy-making. (In the words of one scholar-activist describing the effects of the broadly-based grass-roots Central American Solidarity movement in the U.S. the movement succeeded in inducing in the segments of the power elite "anxiety, confusion and timidity regarding the scale, form and pace of intervention.")[50] For many Greens, the gross disparities between North and South are a preponderant concern, for reasons pertaining both to ecology and social justice. This is well-illustrated by the program for an "ecological world economic order based on solidarity" produced by the Group of Green Economists in Germany, at the core of which are proposals to remedy the North/South imbalance (for example, comprehensive debt cancellation and increased transfer payments) while promoting self-reliant and sustainable development in the South.[51]

If it is especially the Greens in their various radical manifestations who embody some of the most valuable elements of New Left theory and praxis, they are also heir to many of the unresolved problems of the New Left—just as the New Left inherited some of the most serious unresolved problems of the Old. And the same is true in many respects for some of the new social movements. Again, I can do no more here than touch on a number of these problems.

A common characteristic of New Left politics was the almost complete eschewal of parliamentary politics as an instrument of social change. This involved a rejection not only of traditional political parties but of the political party *per se* viewed as an unavoidably hierarchical, bureaucratized and undemocratic form of political organization which could not in the end withstand cooptation by state power. (The failure of the Democratic party to respond adequately to key civil rights struggles was an important factor in this assessment in the United States, as was the evident accomodationism of the PCF in France and its dubious role in the May events, and the entry by the SPD into the Grand Coalition with the CDU/CSU in West Germany.) The attitude of many New Left students toward the official democratic process is encapsulated in the May '68 slogan: "Élections—Piège à cons" (Elections are the trap of fools) and the assertion by the brothers Cohn-Bendit that, "The setting up of a party inevitably reduces freedom of the people to freedom to agree with the party."[52]

A critique of centralized bureaucratic organizations in general, and an analysis of the seemingly inevitable ossification and substitutionism of the vanguard parties of the Old Left gave rise to an overemphasis on spontaneity and a jaundiced view of large structured organizations. American student leftists wedded to the ideal of decision-making by consensus were so suspicious of anything resembling hierarchy that Paul Booth, national secretary of SDS in 1965 was prompted to reflect:

> We have to learn the value of creating permanent institutions to embody the movement. We tend to believe in the false view that structure in itself is harmful—and we should learn how, throughout the movement, to create structures to which people will feel confident in attaching themselves.[53]

But nowhere were these new permanent democratic structures built. And the efforts of some parts of the New Left to reenter party politics in the seventies only contributed to reinforcing the perception that party politics were inevasibly corrupt.

Part of the fallout of this heritage was the refusal by many Greens in Europe and the U.S. to risk institutionalization by forming political parties and the continuing conflicts in the parties once constituted over their roles. In Germany, it was former SDS leader Rudi Dutschke who launched a campaign in the mid-seventies for a broad anti-capitalist alternative party. His initiative failed but the idea of an alternative party took root in the anti-nuclear, peace and ecology movements. Many people concluded that to have real and enduring political impact in a formally democratic society, they could not bypass the parliamentary road. As Petra Kelly affirmed:

We can no longer rely on the established parties and we can no longer depend on the extra-parliamentary road. The system is bankrupt but a new force has to be created both inside and outside parliament...In West Germany it is becoming increasingly important to vote for what we consider right and not just for the lesser evil.[54]

When the Greens made the transition from movement to party they tried to create structures that would protect against the 'iron law of oligarchy' characteristic of traditional mass parties, but which in turn engendered new problems. Hence, the German Greens have been internally divided since their initial electoral successes in the early eighties between the Realos and the Fundis, the former group committed to active participation in the parliamentary process and in coalitions with other parties, especially the SPD, while the latter remains highly suspicious of parliamentary politics, which can create a gap between the caucus and the base, and especially of coalitions, which may lead to substantial compromises on program. The conflict over the rotation principle is a good illustration of how this type of conflict can play itself out in practical terms. In an effort to prevent the creation of an elected caucus removed from the party base, the Greens at the State and federal levels decided to rotate officials after two years of a four year mandate. For some Greens however, rotation meant sacrificing acquired expertise and prematurely foreclosing the special contributions that could be made by particular individuals in the *Bundestag Fraktion*. A wide and lively debate arose throughout the party and various compromises were reached.[55] But whatever protective mechanisms are instituted, there continues a sometimes acrimonious debate over the very role of the parliamentary opposition and the approach to state power which cannot easily be resolved: should parliamentary activity serve merely as a forum for the dissemination of ideas, as a pressure tactic to wrest concessions from the State and rival parties, or as a viable route to radical reform? Although there are certainly some important Greens, such as former student radical and later Sponti Joschka Fischer, a leading realo, who privilege the parliamentary road as the instrument of social change, the majority appears to regard parliamentary activity as one of a variety of means to be employed in promoting the creation of a counter-hegemonic bloc within German society.

The development of the French ecological movement also testifies to changing attitudes towards parliamentary politics. In an essay devoted to the French Greens and the question of state power,[56] Guillaume Sainteny observes that initially in the 1970s many French ecologists were disinclined to any form of electoralism, seeing it as an integral component of the very social and political system they opposed. In the eighties, however, the majority became persuaded of the need to use the mechanisms of representative democracy to alter the balance of forces in order to promote their ideas and encourage the passage of vital reforms, as well as to put pressure on other parties and public bodies to take positions on ecological questions. By the mid-eighties there was a growing current within the Green movement which favoured a strategy for achieving state power. And the Greens were in fact able to score some remarkable electoral successes at the local, regional and pan-European levels in the late eighties.

Like the German Greens, les Verts (founded in 1984) was conceived as an alternative political party as much in its form as in its content, with mechanisms to ensure internal democracy, a high degree of decentralization, and the greatest input from the base. But unlike the other more reformist French Green party, Génération Écologie (formed in 1990 on the initiative of Brice Lalonde, who served as environment minister under Michel Rocard), les Verts have been very wary of coalition politics fearing compromises on program and any loss of an independent identity, and officially adhering to a 'neither left nor right' orientation. However, the *de facto* leader of les Verts, Antoine Waechter, has expressed aspirations of sharing in and eventually assuming state power. In a concession to the realities of electoral politics, les Verts signed an agreement with Génération Écologie to prevent splitting the vote in the legislative elections of March 1993, which in any case saw the Greens deprived of any elected representatives in the National Assembly.

Sainteny concludes: "…at the end of the eighties, les Verts moved from using universal suffrage as a pressure tactic, as a means of protest and as a public tribune to using it as a means of electing representatives to participate in political administration and ultimately of achieving power"[57] (my translation). Based primarily on the declarations of Antoine Waechter, this is probably an overly rectilinear and exaggerated portrait of the evolution of the French Green attitude to state power, but there is no question that electoralism has gradually come to occupy a greater place in Green political strategies.

Greens in the U.S. have shown a continuing ambivalence towards parliamentary politics, undoubtedly exacerbated by the near futility of fielding third-party candidates in a two-party first-past-the post electoral system. However, some Green parties have been formed at local and State levels.

In an article dealing with U.S. Green initiatives to form a national party, Brian Tokar observed that "…many Greens remain concerned that the lure of electoral politics will distract Greens from grassroots concerns, base-broadening efforts and the need to restructure political power."[58] However, he noted that the statement on political strategy passed at the 1990 conference organized by the Green Committees of Correspondence (the major national Green organization) did not exclude electoral strategies but views them as "coequal with direct action, education, alternative institutions and changes in people's personal lives."[59]

In spite of the inherent difficulties of sustaining anti-party parties and participating in mainstream politics while avoiding cooptation, the attitude of many Greens towards the development of permanent structures and participation in parliamentary politics is more constructive than the New Left's total refusal; their efforts to develop various mechanisms to preserve the democratic process within the party, to involve the broad membership in real decision-making and to guard against a lack of accountability on the part of elected officials and the formation of a parliamentary elite represent a qualitative advance. On the other hand, institutionalization may well terminate in the relative demise of the unconventional movement dimension of Green politics and the dominance of a less radical more reformist orientation, as Claus Offe, among others, has argued.[60]

Another problem related to the fear of institutionalization which has bedeviled social movements since the 60s is an allergy to leadership. Here the parallels between the critiques of former 60s activists and current students of the social movements are striking. James Miller and Michael Lerner have written incisively on the destructive effects of the cult of anti-leadership in the American student movement[61]—a phenomenon which had its parallels in Germany, where the hostility to leadership was exacerbated by the association of charismatic leadership with the Nazi past, and in France (it was a different Daniel Cohn-Bendit from the now cautious adherent of Green parliamentarism who wrote in 1968, "...democracy is not suborned by bad leadership, but by the very existence of leadership").[62]

This unqualified rejection followed from the critique of the elitism, hierarchy and centralism characteristic of traditional social democratic parties as well as the traditional parties of the revolutionary Left. (Applied inconsistently it did not prevent students from being wholly uncritical of charismatic leaders of disciplined hierarchical third-world revolutionary organizations.) In its doctrinaire form the aversion to leadership often gave rise to destructive tendencies, such as anti-intellectualism. And the insistence on an impossible equality of talent, often serving as a cover for petty envies, belittled and discouraged some of the most able and competent activists. Moreover, the rejection of official leadership created the possibility of a *de facto* leadership which remained unaccountable, opening the way to more covert forms of manipulation by dominant personalities.

These tendencies have recurred in contemporary social movements, including Green politics. Having interviewed many members of the German Greens in the mid-eighties, Charlene Spretnak and Fritjof Capra were struck by the widespread resentment towards Petra Kelly which stemmed in their reading primarily from her celebrity and the attention she received from the media, as well as from a doctrinal opposition to leadership. They quote one member of the national executive who declared, "Petra Kelly was very important in the formative stages of the party because charismatic personalities are necessary to create stability and to establish new ideas in the public's consciousness. However, that function is no longer needed."[63] Writing about the German Greens, Carl Boggs argues that the Green fetishism of direct democracy growing out of its antiauthoritarianism and desire to distinguish itself from bureaucratized parties, its feminist sensibilities and its desire to insure grassroots input, "reinforces a doctrinal purism at the base, whereby leaders who are politically successful are readily denounced as compromisers and renegades." He observes that "when pushed to its extremes this ideology gives rise to an isolated culture of protest in which concrete action becomes virtually impossible."[64] Connected with the organizational dilemma is a basic theoretical weakness passed on from the New Left to the new social movements: an insufficiently developed understanding of the role of the State and its complex relations with civil society. Taking up from the New Left, the new social movements have espoused a vision of direct democracy requiring small autonomous social units. With the stress on the development of decentralized communities, the new social movements, along with new social theory, have stressed the importance of rejuvenating a civil society which has withered in place of the State. The problems inherent in this perspective are lucidly discussed by Boris Frankel in his book The Post Industrial Utopians. Frankel argues, rightly I believe, that the evolution of capitalist society has rendered any dichotomy of the State and civil society untenable.[65] A rigid separation of State and civil society fails, for instance, to take into account that millions are employed by state institutions which thus form part of the economy. Furthermore, the State not only has a political administrative function but also a socio-cultural function. Frankel notes that in many OECD countries, money derived from state sources accounts for between 28 and 30 percent of household income. And then he asks some searching questions about the implications of these facts for a society of decentralized communities with no central state organizations. For example, what mechanisms will be used to create new sources of income, to ensure working conditions and wage rates, to redistribute wealth and to distribute social welfare in the form of the guaranteed minimum income, and to prevent standards from varying wildly depending on the resources of individual communities.

He also argues that this inadequate grasp of the relations of State and civil society lead, in what he calls post-industrial utopianism, to an inability to elaborate political strategies. Frankel is a sympathetic but probing critic who deserves a careful reading by anyone interested in the strengths and limitations of the radical Green vision as it is most commonly articulated.

However rich the legacy of the New Left is for our time, it must be borne in mind that the material conditions of possibility for the emergence of the post-materialist values underpinning the new politics have changed dramatically. This does not mean that the issues central to the new politics will disappear, but it does mean that any effort to realize the aims of the new politics faces a new and tougher context, one which looks frightfully more like that of the 1930s than it does of the 1960s. While the new social movements have focused their attention largely on 'quality of life issues', to borrow a phrase from the Port Huron Statement, the economic crisis which followed upon the end of the "long boom" extending from the mid-1940s to the late 60s has precipitated a global restructuring of capitalism that has continuing serious ramifications for Left politics. The welfare State and the expanding opportunities for employment taken for granted by the generation of the sixties are a thing of the past. Globalisation has resulted in a new international division of labour. Technology allows capitalism to maintain high levels of production simultaneously with ever higher levels of unemployment. Without tackling these new economic realities and putting forth viable strategies in conjunction with the organized labour movement and the permanent "reserve labour army" the Left will fail to be relevant or to capture the mass support it requires to have any far-reaching practical impact in the long term. I agree with Simon Gunn and others that it is incumbent on the Left to develop a viable economic alternative to the neo-conservative free market. The New Left will have to be as attentive to the problems of the means to exercise control over production, to the relations between work and leisure, to the provision of forms of economic security, as it is to the issues of citizenship and participation, to racism and sexism, and to the environment. And the increased mobility of capital accompanied by the decentralization of production makes it imperative to move beyond localism to a new internationalism. In the present global context: "Any attempt to pursue a programme distinct from that of other States, or independent of the logic and needs of international capital automatically runs the risk of marginalizing and bankrupting the national or local economy."[66] In my view, the Left must attempt to unify itself around a common theme emblematic of and connected in an integral way to a variety of these issues, which can serve to mobilize people in the creation of a counter-hegemony which can effectively resist and perhaps supersede the new consensus forged by the Right. Here the work by the eco-socialist Andre Gorz, among others, on the question of work-sharing can prove extremely pertinent, speaking as it does to the new freedom of capital from labour and forging a solid link between the new politics and the concerns of the labour movement and the unemployed. As Gorz and others have pointed out, the technical possibility of greater free time for the majority of working people, provided it is realized with redistributive measures such as a guaranteed social income and the reconceptualization of leisure in the form of productive non-renumerated activity, can serve as the basis for a renewed Left social project.[67]

The discussion on the subject of the necessity of the redistribution of work is more advanced in Europe than it is in North America and it is a central component of the Green programs in Germany and France. For an excellent brief introduction to the problem by an American scholar, see also Richard Barnet's, "The End of Jobs," in the September 1993 issue of *Harper's*. Again it was the New Left which paved the way for a rethinking of the nature of work in society in its profound questioning of a work ethic that rewards people for diligence in meaningless and unsatisfying tasks and that roots identity in occupational function and status. Klaus Mehnert, a sympathetic liberal observer of the youth movement internationally, concluded his 1976 study of the decline of the New Left with a balance sheet of what the insights of the youth revolt portend for the future. In it he commented insightfully, " Hitherto we have looked on idleness as a vice or as a temporary emergency in a time of recession. Now we must find ways and means of bringing about what one might call creative idleness."[68]

None of these comments are meant to suggest that we replicate the politics of the 30s, in a demand for the resurrection of an interventionist welfare State—although without a concrete and feasible alternative the gains of a century of struggle should not be relinquished without a fight; welfare State liberalism, for all its flaws, offered a better quality of life for most people than the new conservatism with its minimalist State and its fetishized free market. I agree therefore with Michael Rustin's warning about the dangers, especially in the current international context, of an unqualified rejection of welfare reformism.[69]

Furthermore, the social base of the new politics is still relatively narrow—the highly educated, middle class young—and is liable to shrink as educational and occupational opportunities contract. There is a need for a sublation of the terms both of the Old Left, with its faith in an undifferentiated class of workers as the chosen people, and the New Left with its perception, at some stages, that the working class was integrated into the system beyond redemption and had to be written off as an historic force of any moment. Actually, given the variations and oscillations of the New Left in this regard, it is arguably the new social movements which have banished the notion of the centrality of the conflict of labour and capital. There is no doubt that it has been part of their greatest contribution that no credible Left politics can ever view that conflict as the sole contradiction of capitalist or any historic society. On the other hand, the relative neglect of its status by the new social movements as a fundamental contradiction—which can be viewed partly as a case of hypercorrection—will have to be addressed in any new social project.

As Boris Frankel eloquently states it:

> There seems to be a tendency to believe that, just because social movements articulate legitimate values and concerns which are not identical with those of the traditional labour movements, then somehow all those women, gays, greens etc. are not living in the same society, not encountering similar problems to do with war, economic power, public administration, religion, education, poverty, legal rights and other overlapping and interconnecting public issues.[70]

And furthermore, as Stanley Aronowitz suggests, it makes sense to see the labour movement as an agent of social change when it acts like an agent of social change, without necessarily privileging its role among the forces for social transformation.[71]

Of course it is equally true that the organized labour movements must rethink their roles and consider workers as having vital interests beyond the workplace, as citizens and consumers. It is not surprising that German ecologists had relations of mutual hostility in the 70s with that part of the labour movement which rallied to the support of the nuclear industry in defense of the widely rejected power plant program. But it bodes well that some rethinking of along the lines of coalition building with the social movements has already taken place in the trade union movement in North America as well as in Europe.

If the legacy of the New Left is to bear fruit anew, we are compelled to address the totality of social relations and this on a global scale. To make the point in another way, postmaterialist values are not much in evidence in the new Eastern Europe, let alone among the masses of the developing countries—there, basic necessities are the quality of life issues. Finally and at the risk of standing accused of latent or blatant anti-intellectualism, it seems to me that if the Left academy goes on endlessly problematizing, to adopt a phrase from the current jargon, there will be little time and energy left over for the pressing work of synthesis and construction. At the end of the day it is a discouraging commentary on the legacy of the New Left that in 1993 the calls to move 'beyond the fragments' already reverberating in the early 1980s are no less, and arguably more urgent.

Notes

1. Lerner's observation which finds many echoes throughout the sympathetic but by no means uncritical literature dealing with the New Left in both the U.S. and Western Europe is that a sense of exaggerated expectations both about what the New Left could accomplish and about the ability of participants to incarnate in their persons all the high ideals of the movement led especially in face of hostile infiltration to a climate of impotence, self-blame and mutual accusation. Although Lerner overemphasizes psychological explanations for the collapse of the New Left in the U.S. and fails to place the American New Left in an international context—for instance his stress on the peculiarity of excessive individualism of American society as an explanation for the destruction of movements for social change in America begs the question of similar patterns of New Left implosion elsewhere—his characterization of the psychological dynamic and its deleterious consequences warrants attention, especially in view of parallels in other countries and the reproduction of the dynamic in the new social movements. See his "The Legacy of the Sixties for the Politics of the Nineties," in Lerner, ed., *Tikkun:An Anthology* (Oakland: Tikkun Books, 1992), pp. 15-25.

2. It is worth noting that the early histories of the New Left tended to exaggerate the ruptures and discontinuities between the Old Left and the New, particularly in the United States. The relations are much more nuanced in accounts of the New Left in France, Germany, and England, where many New Left thinkers and participants in the student movements were politically active in the traditional Left parties, both Communist and Social Democratic. There have been some efforts to refine the American historical record on this score; see especially, Maurice Isserman, *If I Had a Hammer* (New York: Basic Books, 1987) and Tim Wohlforth, "The Sixties in America," *New Left Review* 178 (1989), pp. 105-123.

3. Régis Debray, "A Modest Contribution to the Rites and Ceremonies of the Tenth Anniversary," *New Left Review* 115 (May/June 1979), pp.45-65. Although his assessment of the overall effects of the extra-parliamentary movement in West Germany is comparatively far less bleak, Werner Hülsberg also points out that the movement helped to create the conditions for the necessary modernization of German society, including educational reform,

more state planning of the economy and greater integration of women into professional life. See his analysis in *The German Greens*, trans., Gus Fagan (London: Verso, 1988), p.42.

4. For variations on this theme see James Miller, *Democracy is in the Streets* (New York, Simon and Schuster, 1987) and Michael Rustin, "The New Left and the Present Crisis," *New Left Review* 121 (May-June 1980), pp.63-89.

5. See Maurice Isserman, "1968 and the American Left," *Socialist Review* (1988/4), p. 97.

6. Stuart Hall, 'The "First" New Left' in Robin Archer, et. al. eds., *Out of Apathy* (London: Verso, 1989), p.26.<

7. For an extended account and analysis of May 86 in comparison with May 68, see Roger Duclaud Williams, "Student Protest" in D.L. Hanley and A.P. Kerr, eds., *May 68: Coming of Age* (Macmillan, 1989).

8. On the Spontis see Betz, *Postmodern Politics*, pp.34-41, and Hülsberg, *The German Greens*, pp.73-74 and *passim*.

9. Todd Gitlin, *The Sixties: Years of Hope, Days of Rage* (New York: Bantam, 1987), p.243.

10. In Germany, for instance, one third of the Extra-parliamentary Opposition's leading figures went on to academic careers. The figure is given in Betz, *Postmodern Politics in Germany*, p. 77.

11. Rachel Bowlby, "60s Feminism" in Sohnya Sayres, et. al., eds., *The 60s Without Apology* (Minneapolis: University of Minnesota Press, 1984), p.36.

12. Lawrence Kritzman, "Introduction" in *Michel Foucault: Politics, Philosophy, Culture : Interviews and Other Writings, 1977-1984*, ed. Lawrence Kritzman, trans. Alan Sheridan, et. al. (New York: Routledge, 1988) p. xiv.

13. Cited in Ibid., p. xvi.

14. The reception of post-structuralism in North America, particularly in the discipline of History is documented and discussed in a sympathetic vein by Geoff Eley in a working paper for the University of Michigan's Program on the Comparative Study of Social Transformations entitled "Is All the World a Text?" (October 1990).

15. See the chapter "The Transformation of the New Left" in Hans-Georg Betz, *Postmodern Politics In Germany* (New York: St. Martin's Press, 1991).

16. Terry Eagleton, *Literary Theory* (Minneapolis: University of Minnesota Press, 1983), p. 142.

17. Gary Peller, "Reason and the Mob: The Politics of Representation," in Lerner, ed., *Tikkun Anthology*, p.164.

18. Ibid., p.165.

19. Barbara Ehrenreich, "Truth, Justice, and the Left," *Z Papers* Vol. 1, No. 4 (October-December 1992), p.64.

20. Michel Foucault in an interview with Gerald Raulet, "Critical Theory/Intellectual History," in Kritzman, ed., *Michel Foucault*, p.41.

21. Illustrating this point, Rachel Bowlby argues that feminism took a conservative turn in the 1980s with the advent of cultural feminism through the work of such authors as Mary Daly which "take on the traditional notions of femininity unmasked as male constructions by the writers of a decade ago and adopt them as positive timeless values that women

should not attempt to give up." See her "60s Feminism" in Sayres et. al., eds., *The 60s Without Apology*, pp.326-27.

22. D.L. Hanley and A.P Kerr, for example, state that "the general ethos of self-expression and confidence in collective or group identities ... were the real hallmarks of May [68 in France]." See their "Elusive May" in Hanley and Kerr, eds., *May 68*, p.8.

23. For more sympathetic treatments of this issue see for example Henry Giroux "Living Dangerously: Identity Politics and the New Cultural Racism," *Cultural Studies*, Vol. 7, No. 1 (1993), pp. 1-27 and Henry Louis Gates Jr., "Multicultural Madness", *Tikkun*, Vol. 6, No. 6 (November/December 1991), pp. 55-58.

24. See Ilene Philipson, "What's the Big I.D.? The Politics of the Authentic Self," *Tikkun*, Volume 6, No. 6 (November/December 1991), pp.51-55.

25. Michael Rustin, "The New Left and the Present Crisis," *New Left Review* 121 (May-June 1980), p.89.

26. See for example Klaus Mehnert's section on "Identity" which draws on the work of psychologist Erik Erikson in *Twilight of the Young* (New York: Holt, Rhinehart and Winston, 1976), pp. 344-49.

27. Todd Gitlin, "Identity Politics," *Dissent* (Spring 1993), p.175.

29. David Rieff, "Multiculturalism's Silent Partner" *Harper's*, August 1993, pp. 62-72.

29. Ibid., p.173.

30. See David Caute, *The Year of the Barricades* (New York: Harper & Row, 1988), p. 461.

31. Gitlin, "Identity Politics," p.173.

32. An example of the manner of dealing with opposing arguments to which Willis refers is marvellously illustrated in a recent interview with Judith Nicholson in the Montreal publication *Voir*. Asked to comment on black American professor Shelby Steele's critique of affirmative action, Nicholson, a journalism student who taught a course in Black Lesbian Culture at Concordia University, incriminates him in the end as an Uncle Tom unrepresentative of the American black community: "La culture blanche male aime bien avoir ses portes-paroles noir. Nathalie Collard, "Diviser pour mieux penser," *Voir* (May 20-26, 1993), p.12.

33. Noam Chomsky, "Rationality/Science" *Z Papers* Vol. 1, No. 4 (Oct-Dec 1992), p.56.

34. See for example the various arguments in Russell Dalton and Manfred Kuechler, eds., *Challenging the Political Order* (New York: Oxford University Press, 1990) and especially the essay in that volume by Karl Werner Brand, "Cyclical Aspects of New Social Movements" in which Brand asserts that the new social movements are the most recent manifestation of a cyclical pattern of middle-class modernization critique—a critique of industrialism, technology, bureaucracy etc., which Brand argues, has ebbed with the advent of a postmodern spirit. Another challenge to the "newness" of the new social movements can be found in Lorna Weir's "imitations of New Social Movement Analysis," *Studies in Political Economy* 40 (Spring 1993), pp.73-102.

35. See for example the saga of *autogestion* related by Lawrence Bell in "May 68: Parenthesis or Staging Post in the Development of the Socialist Left?" in Hanley and Kerr, eds., *May 68*, pp.80-99.

36. This question is addressed by, for example, George Katsiaficas in his *The Imagination of the New Left* (Boston: Southend Press, 1987) and Margaret FitzSimmons and Robert Gottlieb, "A New Environmental Politics" in Mike Davis and Michael Sprinker, eds., *Reshaping the U.S. Left* (London: Verso, 1988), pp. 114-130.

37. Hülsberg, *The German Greens*, p.47.

38. David Caute, for example, refers to the German Greens as "...the only significant political force in Western Europe today who can lay claim to a substantial portion of the New Left legacy." *Year of the Barricades*, p. 459. For an excellent exploration of the thematic continuities between the West German Extra-parliamentary Opposition in the 60's and the Greens, see Geoff Eley, "Germany Since 68: From the APO to the Greens," in *Socialist Review* 4 (1988), pp. 131-141.

39. Jean- Paul Deléage, "L'Ecologie, Humanisme de Notre Temps." Ecologie Politique, No.5 (Hiver 1993), p.12.

40. "Towards a New Politics: A Statement of Principles of the Vermont and New Hampshire Greens," *Our Generation*, Vol. 20, No.1 (Fall 1988), pp.29-30.

41. Ibid., p.30.

42. Deléage, "Humanisme de Notre Temps," p. 13.

43. On this point see Martin Jay, *Marxism and Totality* (Berkeley: University of California Press, 1984) pp. 27ff.

44. "Carl Boggs, "The Greens," *Our Generation* Vol. 18, No. 1 (Fall/Winter 1986), p.14.

45. See for example the book *Ecological Economics: A Practical Programme for Global Reform* authored by a group of German Green economists and translated by Anna Gyorgy (London: Zed Books, 1992).

46. Betz, *Postmodern Politics in Germany*.

47. Ibid. Anti-militarism, which crystallized in the New Left in response to the Vietnam War, is a basic tenet of the Green movement, which itself emerged in the context of nuclear proliferation and gained tremendous impetus especially in Europe from the peace and disarmament movements. And then there is the espousal of internationalism given expression in the by now famous dictum "Think globally, act locally," and a profound commitment to democratic forms of organization which maximize popular participation in decision-making.

48. Dutschke, "On Anti-authoritarianism" translated and reprinted in Oglesby, ed., *The New Left Reader*, p.243.

49. Van Gosse, "Central American Solidarity" in Davis and Sprinker, eds., *Reshaping the U.S. Left*, p.14.

50. *Ecological Economics: A Practical Programme for Global Reform*, trans. Anna Gyorgy (London: Zed Books, 1992).

51. Daniel and Gabriel Cohn-Bendit, "The Battle of the Streets: C'est Pour Toi Que Tu Fais La Révolution," in Carl Oglesby, ed. *The New Left Reader* (New York: Grove Press, 1969), p. 261.

52. Cited in James Miller, *Democracy is in the Streets* (New York: Simon and Schuster, 1987), pp. 253-254.

53. Cited in Hülsberg, *The German Greens*, p.78.

54. For a readable introduction to the politics of the German Greens which deals with some of the internal divisions and controversies see Charlene Spretnak and Fritjof Capra, *Green Politics* (Santa Fe: Bear and Co., 1986). On the question of new attitudes towards parliamentary politics see the interesting exchange between Daniel Cohn-Bendit and Joschka Fischer, a key figure in the German New Left who became a Green parliamentarian and accepted the post of Minister of the Environment in the state of Hesse in 1985, in Dany Cohn-Bendit, *Nous l'avons tant aimée, la révolution* (Paris: Bernard Barrault, 1986), pp. 172-179.

55. Guillaume Sainteny, "La Question du Pouvoir d'Etat Chez les Écologistes" *Le Défi Écologiste* (Paris: Éditions l'Harmattan, 1993): pp. 67-85.

56. Ibid., p. 81.

57. Brian Tokar, "Into the Future with the Greens," *Z Magazine*, November 1990, p.64.

58. Ibid., p. 65.

59. See Claus Offe, "The Institutional Self-Transformation of Movement Politics" in Russell J. Dalton and Manfred Kuechler, eds., *Challenging the Political Order* (New York: Oxford University Press, 1990), pp. 232-250.

60. See Miller, "Democracy is in the Streets" and Lerner, "The Legacy of the Sixties for the Politics of the Nineties," *Tikkun Anthology*, pp.17-19.

61. Cohn-Bendit, "Battle of the Streets" in Oglesby, ed., *The New Left Reader*, pp.261-262.

62. Cited in Spretnak and Capra, *Green Politics*, p.12.

63. Carl Boggs, "The Greens," *Our Generation* Vol. 18, No. 1 (Fall/Winter 1986), p. 50.

64. Boris Frankel, *The Post-Industrial Utopians* (Cambridge: Polity Press, 1987), pp. 202-205.

65. Simon Gunn, *Revolution of the Right*, (London: Pluto Press, 1989), p.16.

66. See Gorz's most recent contribution to this subject, "Bâtir la civilisation du temps libéré" in *Le Monde Diplomatique*, mars 1993.

67. Mehnert, *Twilight*, p.378.

68. See Rustin, "The New Left," pp. 70-73.

69. Frankel, *Post-Industrial Utopians*, p.184.

70. Stanley Aronowitz, *The Politics of Identity* (New York: Routledge, 1992), pp.269-270.

I wish to extend warm thanks to my fellow members of the Thompson House Study Circle: Eugenio Bolangaro, Eric Darier, Steve Jordan, and Qussai Samak. Our amicable if heated debates contributed immeasurably to the writing of this essay. I also want to thank Robert Shultz for his valuable suggestions and encouragement, John Laffey for his guidance and patience, and the Social Sciences and Humanities Research Council of Canada for its financial support.

THE LEGACY OF THE NEW LEFT

by Anthony Hyde

You've asked me to say a few words about 'the legacy' of the New Left—which is to say, the time of my youth—and of course I must begin by noting how discouraging, even distressing, such an assignment must be. For 'legacy' clearly implies conclusion, termination, the dispersal of assets—and worse. Of course I'm aware that time has passed. My capacity for brandy has undoubtedly diminished and some mornings I do feel, attempting to arise, as if I had one foot in the grave. But apparently it's even worse than I'd thought. It seems that I'm speaking to you, like some New Age Spirit, from the other side of the Great Divide.

And perhaps my first task is to face up to this disturbing truth with you. Even if my corporeal presence testifies to some last spark of life, it's clearly a fluke. I'm a hopeless anachronism—indeed, that's why I may be useful. I can testify about a lost time and place, a vanished culture, like an ancient Seminole chief discovered up some ultimate Florida swamp by a go-ahead real-estate man. Brought back to civilization, he must now pass his final years surrounded by graduate students with their whirrip tape-recorders, busy notebooks and all those questions for their theses. And of course it's impossible. Obligatorily, the theses will be written, but really no one will understand a word I say. The gulf is too wide. Almost no one today shares my experience, my traditions, my thoughts, my beliefs, my myths —above all, my feelings.

Let me note a few of those beliefs, just to indicate how hopeless true comprehension must be.

Anthony Hyde was a principle activist with the New Left in Canada, the Student Union for Peace Action (SUPA). He went on to become a best-selling novelist, having authored Red Fox *and* China Lake. *This essay was first published in 1994 in* Our Generation, *Vol. 24, No. 2.*

I believe in liberation. As in liberation movement, as in Liberation Magazine. As in sexual liberation. As in fucking. As, in my case, fucking women. Fucking, screwing, balling, making love not war—call it what you will; but if you don't get that right, you won't get anything right, for that's where everything must begin. Let me recall to mind the words of a fine old chant:

What what what what
What what what what
Whatta ya gonna do, After the orgy
I wanta make friends, After the orgy…
I wanta be your friend
I wanta be your friend
I wanta be your friend, After the orgy ends
I wanta be your friend
I wanta be your friend
I wanta be your friend
I wanta be your friend, After the orgy ends
I wanta be your friend
I wanta be your friend
I wanta be your friend
What are you going to do, After the orgy
I wanna read Blake with you, After the orgy
I wanna eat something too, After the orgy
I wanta be your pal
I wanta be your pal
I wanta be your pal
After we pet and ball, I hope that won't be all
I wanta be your pal…

And so on and so on and so on… Such sentiments—drawn from Tuli Kupferberg and The Fugs, nineteen sixty whatever-the-hell-it-was—can be called mindless, but I fear I still share them today. Men and women are to fuck and the Feminist Thought Police should trade in their pussies for Bibles and bluestockings and admit who and what they really are.

And this gets worse, I'm afraid. Not only do I believe in Liberation and Free Love, but I still believe in Free Thought and Free Speech.

Free Speech. FSM.

You see how difficult this is…. Those initials will mean little to you but they still mean a great deal to me. The Free Speech Movement, Berkeley, the fall of 1964. A great deal started there, with the idea that the university should be the home of free speech and free thought, including political speech and political thought. And I still believe it. Of course, today, very few academics and students believe in free speech, otherwise they couldn't be in universities, for in the United States at least 300 universities and colleges have promulgated Codes on 'word crimes' dictating what people can say. I will quote from one which is particularly poignant to me because it is in force at the University of Michigan, Ann Arbor—which is where all the first SDS people came from. Like most, this code outlaws any utterance:

> …based on race, color, creed, religion, national origin, sex, sexual orientation, ancestry, age, marital status, handicap, or Vietnam era status that has the purpose or effect of creating an intimidating, hostile or offensive environment for academic pursuits, employment, housing or participation in a university activity.

As a practical matter, this prohibition of any meaningful speech in universities probably has little effect, for few academics actually wish to think and not one in a thousand has anything to say. But old habits, you see, die hard. I'll object anyway. I'll think what I want, speak as I choose. The English language belongs to me—not Judy Rebick or Michelle Landsberg, or such Bibles of the politically correct as the *Globe and Mail* Style Book—and it lives in my mouth. Faggot is excellent English. So is fuck. So is Revolution. So is Peace. So is Freedom. So is come, as Lenny Bruce knew. So is bread, as Lenin knew. And all of these words, uttered in public, have been known to create an "offensive environment," indeed civil disturbance. But I'm not ashamed of any of them, nor am I ashamed of my loyalty to the tradition of their free expression.

But there you go—*I'm not ashamed*. Perhaps this lack of shame defines the true dimensions of the Great Divide. I don't feel guilty. Or, to be precise, the only thing I feel guilty about is that I feel guilty at all—what guilt I do feel, I work hard to overcome.

I'm white, for example. And I don't feel guilty about it, not in the least, because I don't identify myself as a member of a racial tribe—I'm sufficiently secure in my own identity—and I refuse to look at others in that way. Even if they desire that I should see them otherwise, when I look at a black person all I see is a black person. Of course this means that I spend a lot of time fighting back nausea, especially when reading liberal newspapers or at dinner parties of a social democratic persuasion. In such milieux you will hear the most astounding things, locutions, for example, *like women of colour*. Let me tell you something. Sane, healthy people don't talk about themselves, or other people, this way. And all they prove is that they've never been sufficiently close to a black woman to share a drink or a laugh, let alone squeeze her sweet black ass.

I'm also male, and I'm not guilty about that either—although clearly, as a white male, I'm supposed to be the root of all evil. Recently I received in the post something called a National Survery of Canadian Men, which asks a series of ludicrously loaded questions about men and violence and then wants me to contribute money to something called the December Fund to "help prevent men's violence against women." Any man who contributes to this fund is sick in the head; rather more than implicitly he is accepting responsibility for, and identifying with, the actions of a madman—the unfortunate who murdered a number of female undergraduates in Montreal in 1989. Well, I don't go along. Again, I define myself as an individual human being not as sexual representative. I've been making love not war since 1962 and what others do with their automatic rifles may be my concern but it's not my responsibility. And the proposition that there's a culture of male violence could not be more ludicrous. Indeed, exactly the opposite is true: the 'problem' is the breakdown of that culture. I belong to the first generation of men in this century—white, educated, North American men I might say—who refused in significant numbers to submit themselves to the inhumanity of war, who explicitly rejected values based on violent death, who insisted that you express your manliness with your cock in bed not with a gun on a battlefield, and who did not confuse the two.

Of course, both the insistence and the refusal were the product of a considerable cultural and social evolution, and it has had equally vast consequences, not least for the American military, and not least for American feminists: who, quite precisely suffering from the confusion between sex and violence my generation of men rejected, have been attempting to reverse this evolution by again tightly regulating sexual behaviour and expression in law, and, at the psychological level, by encouraging repression and guilt everywhere. But the guilt, you see, is their problem, not mine.

And lastly I'm not guilty about being a Westerner, an Anglo-Saxon, literate, a book man. I write novels for a living—complex works of the imagination dependent upon grammar, the dictionary meaning of words, and some cultural reference. I do this in a tradition, a tradition defined by white, western, supposedly repressive males, and I love them all and am ashamed of none of them, including the homosexual blacks like James Baldwin. "No *man* is an island intire of it selfe; every *man* is a piece of the Continent, a part of the Maine… any *man's* death diminishes me, because I am involved in *Man*kinde; And therefore never send to know for whom the bell tolls, it tolls for theee."

If women or people outside the West cannot identify with these lines, that's their loss, and I'm sorry—but they say what I believe and who I am, and I'm not ashamed of myself.

Well, surely I can stop there. I presume I have convincingly demonstrated my own irrelevance—so far as I'm concerned, the word 'legacy' pretty much sums it up. I'm dead. I've just been scribbling notes for my epitaph. Politically, in a world of feminists and gays, of people campaigning for tribal rights of every kind, I find myself in total isolation, and indeed am not politically active in any organized way. Who would come to my meetings? And, as you have doubtless gathered, I sure wouldn't want to go to theirs.

But does that mean that the New Left has had no influence at all?

As I hover spectrally above the current political scene can I recognize nothing of myself? Is there no hint that I passed this way?

The answer, despite my current irrelevance, is yes: the New Left has had its influence, an influence now so completely integrated into current political theory and practice that we no longer recognize it for what it is, or was. And perhaps we are even inclined to devalue this influence for precisely that reason; since we can assume it, why worry about it at all? Indeed, seen from the perspective of the present—though that is a qualification I want you to bear in mind—the legacy of the New Left is not difficult to understand, or even especially controversial. It really consists in a redefinition of politics, of what the word comprehends. This redefinition took place along three lines. First, the subject matter of politics, the issues and questions the word could legitimately include. Second, the definition of legitimate political actors—who could participate in the political process. And thirdly, how politics should be conducted—the legitimate modalities of political action.

Let me take these points in order.

When I first began doing politics it was very narrowly defined, restricted to the 'issues' of elections and the political parties, and was equally expected to stay within the narrow bounds of the formal political process. Time and again, as a young person, you would raise a question, which you considered political, only to have it dismissed; that's moral or spiritual or psychological, your elders would say, not suitable for political discussion at all.

And, coming in the other direction, the inclusion of political themes outside of their accepted sphere would invariably incur suspicion. That was controversial. That was trouble-making. So playwrights and novelists who attempted to deal with political themes would find their work scorned and ignored, and even men of the cloth—timidly raising the question of "peace" from their pulpits—would meet a stony reception from their congregations. Why can't he stick to the Bible? Why does he want to go stirring up trouble?

Remember, this was the Age of Conformity. You talked about baseball and hairdos, and you certainly didn't read *Lady Chatterly's Lover*—it couldn't be legally published. It was a time, wrote C.Wright Mills, "in which issues are blurred and debate muted," in which "the sickness of complacency has prevailed, the bipartisan banality flourished," when even intellectuals indulged in "a celebration of apathy."

Now we attacked all this—and we attacked from a number of directions. First, and crucially—for this was the lynch-pin of the whole system—we attacked the stasis of the Cold War. Happily, younger people will probably not recall how cold that war was, but I can assure you that the epithet was accurate enough. Everything was frozen. A brutal totalitarianism abroad was used to justify a stultifying domestic oppression. Dissent was not quite treason, but it certainly called forth official suspicion, and any questioning of the status quo was seen as offering aid and comfort to the enemy. To think or act, you had to step outside this system—which is what James M. Minifie was trying to do with a book like *Peacemaker or Powdermonkey*. But if neutrality was a hopeless proposition for Canada—the Poland of the Nuclear Age—it was the particular contribution of the early peace movement to discover a small moral patch to stand on, then expand it politically. Bertrand Russell, the Committee of One Hundred, organs like the Bulletin of the Atomic Scientists, and in Canada groups like the CUCND, opened the debate simply by insisting that there had to be some alternative to the MAD status quo—the status quo, that is, of Mutual Assured Destruction. That was a vital step. Once the possibility of an alternative was admitted, defining it established a *political* agenda for the first time in many years.

But we also attacked in the realm of ideas itself—and this was particularly important, given that so many of us were students. We attacked a concatenation of notions whose total effect was to make political thought impossible: "the end of ideology," "value-free social science," a strict division of "experts" and disciplines —intellectual approaches that assumed what they sought, a total integration with the status quo. With C.Wright Mills and Karl Mannheim in our pockets, we worked for an integrated social science which proclaimed and openly debated its values, and attacked the "end of ideology" for what it was—a highly ideological notion bought and paid for by the CIA.

Lastly, as important as anything else, we were ourselves. We were young. We wanted to lead political lives and so we wanted the contents of our lives to be political—in the words of the Port Huron Statement, we wanted "private problems to be public issues." Educational questions, moral questions, sexual questions— these, we insisted, were political questions as well. Sometimes, in discussing the New Left, writers will claim that it was as much a cultural movement as political, but that misses the point: we sought conceptions of culture and politics that were broad enough to include each other.

Well—how much of this has stuck? Surely a good deal. The accepted defini- tion of politics has enormously expanded—think of today's sexual politics for ex- ample—and political questions can be presented and debated in a wide variety of forums, even in Hollywood films—even, God help us, on Oscar night.

The second term of the New Left's redefinition of politics concerned who could legitimately take part in the political process. It's fascinating, looking back at that time, to see how concerned we were with the question of elites. We read *The Power Elite* of course, but some of us even read Pareto and many pored over all those 'community' and 'stratification' studies that were done in the thirties, forties and fifties—by the Lynds, Lloyd Warner, and so forth.

This interest was entirely reasonable. We were concerned with power and were trying to understand how a small group of individuals and institutions had gained a monopoly over it. Above all, we sought clues as to how this monopoly could be broken. For the other side of the coin was equally important. This was the question of agency: which social groups could be mobilized to effect social change? There were a variety of answers—the working class of the Marxists; for C.Wright Mills, the intellectual—but all involved bringing people and groups out- side the political process into it as legitimate political actors. Indeed, the first erup- tion of the New Left into the consciousness of mainstream America was found precisely here, in the Civil Rights Movement, the Freedom Rides of the Mississippi Summer. That movement was explicitly concerned with registering blacks to vote, to bringing them into the political process in at least that nominal way. But, more generally, the organizing efforts of the New Left were concerned to empower those who were dispossessed in the hope that this process would itself create change. We wanted to expand politics, in terms of both issues and actors, and then explode it.

Again, how much of this stuck? Let's not kid ourselves; this country is still ruled by elites, whose best known representative lives on Pennsylvania Avenue in Washington, D.C. But it's probably true that our elites have a little tougher time today. There are more voices heard in the room, more seats at the table. All manner of social groupings now see themselves as political, and individuals are far more likely to see themselves as political actors too.

Finally, the New Left effected an enormous change in how politics is carried on, in the modalities of political action. When we began, politics meant elections contested by political parties of virtually identical political beliefs—"ping-pong" politics, we used to say. It was a politics in which there was no room for new ideas, certainly not ours, and no room for the new political actors we wanted to thrust upon the stage. So we acted differently. At a tactical level, this was apparent at the time. Drawing on the pacifist movement—the Ghandian movement—we staged sit-ins, teach-ins, and innumerable other kinds of demonstrations. We invented a new militancy, and a new style of militancy. We put politics into the streets—and gave street people a variety of tools with which to express themselves politically. We created, through our political action, enough positive examples to show ordinary people that politics was something that they could do, that they had power and could use it. And even now, in these bleak times, you can still see a little of this. The formal political process, however phoney, has had to open up. There are fewer closed doors, more "consultations." And authority must conduct itself with the knowledge that political pressure can come from unexpected quarters at unexpected times, in unexpected ways.

I suppose I should stop here. The New Left's legacy, one can honestly conclude, has been modest, but definite, and after declaring our appreciation we should probably leave the whole enterprise to rest in peace; I'm certainly prepared to let others do the judging.

But there's a problem. As noted, I've been defining the New Left's influence in terms of current, contemporary political life—looking at the New Left from this present, that's what I see. But the present is always changing, which leads to that old truism that nothing is more alive and changeable than history—each day we see it differently. And I'm afraid, you see, that our present is soon to be altered out of all recognition. I stand by what I've said—but I fear it may be transitory, of only fleeting relevance.

The easiest way to explain, perhaps, is to do just the opposite of what I've done till now. That is, I want to note certain aspects of the New Left which can't be found in the current scene, parts of the New Left's legacy which remain unclaimed.

First, we don't have to subscribe to myths about the Flower Children to see that the emotional and intellectual tenor of that period was utterly different from today. The New Left was about openness, self-exploration, discovery. Born into a self-confident time, especially economically, we were prepared, even overjoyed, to challenge every assumption we'd been given. We took a lot of drugs, read forbidden books, and fucked our brains out. We rejected violence. We rejected racial definitions and racial hatred. Looking back at that time, it seems to me that the New Left had only one dirty word—manipulation. Because, you see, we rejected guilt and "power trips"—reflections in our own thought and personal relations of the values and the world we rejected.

But how much of that has stuck? Not much. Look around you. Listen. Listen to rap music—there's a lot to listen to. Lots of protest, certainly. Lots of anger. But not much love. Or think of contemporary, mainstream feminism, building a politics of repression around rape, stalking, abuse—anger and fear and guilt—and finding 'solutions' in censorship and incarceration.

In the New Left, the emotional structure was utterly different from this. Which had a crucial intellectual corollary. For the New Left, ideas were never received; they were always heuristic, exploratory, subject to revision. Others had the Book of the Month. We had the Book of the Week—Goodman, Ellul, Adorno, Marcuse, Gorz, Laing, Althusser. New Left intellectuals would chew through a couple generations of German intellectuals during the spring, then take on the French over the summer. Ideas were exciting, but they were never 'right' and they always led on to others. The hallmark of a New Left political meeting was somebody, probably Judy Pocock, saying, "Yes, but are you sure that's the right question?" Questions, you see, interested us more than answers. We treasured doubt. We were all too familiar with certainty—for that's what oppressed us. To the New Left, the idea of "political correctness" would have been inconceivable, and inconceivably boring.

But now, again, certainty reigns. On the Left—or what passes for it—everything is known. There are no questions. The line is laid down. Thought is used to exclude, to label, to determine loyalty: Communism has failed but Stalinism is triumphant—the accused, by definition, is always guilty. As Doris Lessing has pointed out:

> The phrase Political Correctness was born as Communism was collapsing. I do not think this was chance… habits of mind have been absorbed without even knowing it. It troubles me that Political Correctness does not seem to know what its exemplars and predecessors are; it troubles me more that it may know and does not care.

Amongst militant liberals, the 'end of ideology' has returned, now under the guise of 'rights,' which is just another attempt to deny politics, in this case by carrying it into the 'neutral' realm of judicial decision. At both the emotional and intellectual levels, then, the openness of the New Left has been lost, abandoned.

And there is a very important consequence of this loss. Prepared to question every assumption in our own lives, we were therefore prepared to question the fundamental assumptions of society. That is, we believed in revolution. We had the will—the commitment—to be revolutionary.

You can laugh at that, given what was achieved, but the will, that commitment, was important in and of itself. We did not seek reform. We did not petition or lobby for this law or that, this programme or that, because we assumed that nothing could satisfy our wants but the overturning of all laws and all programmes. That status quo had nothing to offer. We sought revolution; politely, basic social change—or, as we sometimes put it, the transvaluation of values. We were not interested in the problems of blacks or poor people, in a sense even of peace, in a reformist sense; we believed, rather, that mobilizing people around those questions could lead to a wider mobilization—that one could move from those particular problems to the general problem.

Again there was a corollary to this, or an assumption. We assumed that what opposed us, society, was both coherent and comprehensible. And we tried to understand it. Like Woody Allen, we were always 'in analysis.'

By and large, naturally, we failed. For most of the history of the New Left we were so unsure of our understanding that we simply labelled what oppressed us as 'the system.' But our failure to understand that 'system,' though important, was not anywhere near as important as the assumption on which our attempt at understanding was predicated. Indeed, to believe that the world is coherent and comprehensible is to possess one of the most dangerous and empowering ideas of all. It even gave us power—for one thing, the power to have a strategy, to join with others. If the 'system' had a unity, then so did those who opposed it—black people and poor people and people dying in Vietnam had something in common with me; and I didn't feel guilty for them or because of them, I had the freedom to feel sorrow.

Now, of course, it's all different; here is one part of the New Left's legacy you won't find anywhere. There's no commitment to fundamental change or to much of anything else. All thought is fragmentary—and its intention, in any case, is not to understand the world but prove and advertise "political correctness." And the problem is not simply this lack of analysis—worse, no one seems to feel that lack. And at the level of political action this incoherence and fragmentation is perfectly reflected in a banal, divided, reformist politics—feminists, gays, ecologists—which is, with little difficulty, absorbed by 'the system.'

Lastly—at the heart of 'the system'—is the State. The New Left's attitude toward the State, to be historically correct, was ambiguous, but fundamentally reflected the anarchist tradition. This was true about the New Left's attitude toward power in general and you could see it reflected in our organizations, meetings, activities. When it came to running things, we had an expression, "Let's ad hoc it along." The idea of being part of an 'umbrella organization'—for women, Indians, or anything else—would have struck us as bizarre. We sought alternatives to conventional arrangements of power and you could see that reflected in the youth culture of which we were a part—the commune movement, for example. We had an 'authority problem' and were proud of it.

But again, you see, this is all changed. Deprived of the vision and connection to history a movement provides, the Left has lapsed happily into a purely social democratic politics. Half the political groups you see—elaborately organised, most of them—are funded by the State and their real business is engaging in a 'dialogue' with the bureaucracy. The question of agency has long since been settled by today's political formations—the State, the State: the State is the answer and has all the answers.

But now, you see, I've gotten where I wanted to go. Because what we are seeing today is a degradation of the State—a degradation, I believe, that will only accelerate in the future. And this rug will pull the rug out from under the political present we share—and from which we look back upon the New Left.

Most people will probably lament that, indeed struggle against it—against all the coming cuts. Because most people, I suspect, are dependents of the State in one way or another. Moreover, likely believe in it. Believe in the State as a kind of conscience, a controller, a regulator of capitalism. In addition, find it difficult to believe that this degradation is necessary—will try to see it as a thunderous question of ideology.

But I disagree, on all counts.

In my irrelevance, I see the State rather differently. It makes me think of cattle prods and missiles and jails—not pensions and SSHRC grants. No doubt anachronistically, I still see 'the system' as a system—and the State is integral to it; not tacked on; not a conscience, or a source of rationality: but the centre of direction and control. Moreover, I understand that the modern State, absorbing 40%-50% of total output was created by and for war. Expressions like 'the warfare State' are redundancies; war is merely what States do. As one of my favourite Canadian actors put it in a recent outrageous film, "The organizing principle for any society, Mr. Garrison, is for war. The authority of the State over its people resides in its war powers." So true. And the modern State has developed in this century precisely because this century has been a Hundred Years War. This war has had many different names, many different fronts, but its all been the same war, and the modern State was developed to fight it. This principle—war—and its expression—the State—have given the politics of the past century its peculiar unity. Alternating back and forth, Left and Right have really had the same goal. The Right has directed its attentions to building the economic and strategic base of the Warfare State, while the Left has put forward the claims of the Home Front, the comforts necessary to maintain social control. But it's been the same effort. The Warfare State and the Welfare State are one and the same, merely seen from different points of view.

Without doubt the war the modern State has fought has been a terrible war and this horror—and the moral judgements it elicits—tend to make us forget an essential point: our Hundred Years War has been entirely rational. It's been fought to determine who will control the Industrial Revolution, which is conceivably the greatest revolution in the history of man; who will control it, what political arrangements will govern it, how it will be spread throughout the world. To put this another way: the modern State has evolved to meet a particular historical need. But we usually forget this, or deny it. Children, growing up, always assume that their own circumstances apply to everyone else and my generation, growing up after the Second War, has assumed that the continuously expanding State has been both inevitable and eternal. But that's not true. The modern State has evolved at a particular historical moment to serve a particular historical purpose—and now that moment and that purpose are passing.

I hasten to say that I don't believe the war to be over; but its terms of engagement have now dramatically changed. To discuss those changes would carry me beyond the purpose of these remarks, but two points should be noted. First: capital, excluded for decades from Eastern Europe, Russia, Asiatic Russia, and the Chinese mainland is now free to move as it has never been before. And it will move, and it will move as it always moves—toward the highest rate of return. People like Jacques Delors who still believe that capital can be restricted in its movements dwell in a fantasy world—which is to say, the past. Second: labour will also become global. The State can no longer erect barriers against global labour competition. 'Communism' died in the Soviet Union and it has taken 'socialism' with it; economies dependent upon state sponsorship are ultimately doomed—despite the ravings of Pat Buchanan and Audrey Macglauchlin.

Of course, Karl Marx, if he was alive today, would view these developments with equanimity. He never believed for one second that peasants were going to bring about socialism, and the globalization of capital and labour would be, to him, an inevitable step as capitalism moved towards its apotheosis and final negation. But it's hard for us to be so sanguine. What are the consequences of these great changes for Canada? What will happen to the old 'developed' world? How can it compete, carrying the burden of the welfare and warfare machines on its back?

In the final analysis, nothing we can do will change the main trends; there's no doubt of our decline; it's their turn now. But as we struggle to deal with these new realities, it seems to me that much of this struggle will revolve round the State. In my own part of the world, Ontario, about 25% of manufacturing jobs have been lost in recent years while government employment has remained virtually constant. Can such a situation persist? I doubt it. But of course the State will fight to maintain its power and the overall battle will change the face of society. How? I don't know. But I fear the worst, and the worst will likely be fearful. Still, that's not my point here. Because, regardless of how frightful it is, some will chose to resist. And I suspect that such people, looking about for clues, will see a New Left rather different from the one we see today. They may truly be compelled to reinvent the world; the transvaluation of values we talked about may become a pressing necessity. And some of our notions—our attitudes, our stance, our particular attempt to think and feel through the world—may be a help. If it is, the New Left will have found its true heirs.

THEY LOVED THE REVOLUTION
SO VERY MUCH

Interview with Daniel Cohn-Bendit

The symbolic figure of the events of May. He has not changed. Jewish, German, red-haired. Lively, irreverent, wicked, a lover of life, unclassifiable, solemn, sincere. The animator of the Mouvement du 22 mars who became the deputy mayor of Frankfurt and later a Green Party member of the European Parliament.

The following three interviews were conducted in 1993.

Our Generation: How has it been for you since '68?
Daniel Cohn-Bendit: In mid-May, I had felt very alone. The movement was losing from irony. Those close to me were telling me that I had a historic responsibility. Too many were identifying with me, were expecting too much from me. With the general strike, the discourse of the revolutionary groupings was taking over. I was frightened. Something happened. I can say that my deportation saved me. In Germany, I regained a form of serenity. I fell in love. I rejoined a community where I could "live differently," like we used to say. Individually. In France, I would have been the object of desire of all of these groupings, like what happened to Geismar with the proletarian Left. They made a symbol of revolution, of continuity. All this nearly tipped the scales. It happened to Geismar; and so, you can imagine, for me…

OG: You remained in contact with the leaders of '68?
DCB: Yes. They came to see me, as I was forbidden to come until 1978. I was working in a kindergarten. They did not understand. I remember Krivine. He was flabbergasted. He asked me "But what are you doing taking care of kids? and the revolution?" He was serious and perplexed. I was rejuvenating myself. In fact, I am fundamentally anti–authoritarian. I have passed through the alternative movement, pacifism, also the Greens, and I have a son. Blond, not redheaded.

OG: How did you feel in Germany?
DCB: For a long time, I did not have a very clear image. And then, little by little, the content of what I had to say erased the bad reputation which stuck to me since '68. I

am not an ideologist. I even consider ideological debate evil. I developed theses on immigration, for example, against plans from the Left and from the right. Now, I feel I have the support of the media. The book I have just had published in Germany on that subject was very well received, except by the extreme Left and the extreme right. That's all right. Politics have a difficult time classifying me. I was in the pacifist movement. But at the moment of the Gulf War, I questioned myself a lot. In fact, I was against those which were for and against those which were against. We could say that towards the end I was a little bit for. In return, I am absolutely favourable to military intervention in Bosnia. If we leave the Serbs alone, we will find ourselves with Bosnians everywhere in Europe fighting in order to return to their country and we will be carrying a Palestinian problem. Finally, I am a spoilsport of going around in circles on complicated subjects.

OG: What kind of assistant mayor of Frankfurt are you?
DCB: I do not wish to be a professional politician. I refused to collect a salary. Only for expenses. I need 12,000 to 15,000 francs to live. No more, no less. I write articles, I publish books, I participate in television broadcasts on Arte. At my level, to be paid for participating in politics is unnecessary. It's funny, when I travel to other countries due to my job, I have the impression of being some sort of ambassador for Germany. I try to explain what is happening there. It's interesting, but I give myself two more years before moving on to something else. What? I don't know. To leave, perhaps. We'll see.

OG: Without the Mouvement du 22 mars, without Cohn-Bendit, would May '68 ever have happened?
DCB: How can one answer this question? It's yes and it's no. I don't believe that May '68 was absolutely written in History's agenda. A certain number of factors were needed for all that to be triggered, the 22nd of March, in Nanterre. Afterwards, things could still have evolved differently. In these situations, the personalities of individuals play a role, that's evident. Let's say there was a conglomerate of people as well as myself. The media made me into a star. Perhaps it was the new language which struck the journalists. But life is not composed of only. It is not by chance that all began in Nanterre and that first of all, France was going through a fundamental social crisis which made youth rebel and which pulled together all of the elements to prepare the deflagration.

OG: Humour and derision were your favourite weapons. Have you remained faithful to these?
DCB: Irony and speaking the truth are always stronger than the basic confrontation which no one, in general, understands. In '68, facing power, the police, we played at being the more wicked. It was the playful side of things. Facing physical violence is never a pleasure, except for those who like to do battle. Humour was my difference

from the other group leaders who believed themselves to be at the service of the revolution. They remained quite stuck for a long time. To proclaim that sexuality and politics are intimately linked, speaking of "Stalinist debauchery" in a meeting! Neither the ministers of the day nor those who believed themselves to be revolutionary leaders would ever have dared to loudly say things like that. Speaking the truth has its own certain value.

Interview with Alain Geismar

Grey-suited, nervous, in a hurry, the past Secretary General of SNE–Sup, leader of the Proletarian Left, was in the middle of an electoral campaign. Cabinet Director of the Secretary of State for Technical Education, he does not have time to speak of May '68. "Come back after the elections." He did, however, send the following text.

In '68, I was a young physician at the laboratory of the École normale supérieure; I had been working as a teaching assistant at the Paris faculty of sciences. Active against the Algerian war since 1958, committed to the PSA, as well as at the PSU, three or four years earlier I had left this organization to work for trade unionism and had been Secretary General of the SNE–Sup, the teachers' union of higher learning, for a year. Very marked by the war and by racism—what Jewish child would not have been?—my commitment situated itself squarely in the development of "Never again!" I found myself with both feet firmly planted on the Left and I had participated, with good intentions, in the Mitterrand campaign of 1965. I sensed in my generation and the one following it, the outcome of the post-war baby-boom, generous aspirations shackled by the heavy functioning of political and union organizations, themselves trapped in the jolts of the cold war.

'68 ravished me, in the two senses of the term. I willingly allowed myself to be carried away by a movement which I had been accompanying and which I did not wish to leave, even as it diminished. I hoped with all my might that the generosity of the movement, the renewal of social and human relations which it prefigured would penetrate society and that social, cultural and political routines would not resurface completely. The principal effects of '68 were cultural and social, and they transformed personal behaviour well; it is a banality to say this, but we must not forget either that it was at this very moment that the PCF and CGT monopoly of control over working society was run down in lasting fashion. An open Left, not dominated by the PC, became possible, even if we did not understand all the consequences until much later. Power, in '68, was that of maintaining with the CRS the Smig at 600 francs per month in a society in full enrichment. Power, in 1993, is that of compensating to the weakest for the misfortune of unemployment.

In '68, French preoccupations shifted: we brought back that which since always was at the margins of society (women, youth, the elderly, immigrants) to the center of people's and political actions' preoccupations. In no way do I regret this.

The blocking of French society in '68 was internal to our society; much of the current blocking comes from external constraints, from the international crisis, even if this crisis' toughness creates tensing and egoistic or corporate reflexes.

Society is no longer the same, the bipolar cleaving of the world is obsolete, the Left is no longer frozen by the PC and the conservation of the planet is no longer thought of in terms of nuclear war but those of ecology: simplistic comparisons do not make sense.

Interview with Jacques Sauvageot

He abruptly appeared on the scene of May at the head of the student union, UNEF. In 1971, he vanished in the same manner. Today, he is the director of the school of fine arts in Rennes. A long silence is ruptured.

Our Generation: You have not spoken of May '68 for a long time. Why?
Jacques Sauvageot: For all of our generation, it was quite difficult to have our lives behind us. I suffered from this label. I had been considered for the image I had, not for what I was. Although, I had finished my studies in History, Civil Law and Art History, I had trouble finding a job. I became a labourer in order to earn a living. I presented myself to the Nantes municipality, to remove change from municipal parking meters. And then the personnel director proposed a Fine Arts professorial position. Chance.

OG: However, this generation rather succeeded...
JS: It's logical. These people completed their studies: they were called upon to become executives...But, on the political level, there are very few. Except for positions of sweepers. What does Weber do apart from sweeping for Fabius? He must find that the sun's shadow, quite pale for that matter, suffices him. Yes, it blocked us from making political careers. But what we believed! Had I accepted entering the Socialist Party in 1971...I cut myself off from all that. I participated in the free radio movement. And then, I attempted the Democracy 2000 adventure with those who had passed through the Socialist Party. We were to gather together all manner of people in order to completely rethink French political structures. I had succeeded in putting across the idea of total autonomy insofar as socialists are concerned. Not for long. I quickly understood it was manipulation of young party wolves. Their problem is they refuse contradiction. They got rid of me. If a new discussion space opens

up, I begin right away. In the meanwhile, I do like everyone else, I have my good works. And I try not to be too mean in my job. I am a part of those people who have reinvested in their work the creativity which they had wished to see develop itself. I regret nothing. And perhaps we still have the future ahead of us.

OG: Do you still believe in the reality of the ideas of May?

JS: Of course, we are fully in them. What was it that the movement of May was saying? It tolled the knell of real socialism. It sided against authority. And it also said life was not just growth rates. These are exactly today's problems. From this point of view, that movement was quite premonitory. The difference is that in May '68 we ran around with baskets wanting to transform the world. We now have the impression that people remain in their ruts saying: "Most of all, it cannot move." They are afraid because change is in the process of taking place. When it was forecast that the Eastern bureaucracies would disappear, it seemed impossible. It happened for the given reasons: these systems had a stranglehold on liberty, they were inefficient. What was also being said was that liberalism led to catastrophe. We are truly aware of this since quite recently. A quarter of the population is rejected from all. It is necessary to regain a little bit of liberty, equality and fraternity. A bit of generosity. The only question: how to formulate it in political terms?

OG: What remains of the gains of '68?

JS: A bit of the humanitarian, last bastion of generosity. Kouchner, for that matter, does not manage so badly, for a guy who "plays the minister." But as for myself, I am slightly Braudelian. I think that societies evolve in long cycles. May '68 played its role. It crystallized some problems, renewed some myths. But in other countries also, which did not live through this, mores did evolve. I think that the most important was the reactivation of certain ideals. On the level of mores, to the contrary, it can be demonstrated that nothing at all remains. Are you sure that women have really advanced?

OG: Can the idea of the Left be reconstituted?

JS: But it is indispensable! And historic. The socialist ideal has always existed. People have always a need to believe that their situation could improve and that a man was worth another man. We cannot live in this state of despair, with the idea that solely winners win. It is insupportable. We will have to regain the bases of the collective, the idea of '68 of "living differently." To ask again the great cultural and ethical questions. Where is man situated? What is he doing, where is he going, why, with whom? I am convinced that a great philosophical debate will be reborn. It is in the very interest of the actual crisis.

TWO UPRISINGS
One A Protest The Other A Social Revolution

by Jacques Martin

By late April 1968 at Columbia University in New York it was clear that the issues plaguing the university were not going away. The university continued to insist on its right to build a gym on the land occupied by apartment buildings housing hundreds of Harlem's residents, and hundred of students. Neighbourhood residents continued to oppose these development plans. In addition, Columbia University's ties to the U.S. defence establishment via its sponsorship of a branch of the Institute for Defense Analysis [IDA] was angering more and more students and younger faculty as the bloodshed in Vietnam increased in volume and intensity. The IDA's rumored involvement in the death of Che Guevara didn't help matters either.

In the minds of the student radicals these issues were not only connected, they shared the same roots. Consequently, those who carried out those policies were equally culpable. That included Grayson Kirk, president of Columbia, just as much as it included President Lyndon Johnson and U.S. General Westmoreland. That left those who opposed the university's desire to build a gym on land bought out from underneath those who lived on it and its involvement in the war in Vietnam only one route of opposition.

On April 23,1968, after a march opposing the gym construction, Columbia students and neighbourhood residents headed back to the Columbia campus. Enroute, a group of black and white students headed towards Hamilton Hall and took it over by occupying the building. Early the next morning another group of students, including white students asked to leave Hamilton Hall after a consensus

Jacques Martin teaches secondary school in Paris. He is a political activist in the ecology movement in both France and the USA. He was at Columbia University in 1967-1968, but returned to Paris to join the general strike.

reached by the students inside the building, took over the Low Library building which housed many of the school administration's offices. By the end of the following day, a total of six Columbia buildings had been occupied by students and their sympathizers. These occupations continued for several days and nights. Meanwhile, rallies in support of the takeovers took place daily. One rally even featured an impromptu concert by the 'Grateful Dead' who were in town for a series of shows in Manhattan. These rallies were attacked occasionally by right-wing students and professors egged on by plainclothes cops. But those scuffles were nothing compared to the police raid and attack which occurred the night of April 29.

It was this attack which convinced much of the student population who had been previously uncommitted to support the radicals in their demands which had been increased to include a demand that all disciplinary and legal charges be dropped on those involved in the occupations. The radicals' statement that the university would call in the police and beat its own students before it gave up its ties to the military or changed its plans to construct a gym were validated. A strike was called and classes became an empty joke.

Meanwhile echoes started to resound about an insurrection in France, What Columbia students knew was that a demonstration against curfew rules in university dormitories on the Nanterre university campus spread quickly and widely. At Columbia [a microcosm of the U.S.] the corporate powers were more entrenched. Students still protested, only now it is just to get recognition for the degraded status of students and youth in this kind of society. In 1966 at Columbia students took over the Low Library to protest the university's policies which favoured the majority wealthy white student population while at the same time as students and workers in France took to the streets to maintain decent wages for young people. Two years later in both places the university's role in the corporate State was called into question. Daniel Cohn-Bendit summed it up by saying, "...the present educational structure ensures that the majority of working-class children are barred not only from the bourgeois society we are trying to overthrow, but also from the intellectual means to see through it."

In France however, the momentum from the Nanterre campus spread to involve 12 million workers on strike, 122 factories occupied, and thousands of students fighting against a moribund system in which they found themselves. In the late sixties in France real wages were on the rise, but large sections of the working class were still suffering from low pay. This was despite foreign trade having tripled. Unemployment was at half a million, in a period which was considered a post-war boom. Trade union membership had dropped to around 3 million, as opposed to 7 million in 1945. Not many victories had been won in the preceding years. Michelin boasted that they had talked to trade unions only three times in thirty years. So how did everything spread so quickly in France of 1968 when Columbia remained a militant but limited protest?

Nanterre was a university outside Paris. It was a soulless campus built to cater to the increased influx of students. The place was unlike the throbbing cultural live wire of the famous Latin Quarter or Left Bank in Paris. On March 22 1968 eight students broke into the Dean's office as a way to protest the recent arrest of six students of the National Vietnam Committee. Among these was a sociology student, Daniel Cohn-Bendit. He had been part of a group who organised a strike of 10,000 to 12,000 students in November of 1967 as a protest against overcrowding.

In the preceding 10 years the student population had raised from 170,000 to 514,000. Although the State had provided some funding this did not equal the huge influx of students it had asked the universities and colleges to admit. The total area covered by the university premises had doubled since 1962 but the student numbers had almost tripled. Facilities were desperately inadequate and overcrowding was a serious issue.

Six days after the occupation of the Dean's office the police were called in and the campus was surrounded. 500 students inside the campus divided into discussions groups. Sociology students began to boycott their exams and a pamphlet was produced entitled 'Why do we need sociologists?.' The students called for a lecture hall to be permanently made available for political discussions. The lecturers began to split, some favoured the student demands. The university did provide a lecture room, but by the April 2nd a meeting of 1200 students was held in one of the main lecture halls.

March 22nd Movement

After the Easter break agitation was more rampant. On March 22nd a meeting was held in lecture hall B1. It was attended by 1500 students and the resulting manifesto called for 'Outright rejection of the Capitalist Technocratic University' and following this by a call for solidarity with the working class. It was clear that the March 22nd Movement [which had come together as a semi-formal alliance of anti-authoritarian socialist students] was winning the battle of ideas in the campus amongst their fellow students.

The university decided to discipline eight of the students involved, including Cohn-Bendit. They were called upon to appear before the disciplinary committee of the Sorbonne on May 3rd. Four lecturers volunteered to defend them.

The education strike had not interested the Minister of Education. There were major industrial strikes the preceding year at Rhodiaceta and Saviem. In Rhodiaceta [a synthetic fibers factory in Lyons] a strike took place involving 14,000 workers over 23 days. Management went on to sack 92 militants at the end of the year and had also resorted to lock-outs. In June 1967 Peugeot called in the riot police during a dispute and two workers were killed.

From March to May 1968 there were a total of eighty cases of industrial action at the Renault Billancourt car plant.

Red & Black Flags drape the Arc De Triomphe

On Friday May 3rd a few students gathered in the front square of the Sorbonne. The students were from Nanterre and they were joined by activists from the Sorbonne itself. The 'Nanterre Eight' were about to face charges on the following Monday. The eight and some of their colleagues from their campus were meeting student activists from the Sorbonne to discuss the impending Monday.

The crowd began to swell and the university authorities panicked. By 4 pm the Sorbonne was surrounded by regular police plus the CRS riot police. Students were being arrested by the CRS, on the basis that they were spotted wearing motorcycle helmets. News spread rapidly and students came from all over the city. Fighting began to free those who had already been arrested. Such was this battle between students and police that the university closed.

This was only the second time in 700 years that the Sorbonne had to close, the other time being in 1940 when the Nazi armed forces took over Paris. The National Union of Students [UNEF] and the Lecturers' Union [SNESup] immediately called a strike and issued the following demands: re-open the Sorbonne; withdraw the police; release those arrested. These unions were joined by the March 22nd Movement. The original discontent had arisen from overcrowding but it now began to tale on a larger perspective.

On Monday, May 6th the 'Nanterre 8' passed through a police cordon singing the 'Internationale.' They were on their way to appear before the University Discipline Committee. The students decided to march through Paris. On their return to the Latin Quartier they were savagely attacked by the police on Rue St.Jacques. The students tore up paving stones and overturned cars to form barricades. Police pumped tear gas into the air and called for reinforcements. The Boulevard St.Germain became a bloody battleground with the official figures at the end of the day reading: 422 arrested and 345 policemen injured. This day was to go into the annals of '68 as 'Bloody Monday.'

A long march followed on the Tuesday and by outmaneuvering the police Red & Black Flags [red for revolution and black for anarchism] were draped from the famous Arc De Triomphe and the 'Internationale' echoed around the streets. The week continued on in similar fashion and the streets were alive with crowds and talk of politics. By Wednesday public opinion was shifting,

The middle classes were appalled by the brutality dished out to the students by the police and large sections of the working class were inspired by the students' stomach for a fight against the State. On May 10th, Friday, 30,000 students, including high school students, had gathered around the Place Defret-Rochercau. They marched towards the Sorbonne along the Boulevard St.Germain. All roads leading off the boulevard were blocked by police armed for conflict.

Fifty barricades were erected by the demonstrators in preparation for an attack by the police. Reporter Jean Jacques Lebel wrote that by 1 a.m. 'Literally thousands helped build barricades...women, workers, bystanders, and people in pyjamas, human chains to carry rocks, wood, iron...Our barricade is double: one three foot high row of cobblestones, an empty space of twenty yards, then a nine foot high pile of wood,cars,metal posts, dustbins. Our weapons are stones, metal, etc., found in the street,' reported one eye-witness.

Radio reporters said that as many as sixty barricades were erected in different streets. France stayed up to listen to reports on Europe One and Radio Luxebourg.The government had yielded on two of the three demands but would not release those arrested. There was to be no 'Liberez nos comrades!'

The barricades were attacked by the police. They used tear gas and CS grenades. Students and other demonstrators used handkerchiefs soaked in lemon juice and baking soda to protect themselves from the nauseous gasses. Fighting continued throughout the night. Houses were stormed by the police and people were dragged and clubbed as they were thrown into vans. The police, and in particular the CRS,were most brutal in their treatment of the demonstrators.

There were reports of pregnant women being beaten. Young men were stripped and some had their genitals beaten until their flesh was in ribbons. At the end of this battle of the streets there were 367 people injured, and 460 arrested. On May 11th, Saturday morning troop carriers were brought in to clear the barricades and they were booed and hissed as they drove down the Boulevard St.Germain.

On May 13th, Monday the students were released from prison but the spark had already started the forest fire. The trade unions called a one-day strike and a march was organised in Paris for the same day. Over 200,000 people [a conservative estimate] turned up for the march shouting 'De Gaulle Assassin.' The leader of the government was now singled out as an enemy by the people. After the march there was a call for the crowd to disperse and many did, but a large group of students decided that they would occupy the Sorbonne.

The Old Left Up to Old Tricks

The French Communist Party [PCF] had condemned the Nanterre rebels from the start. The PCF future General Secretary, George Marchais, published an article entitled 'False revolutionaries to be unmasked.' In this same article he claimed the March 22nd Movement was 'mostly sons of the grand bourgeoisie, contemptuous towards the students of working class origin' and predicted that they would 'quickly snuff out their revolutionary flames to be directors in their Papa's business....'

But by May8th when the PCF leadership saw the size of the movement they changed their tune and attempted to take control of the uprising. They saw that the example of the students was now being followed in the workplaces. They thought it better to be seen encouraging action than letting the situation escape their control totally.

Once again the Communists had misjudged the situation. The CGT [the Communist dominated trade union] leadership also started to support workplace action, though only after workers had already taken the lead. Louis Aragon, France's most famous Communist writer, was sent to address a meeting at the Odeon. Those of the March 22nd Movement who were present jeered and heckled him throughout with satirical cries of 'Long Live Stalin, father of all the people.' One member of the PCF politburo, Roger Garudy, embraced the students' doctrine of economic self-management, autonomous councils and decentralization. Along with extending solidarity with the aims of the students he also applauded the event of the 'Prague Spring.' He was soon expelled from the PCF.

Mostly, the PCF persisted in classifying the student movement as 'an entire ultra-left, petty-bourgeois cocktail of Bakunin,Trotskyism and plain adventurism....' Around this time an anonymous article was published in the party paper 'L'Humanite.' Its author claimed that the Minister of Youth had 'contacts' with Cohn-Bendit and that money was granted to the March 22nd Movement. This accusation was a complete fabrication and the height of some very strange imagination. This, of course, was neither the first nor the last time the Communists resorted to such slander.

Meanwhile the Sorbonne became transformed overnight as posters of Marx, Bakunin, Lenin, and Mao decorated the old pillars surrounding the front square. Red&Black flags hung alongside the Vietcong flag. Trotsky, Castro and Che pictures were plastered on walls alongside slogans such as 'Everything is Possible,' 'Power to the Imagination,' and 'It is Forbidden to Forbid.' This picture of the Sorbonne gives a good indication of the mish-mash of contradictory ideologies that encompassed the student movement.

A fifteen person occupation committee was elected on May 14th and its mandate was limited to 24 hours. The central amphitheatre was pulsating day and night with political debate. The examination system was condemned as 'being the rite of initiation into the capitalist society.' The March 22nd Movement wanted to 'eradicate the distinction between workers and managers rather than turn more workers' sons into managers.'

The Ecole des Beaux Arts [Fine Arts School] was occupied on May14th. There were meetings every morning at which themes were chosen. Then posters would be produced by silk screening. It was most ironic that these posters became immediately collectors' items and were soon to be found framed in the homes of the well-to-do. The posters were covered with such slogans as 'Mankind will not live free until the last capitalist has been hanged with the entrails of the last bureaucrat." "The general will against the will of the general." Commodities are the opium of the people.' Paris was plastered with such posters.

The political atmosphere of the time led to occupations by radical doctors, architects, and writers. Even the Cannes film festival was disrupted in 1968 when celebrated film makers Jean-Luc Goddard and Francois Truffaut seized the festival hall in support of the national strike movement.

General Strike sweeps France

On May 14th, the workers of the big aeronautics Sud Aviation near Nantes occupied their factory. Then the big Renault auto company's plants at Cleon, Flins, Le Mans and Boulogne Billancourt all went on strike. Young workers at Cleon refused to leave the factory at the end of their shift and locked the manager into his office. The union leadership were stumbling behind the workers. At places like Sud-Aviation the decision to go on indefinite strike was taken by the workers without consulting the union officials.

On May 16th a few thousand students marched to Boulogne Billancourt where 35,000 workers were on strike. The CGT officials locked the factory gates to discourage communication. But workers got up on the roof of the factory and shouted greetings and discussions took place through the iron railings. Solidarity was there and it could not be suppressed by bureaucrats chaining and locking gates.

Industrial Normandy, Paris and Lyons closed down virtually on mass. On May 18th coal production stopped and public transportation in Paris halted. The National Railways were next to go out on strike. Gas and electricity workers took over control of their workplaces but continued domestic supplies. Red flags hung from the ship-yards at St.Nazaire which employed 10,000 workers. The weekend of May 19th saw two million people on strike and 122 factories were reported occupied.

Money withdrawals from banks were limited to 500 francs as the possibility of a Bank of France strike panicked some people. Gasoline supplies soon dried up as drivers stocked up. By May 20th, Monday no cross-channel ferries were in opera-tion and tourists queued for evacuation buses to Brussels, Geneva, and Barcelona.

The Citroen automobile factory which employed a lot of immigrant labour from Portugal, North Africa and Yugoslavia was still in operation. On May 20th as the morning shift headed into work at 6 a.m. they were greeted with the sight of a student picket. As the young foreign workers were puzzling over the students' leaf-lets and whether or not to go into work along came a march of colleagues from a nearby factory. Citroen went on strike.

The textile industry and the big department stores of Paris joined the snow-balling general strike on May 21st, Tuesday. The air traffic controllers at Orly air-port and ORTF French television had already voted to strike the previous Friday. On May 20th ORTF staff issued the following demands: forty hour week; lower re-tirement age; abrogation of the anti-strike laws of 1963; minimum wage of 1000 francs a week; repeal of the government's involvement in the ORTF.

Teachers were on strike as of May 22nd, although many attended school in order to keep in contact with school students as the unions requested.

Within a couple of weeks of the general strike being called, more than ten mil-lion workers were out on strike. As one person put it, 'On Wednesday the under-takers went on strike. Now is not a good time to die.'

Workers displayed a great ability to lead by example. The gas and electricity workers joined the strike but maintained supplies apart from a few brief power cuts. Food supplies reached Paris as normal after initial disruptions. The postal workers agreed to deliver urgent telegrams. Print workers said they did not wish to leave a monopoly of media coverage to TV and radio and agreed to print newspa-pers as long as the press 'carries out with objectivity the role of providing informa-tion which is its duty.' In some cases print-workers insisted on changes in headlines or articles before they would print the paper. This happened mostly with the right-wing newspapers like *Le Figaro* and *La Nation*.

In some factories workers continued or altered production to suit their needs. In the CSF factory in Brest the workers produced walkie-talkies which they considered important to both strikers and demonstrators alike. At the Wonder Batteries factory in Saint-Ouen the strike committee disapproved of the reformist line of the CGT and decided to barricade themselves in rather than talk to union bureaucrats.

The Commune of Nantes

In Nantes, the whole 1968 movement reached its apex. For a week in May the city as a whole and its surrounding area was controlled by the workers, themselves. The old guardians of power and authority looked on helplessly as workers took control of their own lives and the city directly. On May 24th road blocks were set up around the city as farmers made a protest of solidarity with the workers and students. The transport workers took over the road blocks and they controlled all incoming traffic. Gasoline supplies were controlled, with no petrol tankers being allowed into the city without the workers' permission. The only functioning gasoline pump was reserved for doctors. By circumventing the middle man, the workers and farmers made it possible to reduced the cost of food. Milk went down 50 centimes as opposed to 80 previously. Potatoes dropped to 48 centimes per kilo.

To make sure these price cuts were passed on, shops had to display stickers provided by the strike committee saying: 'This shop is authorized to open. Its prices are under permanent supervision by the unions.' Teachers and students organised nurseries so that strikers' children were cared for while the schools were closed. Women played a very active role in Nantes organizing, not only as strikers but also playing a vital role on committees dealing with distribution of, among other things, food.

This all too brief week in Nantes is an example of the working class taking over control of a city and area and running it in a socialist manner, even in very difficult circumstances. We can see that the society created in many ways was an improvement on the one Nantes unfortunately slipped back into after the general strike of 1968 ended.

De Gaulle, now fearing for the survival of his government and slowly watching his power disappear, addressed the country on television on Mat 24th. He spoke of 'a more extensive participation of everyone in the conduct and the results of the activities which directly concern them.' Note rhetoric that comes from a New Left notebook. De Gaulle asked the people, through a referendum, for a 'mandate for renewal and adaption.'

On the same day the March 22nd Movement organised a demonstration of 30,000 who marched towards the Place de la Bastille. The police had the Ministries all protected, using the usual devices of tear gas and batons, but the Stock Exchange building was left unprotected. This was the time to act and a number of demonstrators armed with axe handles, wooden clubs and iron bars and set fire to it.

It was at this stage that some left groups lost their nerve and sense of direction. The Trotskyite JCR turned people back into the Latin Quartier. Other groups such as UNEF and the Parti Socialiste Unife blocked the taking of the Ministries of Finance and Justice. Cohn-Bendit said of this situation 'As for us, [March 22nd Movement] we failed to realize how easy it would have been to sweep all these nobodies away...It is now clear that if, on May 25, Paris had awakened to find that most Ministries occupied, Gaullism would have caved in at once....' Cohen-Bendit was forced into exile later that very night. The students of the March 22nd Movement would not have caused the collapse of Gaullism with this kind of occupation, but it would have raised the consciousness of many of the young militant workers who were inspired by the fighting spirit shown by the students, that, yes, even the State offices could be occupied and held, not only factories. The government could have been ground to a halt, with an ensuing debate on what was a desirable alternative. The students' struggle, although confused and diverse, encompassing too many competing ideologies, had been an inspiration to all. The social dynamite was there and the student uprising was the fuse.

The occupation of the Ministries would have been one step further along the line toward a social revolution. Of the 12 million workers now on strike only 3 million were previously involved in trade unions. The general strike which had paralyzed the country saw workers' demands far surpass those issued by the union leaders. Expectations had been raised by the wave of agitation that was sweeping across the country. The occupation of the Ministries could have brought awareness to people that what could be won here was more than economic agreements with the bosses. The move would have brought the workers closer to the realization that what was at stake here was how the whole system was run and just how fragile it was, and therefore tinkering with it was not enough. In every uprising of the sort witnessed in 1968 there is a need for the libertarian left especially to win the battle of ideas and to fuse those ideas into clear actions so that people are aware of what can be gained, what victories are possible. Had the student movement occupied the government buildings, such an action would have taken a step in this direction and shown the way forward. The workers would have been equally inspired by the occupation of the offices of the State, and would have begun to think about demands beyond pay rises from the bosses.

In the vacuum on May 27th, Monday the government quickly announced a guaranteed increase of 35% in the industrial minimum wage and an all-round wage increase of 10%. The leaders of the CGT organised a march of 500,000 workers through the streets of Paris two days later. Paris was covered by posters calling for a 'Government of the People.' Unfortunately the majority still thought in terms of changing their rules rather than taking control for themselves.

De Gaulle and his entourage had been so scared by the possibility of revolution that he flew to a military airfield at Saint-Dizier and talked with his top generals, making sure that he could rely on them if he needed the army's help to maintain his power. On May 30th, he once again appeared on French television abandoning this plans for the referendum and promising elections within 40 days.

De Gaulle in typical fashion promised tougher measures if, as he put it, 'the whole French people were gagged or prevented from leading a normal existence, by those elements [Reds and Anarchists] that are being used to prevent students from studying, the workers from working....' Following De Gaulle's address the CRS were sent to disperse the remaining pickets from workplaces.

By June 5th, most of the strikes were over and an air of what passes for normality within capitalism had swept back over France. Any strikes which continued after this date were crushed in a military style operation using armored vehicles and guns. In isolation those pockets of militancy stood no chance.

Snatching Defeat from the Jaws of Victory

All street demonstrations were banned and once again the PCF sought respectability by using its influence to destroy what was left of the action committees. By the end of June the universities were regained and the Red & Black flags were torn down in front of the Sorbonne. In this climate of defeat and demoralization people turned back to the certainties of the political center. In the elections the Gaullists captured 60% of the vote. Their grip on the reins of power was reinforced.

In 1968, the same political and economic system as seen in France, existed in most countries in Western Europe. Yet, during the events of May that system in France was in total turmoil and De Gaulle had foreseen that he might have had to use the army to crush the movement of the people. The streets of France could have flown with blood as they did in Chile five years later.

Cohn-Bendit and the March 22nd Movement aspired to a classless society based of self-management of the economy where the division between order-givers and order-takers disappeared. But obviously this vision of a future society was not shared by others on the Left and the part they played was to place obstacles in the way rather than to overcome the ones that already existed.

Where the power of the State had been broken, the working class led by example, as in Nantes where they showed themselves capable of taking over and managing their city directly instead of through representatives or intermediaries. The most active strikers were more progressive and far sighted than their union bureaucrats. Workers showed that there was more to attain than simple demands.

The Legacy and Lessons

Why did France 1968 ultimately fail to have a social revolution? There was no coordination of ideas or tactics when events reached a crucial stage. There was no ongoing multi-sectorial forum of debate for both students and workers, no venue where delegates from various workplaces and institutions could commonly recognize as the place where questions of today and tomorrow could be discussed, openly and democraticly, where pro tem coordinating bodies could be elected, revocable at all times, where the future society could be debated. The influential, well funded PCF believed that their power would increase in the elections and so were hostile to all movements outside of its control. The small PSU was not a major player. The trade union leadership helped pacify the workers by restricting the focus of workers to 'bread and butter' demands and away from the wider political issues.

Many people had fine aspirations but not much idea of how to achieve those aims. Too many things were left to chance and the whole movement seemed to stumble on from day to day like a blind person desperately trying to find the light of freedom that must exist at the end of the tunnel. What lessons can we learn from the event of the general strike of 1968? We saw an advanced capitalist society being brought to the edge of revolution, questioning the whole system.

The general strike spread very rapidly as the working class, fused by the energy and bravado of the students, raised demands that could not be realized within the confines of the existing system. The general strike displayed with beautiful clarity the potential power that lies in the hands of the working class. However, the situation needed more co-ordination and organization. What does this mean ?

No one anticipated the 1968 general strike in France. No one prepared for such a general strike, including none of the French revolutionaries. Therefore there was no general understanding among the French Left in part and certainly in the whole, as to what to do concretely under revolutionary circumstances. Once the beginning unfolded, there was no educational campaign undertaken that extended a libertarian sensibility on what can happen, and how, building on those instincts that were manifested among both students and workers. There was no general call to organise the general strike along libertarian lines: setting up neighbourhood or community councils in various boroughs in various cities that could be federated, where debates and decisions could be taken among people who lived and worked in the boroughs, sending mandated and revocable delegates to other meetings to assure coordination; setting up workers councils in any workplace where debates and decisions could be taken with the same structure and intention as the community councils, plus a federation within or without the existing unions to jointly discuss starting up the economy on the basis of self-management and start production for needs rather than profit; and finally there was no attempt to constitute a general assembly of all these thus constituting a Commune in a more advanced form from that of 1871. An international call could then have been sent out for solidarity.

The Columbia University uprising was both a student and community-rooted action. Yet it did not spread to the rest of New York City. The students did not or could not reach out to the other universities, colleges and schools for solidarity. The blacks of the residential buildings which were threatened by the proposed Columbia new gym did not or could not reach out to the rest of Harlem and beyond in New York inviting and getting the solidarity of other blacks and in general other New Yorkers. In a word, the outreach was not there. The connection with the trade unions or working people was not made. The Columbia action, as important as it was in itself and taking place in a city the importance of New York, the seat of finance capital, became one of several radical actions in the U.S. in 1968. It is a case study of an American protest which did not go further. The new left slogan 'From Protest to Resistance' did not apply here. The resulting frustration among the young militants lead some of them into the Weather Underground and terrorism.

FUGITIVE RADICALS

And Then There Were Two

The imprisonment in Boston of sixties' radical and bank robber **Katherine Ann Power** left only two major anti-Vietman War players still at large.

On the Run

Leo Burt: Allegedly one of four people involved in the 1970 bombing of the Army Math Research Building at the University of Wisconsin that killed one and injured several people.

Joanne Chesimard: Former head of the Black Liberation Army, convicted of killing a New Jersey state trooper. He escaped from prison in 1979.

In From the Cold

William Ayers: Surrendered and pleaded guilty in 1980 to possession of explosives. He served no time. Today he teaches early-childhood development at the University of Illinois.

Silas Bissell: Has legally changed his name to Terry Jackson. Was arrested in 1987 in Eugene, Ore., on a federal charge of attempting to bomb a University of Washington ROTC building in 1970. Served 17 months in a federal halfway house.

Judith Bissell: Convicted in 1979 of possession of explosives, several years after she separated from her husband. Released from prison in 1982.

Katherine Boudin: Convicted in a 1981 holdup of a Brink's truck in Nanuet, N.Y., during which two policemen and a Brink's guard were killed. At time of her arrest she was a fugitive wanted for questioning about a 1970 explosion in New York City. Serving 20 years to life.

Bernardine Dohrn: Surrendered in 1980 and pleaded guilty to aggravated battery and bail-jumping charges stemming from anti-war protests in 1969. Served seven months in prison for refusing to co-operate with grand jury investigating the Brink's robbery. Now works with law-oriented organizations in Chicago.

Judith Clark: Serving 75 years to life for the Brink's robbery.

David Gilbert: Serving 75 years to life for the Brink's robbery. Married Katherine Boudin at his sentencing.

Susan Saxe: Arrested in 1975 for the 1970 bank robbery in Boston. Served six years and was released.

Cathlyn Wilkerson: Turned herself in and pleaded guilty in 1980 to possession of dynamite in connection with a fatal explosion at a "bomb factory" in New York City. Got a one-to-three- year term in prison,

David S. Fine: Arrested in 1976 for the University of Wisconsin bombing. Served three years of a seven-year term. Now works in a law office in Portland, Ore.

Brothers **Dwight** and **Karleton Armstrong:** Arrested in the same bombing. Karleton was arrested in 1972 in Canada, served eight years of a 14-year prison sentence and was paroled. Dwight was arrested in Toronto in 1976, served three years of a seven-year prison term and was paroled.

THE DEATH OF SDS

by Mark Rudd

It's probably not a great idea to pursue an hallucination all the way to the end. Most likely the results will not be what you thought they would be, but 35 years ago we weren't playing the probabilities.

There was this beautiful hallucination back then, roughly 1967-1970, that the world was about to be remade; that this monster of militarism and injustice was about to fall; that young people in this country would join with people all over the world to end imperialism and make a new world. I get shivers just writing these words.

Students for a Democratic Society had been growing almost effortlessly since 1965 when the U.S. attacked Vietnam with ground troops. By 1968 there were over 300 autonomous chapters on college campuses, high schools, and even post-college; the number of active members may have been more than 100,000 (though dues-paying national membership was much smaller). Our official uniting slogan was the ambiguous "Let the people decide!" but most SDS'ers considered the organization "radical" in the sense that we wanted to get to the roots of the problems of war, racism, poverty, that is, we opposed capitalism. Our 1962 founding document, "Port Huron Statement," was radical for its time in rejecting the cold-war and the anti-communism which propped it up, though its solution was to create a left-wing of the Democratic Party. By 1968 most SDS'ers had

Mark Rudd was a leader of the 1968 Columbia University strike against the Vietnam War and racism, the last National Secretary of Students for a Democratic Society, the largest radical student organization in the USA in 1969, and founder of the Weather Underground, a revolutionary guerrilla group in the seventies. He was hunted by the F.B.I. for seven and a half years, until 1977. He is currently an activist and teacher in Albuquerque, New Mexico.

rejected party politics and the liberals that gave us the war and perpetuated racism in this country. We were moving to the left "from reform to revolution."

The amazing, dizzying events of 1968 pushed us even further: in Vietnam the Tet Offensive of January-March showed that the U.S. government and military had been lying about winning the war and turned a majority of Americans against it; the assassination of Martin Luther King in early April gave rise to riots in dozens of cities and the belief that the Black Power movement was ascendant; the occupation and strike against the war and racism at Columbia University (which I participated in) provided a model for further student militancy ("Create two, three, many Columbias!" was a slogan); the student-worker general strike in France known as "May-June" almost toppled the conservative deGaulle government; the assassination of Robert Kennedy, a potential anti-war candidate, followed by the Democratic National Convention in Chicago in which the police rioted against anti-war demonstrators as the Democrats nominated a pro-war candidate ("The whole world is watching!"); the massacre of students in Mexico protesting the Olympics, the invasion of Czechoslovakia by the USSR. All of this left us breathless and believing that massive change was imminent. Our movement was growing. (For more on the impact of 1968, check out Mark Kurlansky's book, 1968: the Year that Rocked the World.)

But where to go? How to get there? Could students make a revolution alone? Was there some useful theory of revolution? How would revolution happen? We needed ideas and a plan, but even more, we needed a framework for thinking about the world and social change, we needed an ideology.

Marxism had already given us what appeared to be an extremely useful analysis of the war, racism, and the class structure in this country. The war was part of the grand scheme for global domination that the U.S. had been implementing since the end of World War II. U.S. imperialism needed labor and markets and natural resources (such as oil) and military bases with which to impose its rule. Opposing it were national liberation movements such as Vietnam's and Cuba's which were strong enough to not only challenge U.S. control but also to actually achieve liberation and revolution. We noted, of course, that these victorious revolutions were led by Marxist-Leninists. The Cubans and the Vietnamese, whom we met, were among the coolest people in the world, we thought.

Adding to the attraction of Marxism was the fact that our professors despised it: they were mostly liberals who had no explanation for the war other than as a well-intentioned mistake on the part of liberal Democrats such as Kennedy and

Johnson. They were part of the structure of class privilege which universities were created to uphold! Screw them!

Once deciding to head down the Marxist road, things started getting dicey. We were faced with a further question: which brand of Marxism should we adopt? It was as if you suddenly had a vision that Jesus was the Way, then you looked in a yellow pages to figure out which church to go to on Sunday. What a mess!

Back in 1962, in the Port Huron Statement, SDS had rejected a cornerstone of the cold war, anti-communism. In so doing we had not only opened ourselves up eventually to Marxism, but to actual infiltration by members of communist parties whose goal was recruitment. The fastest-growing party at the time among college students was the Progressive Labor Party (PL), a pro-China Maoist party which had split from the old Soviet-oriented Communist Party of the United States. China was then in its Cultural Revolution, its revolution was still young and vibrant and attractive. "Long live Mao Tse-tung thought!" PL, by late 1968, early 1969, seeing a good thing in SDS, had infiltrated many of the most active chapters of SDS, such as Columbia's, and had even taken over whole chapters, such as at Harvard. They were pushing as a strategy for SDS something called, "the Worker-Student Alliance," which postulated that students should unite with the true revolutionary power in this country, "the workers," in order to make the revolution. Why were they revolutionary? Because Marx had told us so back in 1848. There's the religious aspect for you.

I knew PL was just blowing wind. After being kicked out of Columbia in May, 1968, I had become a regional and national traveler for SDS, going to chapters around the country to help them get organized. I constantly spoke about the events at Columbia, how it was necessary to support black students (SDS was mostly white), how militancy and a radical analysis gained us support. I found many other non-PL SDS'ers who believed as I did, and together we formed an anti-PL faction which put forward a competing vision of revolution based on what we saw happening around us, in this country and around the world: that national liberation movements such as Vietnam's and the black liberation movement in this country were actually leading the struggle, and that we white students should organize support for them. Fixating on "the workers" was racist in that PL didn't want to see non-white people as the revolutionary agents. (In retrospect our faction has been called "Third Worldist," and there's a certain element of reverse racism which is itself quite racist contained in our beliefs).

One other thing we noticed was that SDS membership and activity was increasing at state schools, which drew on less elite populations than the Ivy League; Kent State SDS, for example, composed of workng-class and lower- middle class students, was a model of militancy in 1968 and 1969. This led us to flesh out a strategy to compete with PL's Worker-Student Alliance: we would build a Revolutionary Youth Movement (RYM) which would unite college students and non-student working class young people to support third world revolution. Our great strategic theory was embodied in a paper, "You Don't Need a Weatherman to Know Which Way the Wind Blows," prepared for the 1969 SDS National Convention in Chicago. Taken from a Dylan line, the title means you don't need dogmatic Marxist theory (PL) to figure out what's happening in the world, just look about you.

It was at that SDS National Convention in June, 1969, that the whole thing came to a head. PL had brought every single member they possibly could; my faction, the RYM, did similarly. For days we battled verbally, then an unplanned incident blew the convention apart. The SDS National Office (a RYM outpost) had invited the Black Panther Party to address the Convention. PL didn't like the Black Panthers because they didn't recognize any other party than their own; how could there be two Marxist parties, both with the Truth? And the Black Panthers didn't like them.

A Panther leader was at the podium attacking "armchair Marxists" when he suddenly started talking about women's liberation, the power of love, and "pussy power." This stupid statement played perfectly into the hands of PL, who started chanting, "Fight Male Chauvinism! Fight Male Chauvinism!" From there it was pandemonium in the hall, as we just as vehemently chanted back, "Fight racism!" The next day, the Panthers demanded that SDS expel PL for its racism in not supporting national liberation; the RYM faction then led a very angry walk-out from the convention, thereby splitting the organization.

We elected our own officers and took over the National Office. I was elected National Secretary. We also called for a National Action in Chicago, demonstrations to coincide with the opening of the trial of the Chicago 8, who were indicted for conspiracy for the demonstrations the previous summer at the Chicago Democratic Convention. The action would be militant and openly anti-imperialist: "Come to Chicago to fight the pigs!" we advertised, "There's a war going on in the world!" The date planned, Oct. 8, was the second anniversary of the death of Che Guevara in Bolivia.

The story of what happened at what became known as The Days of Rage has been told elsewhere, including the 2003 documentry, "The Weather Underground." What's significant for this story, though, is that the SDS chapters rejected en masse support for the action. Most chapters had been independent, neither PL nor RYM, and didn't participate in or even understand the argument. The effect of the split at the June Convention was to cut them off from the National Office. We in what became known as Weatherman had lost our base. But we kept going without one.

The effect on SDS as a whole was disaster. By the beginning of 1970 the national organization had ceased to exist. We in the Weatherman leadership had made a decision that SDS wasn't radical enough, that it was an impediment to the building of a revolutionary movement in this country. We needed an underground guerilla army to begin the revolutionary armed struggle. So we disbanded the National and Regional Offices, dissolved the national organization, and set the chapters adrift. Many chapters kept organizing, in their own ways, against the war and racism; demoralized, others disbanded.

We couldn't have done the FBI's work better for them had we been paid agents, which I know we weren't. We were just stupid kids too in love with our ideas to realize they weren't real. We believed they were real because we thought them. That's the essence of the downside of idealism. (You don't have to look very far to see idealism at work today. Just look at the neo-cons' war in Iraq to see people believing the truth of their own stupid ideas).

The war was still raging in 1969, despite the fact that the war planners knew the U.S. couldn't win. The carnage would continue for six more years. SDS had been the largest student anti-war organization in the country. When the U.S. invaded Cambodia in late April, 1970, thereby openly widening the war beyond Vietnam, there was no national student group to coordinate and send resources to the hundreds of protests and demonstrations that broke out. A few days later, when the Ohio National Guard murdered four students at Kent State, and three million students went out on strike, the largest student strike in U.S. history, SDS didn't exist to help inform the millions about the imperialist nature of the war. I myself was sitting useless on a park bench in Philadelphia, having just escaped a run-in with the FBI, reduced to reading in the newspaper about the protests and student strike while contemplating the stupidity of my ideas. I hope you never have to go to those lengths to learn a necessary lesson.

Many veterans of the anti-war movement speak about the death of SDS as some sort of inevitability. I have heard people talk about the organization as having been "played out," whatever that means. My recall is that my comrades and I in the leadership of Weatherman made specific bad decisions based on our evolving and deepening ideology toward the chimera of revolution and the strategy revolutionary guerilla warfare. One thinks of the roads not taken. We could have chosen to fight to maintain the organization, to strengthen its anti-imperialism and anti-racism among students, to build the largest possible coalition against the war. Perhaps we could have ended the war sooner, who knows?

Be careful when you're tempted to believe your own shit.

But we're fortunate that ideology is not the problem now. Outside of a few hard-core anarchists I've heard who say really dumb stuff like, "We don't want a movement, we don't want any movement, we want autonomous communities of struggle," activists don't kill each other and their work over whose ideas are the best. This old way of behaving is basically kaput, thank god. But the opposite problem prevails: not enough ideas about where we're going and how we're going to get there. Vision and strategy. One good thing about SDS, which was also our downfall, was that there was no shortage of ideas.

THE LEGACY AND LESSONS OF THE 1960s

by Katherina Haris

1968 was one of the most significant years in history from the beginning of the 19th century until today. The origins of what happened and why as well as the consequences of 1968 are still being accessed today.

What happened took place within a year and on a global scale, a rare occurrence in human history. Large social movements and what they promoted sweep across the United States and Canada, many countries in Western Europe, several countries in the Soviet bloc, in Mexico and Japan. The nodules of these social upheavals were the universities, comprising students and oftentimes teachers. This social class was not the only strata of society involved in the upheavals, as a result of which the impact made was traumatic for the respective power elites. 1968 and the build-up during the decade which preceded it, resulted in a dramatic year because the movements involved were of long duration expressing profound social changes and conflicts with long-term consequences. What is the legacy of this decade and what can we learn from a distance of more than four decades ? This legacy is particularly important for us to appreciate and understand because since the mid-1990s, a new global social movement has emerged challenging the direction and impact of the world economy.

As in 1848 in Europe, or in the initial spread of socialism and anarchism in other periods, ideas and types of actions, aspirations and sensibilities, spread across national borders, from continent to continent, in what appeared to be a searching movement of global solidarity. In fact, in 1968, the separate movements developed their own particular combinations and fusions of cultural and

Katherina Haris is a sociologist with an activist research group in Hamburg. She has lectured in England and in the USA. This essay was translated from the German by Stephen Markham.

social themes, were often differently composed, and inserted their own general contemporary elements of protest in their own specific historical traditions. The simultaneity of the movements took place without concealing different historical and cultural modes which were temporarily united culminating in 1968. Much of the excitement, of the sense of worldwide upheaval, was provided and tied together visually and in the imagination by the media—television, especially, with its dramatic and instant images, but also the proliferation of rapid analysis, interviews, manifestos, in daily newspapers, weeklies and monthlies, pamphlets and posters, and later in books. Recall that all this was before the Internet.

The fact that in many places it was a movement of the educated accounted for a special and often puzzled response from the media—whose managers and workers had, often enough, a common culture with the groups involved in protest. There was also the factor of travel and prolonged residence for many in the various countries. It was a period of 'on the road,' and continuous hitch-hiking. Many European students were in North American when the civil rights movement and the protests against Vietnam took place, and students in Europe had been influenced in the early sixties by contact with the European New Left in London, Paris, Frankfurt and Milano. Workers in Portugal, Spain and Italy often had first hand knowledge of developments in France, Germany and other European countries. Those who lived in Czechoslovakia and the authoritarian regimes on the Iberian Peninsula sometimes traveled and were often visited by many tourists making contacts with persons with other experiences.

The channels of communication were often open, resulting in all sorts of messages going back and forth. It would be exaggerating to say that the new culture of consumption, made possible by economies of mass production, created behaviour patterns which were less tied down to work for the sake of work and survival, and more in the direction of enjoyment and relaxation as in 'doing my own thing.' The spread of 'life-style' questions of all sorts which included clothing, and the consumption of soft drugs, opened a whole new perspective on quality of life issues. The new movement of the 1960s, was a youth movement, and as such it introduced without any restrain a wide range of new sensibilities, new cultural and social experimentation, all of which were rapidly internationalized. Thus an impression was created of a global movement of youth, an impression which had the effect of a self-fulfilling prophecy. Underlining such cultural changes in attitude and behaviour were a series of political and economic demands, the combination of which delegitimized the power elites in various countries. The world, at that time, was dominated by two superpower nuclear blocs—the U.S. and its NATO allies and the SU and its Warsaw Pact allies—but these were being undermined internally by a growing awareness of intolerable contradictions. The movement of American blacks for civil rights was a drastic repudiation of the claim that the U.S. represented a morally advanced society. The war in Vietnam and its visible horrors generated revulsion all the more profound for the sanctimonious hypocrisy of those who defended it. The U.S. was viewed as a sick society that murdered its best leaders, Martin Luther King Jr., and the two Kennedy brothers. Along with this impression was a wide spread discrediting of liberalism as a route to social transformation. Nevertheless it was a society under great scrutiny because a whole generation of blacks and whites were in social and political motion across the country, using ideas and actions which were inspiring.

The SU under Brezhnev was widely viewed as repressive, regressive, and sclerotic. Its leaders were depicted, correctly, as mediocrities that had been frightened by Khrushchev's initiation of a discussion of Stalinism. Significant trails of dissidents, the appearance of the scientist Sakharov, literary ferment, preceded the Warsaw Pact's invasion of Czechoslovakia in August 1968 terminating the project of 'socialism with a human face.' Along with this impressive was a wide spread discrediting of Marxism-Leninism as a route to social transformation. The political map of concerns included Spain and the alliance between the old fascist Falangists and the Catholic Opus Dei technocrats, Mexico and the predictably elected corrupt Party of the Institutionalized Revolution, France with its messianic nationalism and General De Gaulle and the State/corporate managerialism which it promoted, the post World War II social pact between political parties which assured social peace in West Germany, Japan with its monolithic union between big capitalism and gangsterism.

All these corners of the world made any claims of exceptionalism untenable. For awhile, it seemed that John F. Kennedy, Nikita Khrushchev and Pope John XXIII might combine in an alliance of change. The rhetorical fallout from the Vatican Two Council for left Catholicism echoed far and near, but the U.S. and SU superpowers reverted to a condition in which their regimes were their own caricatures.

Meantime while for some of the rebellious youth, the images of the dead Che and the living Fidel, of moralistic Maoism and the Cultural Revolution in China, the doctrine of Franz Fanon, were attractive as alternatives. This tendency among some young people was fed on myth, not on accurate information which great distances between the scenes of social action in one part of the world and the Third World countries generated.

As a dramatic confrontation with the past and present unfolded during the sixties decade, certain powerful themes emerged across a number of countries. Anger was widely expressed against the older post World War II generation, which fed a pervasive anti-authoritarian attitude and behaviour. During a decade of seeming material abundance the paradox of anti-materialist values arose which merged with life-style choices of all kinds. The economic goals of 'production for the sake of production,' and 'consumption for the sake of consumption' were seriously questioned. Progress defined in terms of the accumulation of materials was not only scrutinized in the light of human criteria but attempts were made to replace this with enjoyment, personal fulfillment, new cultural expressions, more often times then not conveyed by forms of individualism which promoted the rights of the individual which liberals found difficult to understand.

The word and general concept of *radical* was restored for general use. It also was a substitute for words like 'left,' 'leftist,' 'social democrat,' 'liberal.' An all-out attempt was made to go to the 'root' of the malaise of our society.

What followed was a radical egalitarianism in practice so that hierarchies of all kinds, large and small were rejected as politically and morally unacceptable. Thus all conventional and traditional organizations were looked upon with great suspicion as they were deemed vehicles which crushed human potential. Political parties by definition were rejected, trade unions were looked upon with reserve, and instead 'The Movement' with all its diversity and contradictions but with its singularity of purpose of changing society fundamentally, which could include social revolution, replaced all forms from the past. The movement was thus millenarian.

One part of the movement, largely in North America, was highly spiritualist. Moral energies condensed into aspirations for immediate experience and gratification at the same time joined ideas of a new beginning, of secular transcendence. Mystical groups emerged out of the sub-movement of the 'counter-culture' which fled from the possibility of contact with the world of political and social change in urban centers. Rural communes were set up widely as a psychedelic generation sought refuse from a corrupt society.

There were on the one hand the hard-nosed fighters who sought to change society in a confrontational or 'speaking truth to power' manner and on the other, those who sought to show alternatives to this society as examples of what to do. The secular protest movements of the sixties exhibited aspects of both these wings. Either way they were often, closer to the process of social creativity (that is, the irruption into history of long-accumulating psychological and social demands), than to the standardized modes of belief and behaviour we usually understand as politics.

All of these phenomena, however, were connected with the standardized and traditional politics the movements rejected. Indeed, the movements often defined themselves by what they were not: they were not authoritarian, bureaucratized, centralized, and dependent upon precedent and tradition. Of course, they rejected chauvinism and enthnocentrism, emphasized solidarity. What is striking is how relatively little use they made of the rhetoric of the American and European movements for social reform based upon the traditions of Enlightenment and Progress. The old and established ideologies were roundly rejected. Liberalism, social democracy, Marxism-Leninism, and those of the right were all disregarded.

Among the youth in Germany there were those who sought a renewal of certain forms of Marxism such as that of the Frankfurt School. In France there was a search for a libertarian Marxism which was fed by 'council communism' and some forms of anarchism. In Britain, some left-wing intellectuals and activists, formerly of the New Left and who had resigned from the Communist and Labour parties, still maintained a working relationship with strands of Marxism, seeking some kind of renewal from the socialism of William Morris, Robert Owen, and G.D.H.Cole. One feature was common throughout: there was no interest in Bolshevism or Leninism, until a small minority began promoting it after 1968. In North America, there was no such interest in any of the above, except in a couple of 'Europeanized' cities.

Currents of the authoritarian left emerged only after exhaustion and despair were prevalent at the end of the decade of the sixties. And this took place almost at the same time as many new movements were born, the women's liberation movement, the new environmental movement, the gay liberation movement and others. The one exception to this earlier general trend was a very open process in the Soviet bloc, where the protesters to a large extent consisted of reformist or revisionist projects for a renewal of Marxism. These kept the linear sense of Marxism, presenting themselves as truer to Marx's intentions than the deformed Stalinists and neo-Stalinists they opposed.

We come to a central aspect of the movements of 1968, their insertion into their respective national cultures and histories. If some of the movements were beginning to use ideas other than those of linear progressions, they were nonetheless themselves the results of historical sequences. With the help of hindsight, we can now see them much more clearly.

The movements, largely defined themselves by what they were not. That entailed defining themselves in opposition to established organizations such as political parties and trade unions. Exquisite generational conflict was nowhere as evident: the young accused the old, or those older than themselves, of having compromised, even betrayed, their original values, of having settled into compromise, cynical or merely resigned, with existing systems of power of which they had become indispensable pillars.

In France, the student revolt was not organized by the student section of the large Communist Party or by the established student organizations. It was begun by the Situationists and anarchists, in effect modern exemplars of anti-authoritarianism and the politics of the Surrealists and Dadaists, aided by some of the Trotskyites.

The vast expansion of university youth had created a new academic 'proletariat' anxious about the future and aware that it was not destined for interesting forms of employment. When university protests provoked absurdly repressive tactics on the part of academic authorities, the conflict generalized to one of educational policies and philosophy of government and quickly into a questioning of the Gaullist State as such. General De Gaulle himself had said in his New Year's address to the nation that France was bored, but even De Gaulle [for all of this insight] did not envisage how volatile and dramatic the response to boredom would become that year (1968).

The student revolt acted as a fuse for the explosion of multiple discontents. When the students fought the police in the Latin Quarter, young workers from the industrial suburbs joined them. It was these young workers who led the rank and file in occupying factories—to the astonishment of the union leadership and above all of the Communists and socialists.

When a general strike swept across France, with working people in both the private and public sector occupying companies and government offices, the authority of the State was for a time reduced to commanding the police guarding De Gaulle in the Elysee Palace. All of France seemed to be in a popular festival of rebellion. Debates raged at the general assemblies at the Sorbonne and radiated outward through society at large. Slogans like 'all power to the imagination' or 'it is forbidden to forbid' expressed the strong libertarian character of the movement. Meanwhile in Nantes, Catholic unions organized, for a brief period, self-government for the city's economy for a brief period. France, it should be remembered, under De Gaulle was not ruled by the traditional right-wing but by a new technocratic elite administering an expanding welfare State.

The Communists, largely through the unions they controlled were part of this arrangement, the more so as the Soviet Union had every reason to wish De Gaulle to remain in power indefinitely because he stood aside from the Americans on certain key issues. De Gaulle and his government were at first completely bewildered and disoriented by the collapse of the State, but moved swiftly with a strategy to regain control. They restored the sovereignty of consumption by arranging for supplies of gasoline to be delivered to the nation's gas stations. The French army played transportation system.

The strategy included negotiating a new wage bargain with unions, led by the Communists. De Gaulle made it clear at the end that the army would, if necessary, intervene—frightening the Jacobin party of the left which had announced its readiness to assume power [Pierre Mendes-France, Francois Mitterrand, and Rocard] but which was then surprised to find that almost no one listened to them. In the end, the social revolution collapsed as quickly as the dominatant institutions of society had seemed to dissolve.

During the upheaval (the massive general strike which included millions of people), alternatives to the traditional institutions did not emerge. The workers, did not re-start production in factories or in other work places under the direction of democratic workers councils exercising workers' control of what was to be produced and how. The students did not start schools and universities anew with programme designed and directed by new student-faculty councils.

In June 1968 De Gaulle won a large electoral victory. Unlike the American movement, the French one had temporarily achieved an alliance of students and workers—but it did not prove to be a building block toward the social reconstruction of reality. The French movement also exhibited some continuity with the traditions of the French Left, and the role played in it by somewhat older veterans of the mass protests against the Algerian war [1954-1962].

Nonetheless, the spiritual goals and expressiveness of much of the protest were very different from the Jacobinism or proto-Bolshevism of the French Left with its heavy emphasis on political organization, control of a highly centralized State, and the abstract notion of national citizenship.

The Federal German Republic has experienced a lot of protest before the mid-sixties: the movement against rearmament and against nuclear weapons and the presence of the American military; demands that former Nazis in high places be removed; the turbulence around the government of Conrad Adenauer's seizure of the offices of the mass circulation magazine *Der Spiegel*. Tension existed between the protest movement of young Germans and the large Social Democratic Party. What was particular to the sixties was the generational character of the protest.

Again, a movement had begun against restriction in the universities, an especially unreformed institution in post-war Germany, with many senior professors who had served educational ministries from Kaiser Wilhelm to the Nazis, followed by the allied occupation into the current situation. The protests spread to a bitter critique of what was termed the restoration, that is, the consolidation of bourgeois and capitalist power in a restored West German State.

Theories of restoration were, perhaps, far too simple as they ignored the important role of the Social Democrats in guaranteeing minimal democracy and decency in public life; but at the same time the critique pointed to the Social Democrats' and the trade unions' most vulnerable point, their acceptance of a class and political compromise in a country thoroughly integrated in the NATO alliance and its nuclear strategy. There was then, a direct continuity between the movement against rearmament, the sixties protest, and the later movements of the late seventies and eighties against new U.S. nuclear missiles. Adenauer and the power elite of the country celebrated openly the U.S. as a model, and when a considerable segment of Americans in their turn provided young Germans with a model for systematic protest and dissent they were shocked.

The New Left and protest movement showed an unparalleled coherence. An original and sophisticated movement formation was created called the 'Extra-Parliamentary Opposition' which was not exclusively composed of students. There were members of the intelligentsia, older as well as younger Left-wingers like the writers Bolle and Grass, and critical social democrats and unionists, a number of Protestant theologians, and a smaller number of Catholic ones. As elsewhere, the movement defined itself in contrast to and in opposition to a major and tradition-laden grouping, the Social Democrats. No doubt, a great deal of the psychological energy for the movement came from an effort to keep a critical distance from the complicity with the Nazis period which marked the older generation. Even the resistance figure, Willy Brandt [who was later to do so much to integrate the protest generation in German society] had served as Foreign Minister under Chancellor Kiesinger, who had been a Nazi. The Extra-Parliamentary Opposition in theory and practice however did not become massive enough, and disruptive enough to attract on a longer-term basis a major section of the middle and working class and thus detach them from the existing social order and loyalty to the State.

Italy

The country where there was a more enduring alliance within a movement between students and workers was Italy. There was the outline of a common programme although defined by opposition—to the rigid large Communist Party and the Socialist parties. There was also the particular phenomenon of Left Catholics. In Italy, however [in 1969 especially] there was an independent section of the working class which came from the southern part of the country and therefore were more disadvantaged, who sought wage parity in contractual relations, and developed a critique toward the official union organizations.

The Communist Party, which was more open than other more Stalinist such parties elsewhere, attempted to integrate the newer cultural themes, the ideas of participation and base democracy, articulated by the movement, and in particular avant-garde thinking groups like Il Manifesto. Open or not, however, these new ideas still clashed with the Leninist traditions of the Communist Party, but even more, with the party's determination to present itself before the Italian electorate as a force for stability and clean government.

For a time in the seventies, the Communists were able to use the energies of what had been the protesters for their own project of appearing to integrate some vanguard ideas of the new Italian culture. That they sought to integrate these in a political programme which rested on an alliance with a Catholic party which had only partially and reluctantly accepted the reforms of the Vatican Two Council is a measure of the contradictions which were to bring the Communist Party a third of the vote in 1975, only to begin an unstoppable decline thereafter. *The Partito Radicale* ...

The Soviet Bloc

The protest groups in the Soviet bloc had appreciably simpler goals—by contrast with the diffuse ideas of total transformation of advanced industrial capitalist societies were in Western Europe and North America. They clung to the idea of reforming the system from within, and sought to mobilize significant parts of society behind a programme of modifying what was, in one or another way, neo-Stalinism. This choice has several sources including a very practical one: that of a heavy handed secret police and State repression apparatus. The events in Czechoslovakia before the Warsaw Pact invasion in August, 1968 showed how much potential there seemed to be in the Communist parties themselves for reforms which would bring greater national autonomy, more freedom from doctrinal thinking, and the beginnings of a genuinely new political culture.

The protest groups in both East Germany and Poland were inspired only in part by what was happening in the West—more likely it was the attempt of Czechoslovakia to develop 'socialism with a human face.' The Czech Communist reformers did succeed, for some months, in uniting intellectuals and workers—something neither East Germans nor Poles were able to do. The brutal crushing of the 'Prague Spring' led immediately to a renewed repression in East Germany and Poland.

In East Germany, the internal reformers settled into passivity and resignation: there seemed to be no chance to mobilize a working class unwilling to take risks. Smaller groups of dissidents, in the Protestant Church and among intellectuals, did turn west—to the newer sensibilities of the protest movements. Later, these currents were to condense into what was called the New Forum. In Poland, the intelligentsia concluded that nothing could be accomplished without the working class—and began the arduous process of rapprochement which led to 'Solidarnosc.'

In the Soviet Union, by contrast, there seemed to be no hope of popular opposition to a regime which had become identified with the nation. The handful who protested in Red Square against the invasion of Czechoslovakia were attacked not by the police, but by, what appeared to be ordinary Soviet citizens. Sakharov and the literary dissidents, the human rights protesters, began their long and isolated struggle—while in the research institutes of the Academy of Sciences and the Communist Party, the loyalists took the first hesitant steps on the road to reform from above.

Spain

In Western authoritarian regimes like Spain, 1968 hardly brought an intensification of the worker-student alliance formed earlier. General Franco's technocrats had supposed that by expanding the universities and aligning the economy with Western European capitalism, they would incubate a generation of satisfied careerists. The students, however, insisted on what the West Europeans took for granted, rights of citizenship—and, in their opposition to the conformism and narrowness of their parents, found allies in a working class struggling for minimal standards of material existence and maximal ones of dignity. The focus of Catholicism on a peculiarly narrow code of repressive morals brought students together in their pursuit of personal and political freedom. Spain in 1968 was a country with an active underground where all sorts of social and political forces were rehearsing their eventual emergence given appropriate conditions. The mentality among the power elite who thought that Barcelona, Madrid and Seville could exist indefinitely in an ossified straight-jacket while Paris, Milan, Frankfurt and London were already preparing new direction which would take the new generation into the 21st century, was simply unrealistic. A disquiet also existed in Portugal next door with an underground that was also biding its time, only to break-out in a dramatic and remarkable social revolution in 1974, the 'Revolution of the Flowers.' It matched in scope and depth the social revolution in Spain, 1936-1939. Many of the forms, ideas and experiments that took place showed roots in the sixties.

North America

On the North American continent, apart from what took place during the sixties in the U.S., there was a remarkable and bloody revolt in Mexico in 1968, and a significant social movement in Canada which left a strong lasting influence. In the US, the movement was a revolt against the political establishment, incarnated by the Democratic Party and President L.B. Johnson.

The Cold War, with all the anxiety it produced, re-enforced the conservative and reactionary forces in American society in which big capital, the trade unions, and the technocratic elite—led by a political power elite which continuously bargained foreign policy issues with domestic issues—thus creating a highly manufactured national consensus along with its narrow electoral liberal democracy with an equally narrow plebiscite held once every four years.

The revolt of Southern blacks against the humiliation of segregation, followed by the revolt of Northern blacks against permanently inferior economic and social status showed to progressive whiles, especially younger whites on the university campuses, that their country's achievements fell far short of the rhetorical promise of its egalitarian philosophy. The role of the U.S. in the nuclear weapons and military hardware build-up in the Cold War, the war in Vietnam and southeast Asia, with conscription, sucking up the lives of the young, was seen not as an accident or a mistake as many liberals of the political center and left believed, but as an inevitable consequence of a society dominated by materialism, greed and powerlessness for the vast majority. Johnson's efforts to integrate blacks, and the impoverished generally, in economy and society through ambitious programmes of social reform represented the most serious attempt to enlarge the American welfare State since Roosevelt, but it was interpreted by the "Movement" as confirmation of their worst suspicions: the U.S. was not a just society, and government had the fiscal latitude to change conditions if the will was to do so.

The very modalities of government reform, the use of the ordinary political system to achieve an increase in redistribution, quickly drew their opposition. Johnson's reforms were understood to entail strengthening what was now termed the warfare-welfare State and it was this State the movement rejected. What was rejected was 'corporate liberalism' or 'liberalism' used by Americans to mean 'progressivism' and piecemeal reforms. Insofar as it was 'corporate' it involved bargaining among and control by trade unions seeking social compromise, capital attempting to expand markets while keeping its power, and a techno-bureaucratic class devoid of morality or a sincere interest in a just society. The difficulty was that large sections of the rest of the population, the so-called middle America, was attached to the American State through nationalism.

Motivated by chauvinism and racism, they were eventually drawn to oppose the social movements—which never made permanent or serious inroads in a large enough percentage of the middle class, the working class, and especially its trade unionized component. Misled by the initial white sympathy for the blacks and by a broad sentiment of popular doubt about the Vietnam war, the "Movement" supposed that it could fundamentally alter the culture and structure of American life quickly. Richard Nixon's electoral triumph in 1968, with the Democratic Party electoral base vote split between Johnson's Vice-president Hubert Humphrey, Nixon and the racist southern state governor George Wallace, allowed the Republican Party to win the White House.

The Movement was made up of a significant percentage of university students, perhaps up to 10%, of young persons already in the labour force mainly in temporary or white collar employment, and those sections of intellectuals restive about their integration in a techno-bureaucratically structure part of the economy—or, like university teachers in the humanities, social sciences and natural sciences. The Movement had little or no connection with either the Democratic Party , the fragments of the American Left in the U.S. Communist Party, various socialist groupings, or sects. Its main agenda was protest and preventive. Prevent Johnson, Kissinger, and Nixon from intensifying the Vietnam War. With the Nixon election of 1968, the Movement broke rapidly into several components. Those who had pursued spiritual liberation, new inner experiences, and new dimensions of personal existence withdrew either to bohemian enclaves in certain city neighbourhoods, or to experiment with various drugs, or short-lived rural communes.

The blacks launched themselves in the desperate pursuit of 'black power'—a serious illusion in a society in which they were about 12% of the populace, scattered across of vast sub-continent of a country. Women, disaffected by the patriarchal leadership of the movement, revived American feminism, the third wave. Some political groupings descended into dogmatism and sectarianism finding easy answers to their frustrations in one form of Marxism-Leninism or another, eventually moving into terrorism.

The rationalization of these activists was that the American majority [including the working class] was integrated into consuming the spoils of Empire, and so infected by nationalism that they could not be dislodged. Thus they concluded the challenge at hand for them to try to unite with Third World peoples outside the U.S. and minorities within for an ultimate attack of some sort on the privileged and deluded American majority.

Some still pursued the original goals of the movement, and did in 1970 mount an impressive nation-wide strike against the Cambodian invasion—but many sooner or later rejoined the Democratic Party, to follow the unsuccessful leaders of its left-wing, George McGovern, Edward Kennedy, and Jesse Jackson. American, Canadian and West European politics are very different one from the other.

Canada

In Canada, the sixties also swept up a new generation of activists that spread their actions across this vast country working with aboriginal peoples near the west coast to the black population in and around the Halifax area on the east coast. Attempts were made to mobilize and help organised powerless people in a number of locations, and to bring all such projects together along with campus radicals and those who constitute the political Left, excluding the authoritarian Marxist-Leninists. The Movement gained an enviable reputation even though it was not a mass movement. It was multi-issued, dealing with urban and rural poverty, opposed Canadian complicity in the Vietnam war by government collaboration with the Americans or the military industries feeding the U.S. war machine. True to its origins the Movement continued to oppose nuclear weapons on Canadian soil, gained a working relationship with the Quebec nationalist student union and together expressed solidarity with the civil rights movement south of the border. All of this work it influenced both the left-wing of the Liberal Party and the social democrats in the New Democratic Party.

The objective nevertheless was to form and sustain an extra-parliamentary opposition. The political elite in the Federal government feared the outcome to the extent that it created a programme and organization called the Company of Young Canadians which both divided and co-opted a good part of the Movement's leadership. Nevertheless, the Canadian movement, as well as its 1968 upheavals in Vancouver/ Burnaby and Montreal, had its impact on society.

The birth of the Green Party in Germany as well as in other countries shows a clear continuity with the sixties in terms of some key ideas and approaches to politics. The massive opposition to a new generation of nuclear weaponry in the 1980s in Germany, in Western Europe in general as well as in North America demonstrates this continuity. This movement also, in turn, had serious echoes in East Germany, Hungary and Poland, as well as the SU, with the additional important element in that it argued for a non-aligned politics. In France the highly centralized political State was slowly opened up to some regional and urban decentralization.

In the U.S., third wave feminism, multi-cultural,multi-ethnic, and multi-racial identity politics which were redefining American society, were the direct result of the fragmenting of the movement at the end of the sixties. In this the politics of the self continued. In the Soviet bloc, Solidarnosc was born and helped by the New Left in the West, the revolution of 1989 in Czechoslovakia and the methods used to initiate this basic change echoed many creative ideas from the sixties and 1968.

Recall that 1968 represented the apogee of anti-authoritarianism of the Movement, often spilling into anarchism. The Movement demanded participatory democracy, its demand for transparency and public scrutiny of those who had political power, insisted that the State had to earn legitimacy.

The basic idea went even far beyond the borders of conventional politics [elections and representation]: a whole new openness to public consultation was insisted upon. The process of redefinition and social relocation are still going on—as in relations between the sexes, within the family, between generations. The unquestioning submission to authority was over, as the clamor of human rights and civil liberties became deafening. The trade union organizations had become structurally or organizationally ossified, even though often these same hard forms defended at least minimally the interests of its worker members in the face of aggressive capital.

The sixties Movement was deeply suspicious of these forms. The sources of that suspicion are to be found in the movement's insistence on spontaneity which had many sources: separation from cultural history of society in an epoch of considerable social mobility, the psychological impact of mass media and its message of instant gratification, and more flexible and attentive personalities resulting from new child-rearing practice. No doubt affluence had its psychic effects, too.

It is possible that not only in the U.S. but also in other countries, despite their socialist and trade union traditions, despite Jacobinism and its emphasis on organization and the conquest of the State as an indispensable precondition for the transformation of society, the sixties Movement was a revolution which redefined politics and power. The Movement's eye was on the super-structure first and foremost.

However, in spite of the Mmovement 's rejection of consumer society, of the mass market, the activists were often honouring limitless consumption—expressed as ideas of instant gratification, directness in all human and social relationships, and the end of institutional constraint. Perhaps this is an exaggeration, but let us take it as a metaphor. The political Right responded to the crisis of the idea of progress, the view that history is the unfolding of reason, with the cynical defense of the minimal attainments of civilization and a large shrug in the face of brutality, exploitation, and the absence of human autonomy. The Movement of the sixties responded by demanding that history be telescoped or collapsed, that progress be realized at once—a denial of any theory of history. Nevertheless the movement played a central and immediate role.

The Movement of the sixties attacked the State, although in North America it only had a vague idea of the need to fundamentally change the market capitalist economy. In Europe, the movement did both, but was unable to re-start a new economy once it shut it down, in France for example.

The Movement also was concerned with cultural institutions, structures of authority throughout society but again disregarded some significant exceptions regarding the market-place. It made a historicaly significant change in educational philosophy and practice. It had a powerful impact on psychology and psychiatry. However, the emancipatory and libertarian streams that were fostered affected only part of society, and their impact was limited to those who theoreticaly had the power to shut down the economy and force deep changes—the unionized labour movement. This latter movement, at its best, sought to transform society by taking over the economy only to be defeated many times by ignorance, greed, chauvinism and servility to authority.

The sixties Movement represented an effort to spread internationalism and solidarity, a pre-condition to an ultimate basic change of society that re-defined political as well as economic power. The economic power elite however understood all to well the importance of the State. The Right learned a lot from the sixties: witness Thatcher, Reagan and the Trilateral Commission and their cohort of rapacious speculators, ruthless political managers, and ideological thugs. They created a structure, artifically, a Darwinian system, and then pointed to it as evidence that ideas of a cooperative and just social order were infantile fantasies.

We now face a global crisis that has several features. The combination of a globalized labour market and the profound changes in the technologies of economic production. The ravenous growth of consumption is seriously depleting Nature, world-wide. Sooner or later natural disasters are going to become more than news stories on the 6 o'clock news which will impact negatively on both economies and societies in general. The welfare State has been rolled back in certain countries, while in others, the call for meaningful work seems wiped from public discussion. In other areas the values of the sixties are very relevant. Where work is limited, new ideas of income and psychological gratification, new conceptions of self-government, new solidarities are necessary more than ever. The cry for work-sharing, and reduction of working time continues to be necessary more than ever. The link between work and income, income and social status, still needs to be rethought. As long as the productivist ethos of big capitalism prevails, along with a simplistic Darwinian individualism disguised as the realization of philosophical liberalism, rethinking will be impossible. Here the sixties have generated ideas which require new political and social institutions if they are to be given concrete form—an institutionalization unthinkable in the sixties, given the very nature of the decade. It is a task for all.

It is difficult enough to develop enduring solidarities within a country. Selfishness and materialism are so deeply embedded now in western civilization, and spreading so rapidly throughout the planet that they are becoming deeply embedded in the popular psyches of most people.

The Movement of the sixties has multiple relations with the Third World. For lack of historical analysis, many in the Movement created colourful myths of its Leninist political leaders like Che, Fidel, Ho, and Mao. In protesting and stopping the Vietnam war and later the war in Nicaragua, as with the Algerian war before that, they expressed concrete political solidarity with these struggles for national liberation.

The Movement began with ideas of long-term economic solidarity with the societies suffering from disease, famine, poverty and, of course, exploitation brought on by their own elites and by powerful economic interests in the Northern Hemisphere.

Many government and U.N. reports reflect the rhetoric of the sixties. If the richer countries are to contribute to the development of the poorer ones, new models of development will have to be invented. The sixties notions of altered patterns of consumption, however rudimentary and schematic, are indispensable for any viable future for both developed and developing economies. The connection between the new environmental movement and the sixties is complex, but keeping in mind some of its major thinkers we now know that any new politics will have to be ecological, ethical and participatory.

A number of key questions remain. How is political power to be decentralized in society? How is the economy to be detached from the complex of uncontrolled greed of the market-place toward the production for real and not manufactured needs? Liberal and Jacobin ideas of loyal citizenship assume modern centralizing power elites.

The sixties Movement presented experiments in new forms of participation, but almost never engendered consistent and long-term projects for political institutions which would be based on a new rapport between the heavy concentration of power and the need and demand for autonomy of those who would otherwise be crushed or ignored by the agencies of power.

Some of the ongoing discussions of civil society are at the level of incantation: civil society is no more an independent or self-conscious entity than is the working class of Marx. The problem is less to allow civil society to express its freedom than to pretend to create areas of freedom within the State or the market. It is significant that many who were active in the sixties have now taken up ideas of civil society—add to this the new understanding of the place and role of social movements and we have a renewed attempt to overcome the fragmentation of movements and organization that dominated the 1970s.

The sixties taught us much both in the immediate and enduring impact of its successes and also its failures. The messianic character of the Movement is not to be underestimated or disparaged because it was onlyone sign of its seriousness. Without continuous infusions of moral energy, any movement for social transformation is bound to become a routine and, indeed, more easily corrupted.

The sixties were preceded, made possible by decades of patient and deliberative discussions of the highest quality in darkness and in light. An ongoing equally patient examination of the legacy of the sixties is a precondition for another leap forward of hope and moral imagination which began with the anti-globalization movement of the nineties and now the 21st century.

DEMOCRATIC IDEALISM
SDS And The Gospel Of Participatory Democracy

by Gregory Nevala Calvert

While SNCC took the lead in the new student activism of the 1960s, others were quick to follow. In particular, the growth of the Students for a Democratic Society (SDS) was conditioned by the sit-ins and the emergence of SNCC in 1960. SDS, which was to become the largest organizational expression of the New Left, was given both tactical and organizational inspiration and models by SNCC. Nonviolent direct action and a decentralized approach to organization were directly derived from SNCC's experience and guided the early development of SDS. Furthermore, this fruitful interchange between the predominantly black southern student movement and the white northern student movement informed both the strategies and the political philosophy of SDS. The broad principles of the politics of participatory democracy that SDS articulated in its *Port Huron Statement* of 1962 were drawn in part from its symbiotic relationship with SNCC during the first two years of the decade. Thus the political theory of the New Left emerged in part from the grassroots experience of the student-led wing of the civil rights movement.[1]

Northern Students and the Sit-in Movement
The nationwide effect of the sit-in movement in the South in the spring of 1960 was dramatic and far-reaching, particularly in regard to its impact on northern white students. By the end of the spring of that year, according to Kirkpatrick Sale's account in SDS,

Gregory Nevala Calvert died of complications from diabetes in Albuquerque, New Mexico in 2005. This essay first appeared in his book Democracy from the Heart *(Communitas Press, Eugene, 1991). He held a PhD in Political and Social Theory, and was a Woodrow Wilson graduate fellow at Cornell and the University of Paris. In 1966 he was National Secretary of Students for a Democratic Society and the National Mobilization Committee to End the War in Vietnam.*

...students at perhaps a hundred Northern colleges had been mobilized in support, and over the next year civil-rights activity touched almost every campus in the country: support groups formed, fund raising committees were established, local sit-ins and pickets took place, campus civil rights clubs began, students from around the country traveled to the South.[2]

As Aldon Morris puts it: "No previous actions of the Southern civil rights movement had generated this kind of widespread activism among whites across the nation. In effect, the 1960 sit-ins generated the activist stage of the modern white student movement."[3] It had been shown "that the typical [white Northern] student was affluent, excelled in scholarly pursuits, usually majored in the social sciences and had liberal-to-radical political values."[4] Furthermore, "they were dissatisfied with the huge gap between America's democratic rhetoric and its actual practices." Morris goes on

...to answer the question of why that discontented group of affluent white students became involved in the politics of protest. That group entered into the politics of protest because the sit-ins were dominated by black students provided them with a visible protest model, which demonstrated how they could proceed tactically and organizationally. It was an especially attractive model because the white student shared two important characteristics with the sit-in demonstrators: both were students, and both were young.[5]

In the North, the newly reorganized Students for a Democratic Society was profoundly affected by the sit-in movement and the development of SNCC. Both the tactic of nonviolent direct action and the decentralist organizational style of SNCC provided models for SDS and thus shaped the emergence of the New Left from its inception. SDS leaders like Robert Alan ("Al") Haber and Tom Hayden were taught the methods of nonviolent direct action by black activists at conferences and workshops. Haber served as liaison with SNCC and was influenced by SNCC leaders whose top-level meetings he attended. He recalls that "Ella Baker provided a bridge between the black student movement and the emerging white student movement."[6] Morris points out that "SDS, like SNCC, emerged as a loosely structured organization that emphasized local autonomy and direct action rather than strong centralized leadership. In this sense Ella Baker was the 'mother' of both SNCC and the activist phase of SDS."[7]

Despite the importance of SNCC's example and inspiration for SDS, it is, however, important to realize that SDS made its own unique contributions to the Movement. Among these, none was more important than the articulation of a new vision of democratic radicalism in its famous *Port Huron Statement*. If there was a single manifesto that shaped the language and thought of the American New Left, it was this document prepared for SDS's first real national convention in 1962.

Vision and Values

The 59 young people who gathered at the United Auto Workers' camp at Port Huron, Michigan, in June 1962, had all been deeply influenced in their political development by the civil rights movement. None had been more impressed by the experience of SNCC than Tom Hayden, whose wife Sandra "Casey" Cason was a SNCC organizer and a member of the SNCC Coordinating Committee. The central concern of this national convention of Students for a Democratic Society was the final scrutiny, revision, and adoption of a document on which Hayden had been laboring for several months. What was produced came to be known as the Port Huron Statement, and it served not only as a manifesto for SDS but as a founding document for the American New Left as a whole. It contained, among other things, the guiding principles of the political discourse which was SDS's most enduring contribution to political life and thought in the United States and abroad, the gospel of participatory democracy.

However incomplete and ambiguous this presentation of the concept of participatory democracy proved to be, it did accomplish one vital task: it gave the emerging New Left a new language for talking about politics and social change. By breaking with the stultified rhetoric of Marxism and the hollow platitudes of liberalism, it opened up the possibilities of thinking about political and social problems in new and creative ways. It opened the horizons of political thought to the potential of a new vision for democracy.

Tom Hayden's political ideas were not formed entirely by his experience in the civil rights movement. There was a complex interaction between Hayden's experiences as an activist and his intellectual quest as a student. Perhaps the most difficult part of his development to decipher is the way in which values came to occupy a central place in his political thought. It was this characteristic that suited him so eminently for the job of framing a manifesto for the New Left, because it was precisely this issue of the primacy of values that distinguished New Left political thought from its Marxist and liberal predecessors.

Hayden's political development was almost synonymous with the growth of the early SDS. When the organization changed its name from the Student League for Industrial Democracy to Students for a Democratic Society in January of 1960, its parent organization (the League for Industrial Democracy) hired Al Haber as Field Secretary. Haber was an older professional student of sorts in Ann Arbor, Michigan, who soon recruited Hayden, editor of *The Michigan Daily*, to the new organization. While Haber represented the tradition of Jewish radicalism which had been a dominant force in the Old Left (Haber's father was a well-known econo-mist and labor arbitrator whose political sympathies lay with Norman Thomas and the Socialist Party),[8] Tom Hayden was the product of a distinctly different back-ground—unconnected to the history of the American Marxist left and the labor movement. Thus Hayden was heir to neither the Stalinist nor social democratic wings of the Old Left (the Communist and Socialist Parties), nor was he weaned on the predominant discourse of the left-wing intelligentsia, Marxism.[9]

Hayden, born December 11, 1939, came from a conservative Catholic back-ground in Royal Oak, Michigan, and was actually baptized by the right-wing priest, Father Coughlin, whose reactionary demagoguery was eventually silenced by the Church. There seems little doubt that Hayden's early values were deeply influence by his Christian faith and his Jesuit teachers. By the time he entered the University of Michigan in the fall of 1957, he had, however, broken with his traditional Catho-lic upbringing and set out on an intellectual, spiritual, and political odyssey that would make him the key figure in shaping the discourse of the New Left. Hayden's search for a broader understanding of human values led him to the works of Albert Camus, and existentialism provided him a framework for the exploration of values in a non-theistic framework. The existentialist path was a way for many of Hayden's generation to reconcile their attachment to deep moral and spiritual val-ues, which were often learned in a religious context, with the loss of their religious beliefs. It was a shaky undertaking, but it worked for a time for many young Ameri-cans who were to become activists in the New Left. It gave them some basis, other than the Judeo-Christian tradition, for justifying their moral convictions and for the expression of their humanistic values.

Existentialism was by no means the only intellectual influence at work in Hayden's life. The work of the renegade American sociologist, C. Wright Mills, played an important role in giving Hayden a sense of social theory couched in a lan-guage of native American radicalism. Mills recognized the importance of under-standing Marxism but was not a doctrinaire radical and his leading works, *The*

Power Elite and *White Collar*, provided a fresh look at American social structures and dynamics that was free of the dead hand of Marxist dogma.[10] Finally, in the area of political theory, Hayden seems to have been deeply influence by what James Miller, in *"Democracy in the Streets,"* calls "the tradition of civic republicanism that links Aristotle to John Dewey."[11] While it is possible that Miller overplays this theme, it is vital to understand that Hayden's political ideas were indeed shaped by the classical tradition of political theory in the Western World which, beginning with Aristotle, had seen politics as a branch of ethics and made the issues of civic virtue and a virtuous citizenry central concerns of political thought. It was this tradition which modern liberalism and Marxism had largely displaced with their differing versions of "social science."[12] The central role of moral action and the privileged position of values in Hayden's thought clearly link him to this classical tradition.

Finally, it is difficult to judge how deeply Hayden was influenced by the philosophy of the civil rights movement. Certainly a commitment to nonviolence is explicit in the *Port Huron Statement*, and there seems no reason to doubt the sincerity of Hayden's statement of that commitment. Whether he absorbed much of the philosophy of Satyagraha is unclear. It is, however, true that he was deeply impressed by his contact with the radical pacifists around *Liberation* magazine and took their ideas seriously.

In terms of the cultural currents of the times, Hayden was clearly affected by some of the Beat Generation writers. It was the reading of Jack Kerouac's *On the Road* that inspired him to hitchhike across the country in the summer of 1960 and led to his direct contacts with the radical activist community in Berkeley, California.

In assessing the influence of the civil rights movement in Hayden's political development, it is important to recognize that his direct involvement was the primary educative factor. Just as for most other young radicals of the 1960s, activism proved a more powerful force than books in the shaping of Hayden's life. His first engagement with the civil rights movement involved writing an editorial in *The Michigan Daily* (the University of Michigan's student newspaper) supporting picketers in Ann Arbor who were organizing demonstrations of solidarity with the southern student sit-in movement. The idea was suggested to him by Al Haber, and it did not represent an activist stance on Hayden's own part. He was still in the role of supportive journalist.

Interestingly, it was an encounter with Martin Luther King, Jr., that seems to have most directly affected Hayden's attitude toward activism. After traveling to Berkeley in 1960 and meeting extensively with activists there, Hayden's West

Coast itinerary then took him to the Democratic Party Convention in Los Angeles. There he met King in person. He later said:

> Meeting King transformed me. There I was with pencil in hand, trying to conduct an objective interview with Martin Luther King, whose whole implicit message was: 'Stop writing, start acting.' That was a compelling moment. It seemed so absurd to be a student writing about students taking action, as opposed to becoming more of a committed writer and thinker, with commitment coming first.[13]

Commitment (*engagement* in French) was one of the keywords of the existentialist vocabulary. It was natural that Hayden would use it to describe the gripping effect of this meeting with King. It forced the marriage of values and action. As such, it represented very clearly the moral tone of the new political activism.

On his return trip to Michigan, Hayden stopped at the University of Minnesota to attend the annual congress of the National Student Association. Al Haber was there, pushing successfully for the adoption of his position paper, "The Student and the Total Community," as an NSA policy statement supporting student activism. But, perhaps more importantly, Hayden came face-to-face with a group of students who were to represent for him the new ideal of existential commitment to radical political activism. They were the delegates from the newly formed Student Nonviolent Coordinating Committee. Among them was Sandra "Casey" Cason who would become Hayden's wife. Cason was a white woman from Texas whose political activism was informed by a deep religious faith. A student at the University of Texas in Austin, she had become active in civil rights work through the YWCA. But she had also become deeply involved with a radical Christian "intentional community" call The Christian Faith and Life Community, an offshoot of the Wesleyan (Methodist) Student Fellowship in Austin. Under the charismatic leadership of the Reverend Joseph Matthews, this group preached a form of Christian existentialism and political activism that emphasized both living in community and intense involvement in the world.[14] Cason and her colleagues in SNCC provided a powerful role model for Hayden on his road to activism.

Over the next two years, Tom Hayden became an example of what was to happen to thousands of other American students of his generation. For the first time in American history political activism became the central focus of student life. The ivy-covered walls between the "Ivory Tower" of academia and the "outside world" came tumbling down and a new vision of *the student as democratic citizen* was born.

After his return to the University of Michigan in the fall of 1960, Hayden's new enthusiasm for a commitment to radical activism was expressed in a series of editorials in *The Michigan Daily*. He took some of his cues from David Riesman's *The Lonely Crowd*, Vance Packard's *The Hidden Persuaders*, and William Whyte's *The Organization Man*, three popular sociological portraits of mass society, bureaucracy, and manipulative consumerism. "In recent times," Hayden wrote, "spokesmen as disparate as Riesman and the existentialists have been concerned with the actual breakdown of dogma and tradition and the resultant society which seems directionless, decisionless, amoral."[15]

The real questions that seemed to be haunting Tom Hayden were: "How can one create a democratic theory of politics and society which paces values and morality first?" and "How can one justify individual commitment to social justice and political action outside of a traditional religious framework if it is not a matter of narrow self-interest?" He saw the new political idealism as being nurtured eclectically by "Mill and classic liberalism," "Jefferson's attitudes on liberty," "Gandhi's principles of non-violent action," and "Camus's concept of the human struggle and commitment." Students were the forerunners of a "revolution that would reduce complexity to moral simplicity, that would restore emotion to religion, that would in fact give man back his 'roots'." Student activists had shown a "new willingness to take up responsibilities of the individual to the democratic order."[16]

Hayden also founded a student political party on campus. VOICE, as it was called, was directly modeled on the UC Berkeley's radical campus organization, SLATE, which Hayden had studied first-hand during his summer travels. VOICE joined national and campus issues and ran candidates for student government. Then, in February, 1961, Hayden had his first real experience of the Southern civil rights movement. He traveled to Fayette County, Tennessee, and reported on the struggles of black sharecroppers who had been evicted because of their determination to register to vote. He had his first experience of dealing with a "mob" that chased him out of town. This experience and his increasing involvement with activist Sandra Cason drew Hayden further into the civil rights struggle.

Hayden was also being drawn, or dragged, into SDS. Susan Jeffrey and Bob Ross, SDS members at the University of Michigan who came from Jewish social democratic backgrounds (like Al Haber who was now busy working in the New York office) actively recruited Hayden despite his great reluctance to become involved in any organization linked to the traditions of the Old Left. Of Jeffrey and Ross, Hayden recalls:

Their view was that things weren't happening unless you were signing up people to become card-carrying members of this organization-in-the-making, the SDS. My view was that things were happening very well, thank you, without any assistance from these groups out of the morbid traditions of the Left centered around New York City.[17]

He was also being recruited, unsuccessfully, by Michael Harrington of the Young People's Socialist League. Hayden felt that the use of the word "socialism" was unsuited to the American political tradition and would alienate the American public.

Hayden finally opted for membership in SDS with its nonsectarian democratic rhetoric and style. He was a vitally important recruit in providing a link to constituencies beyond the narrow social base which hampered the growth of other left-wing student organizations. In addition, he married Sandra Cason whose work with SNCC in the South had been a source of deep inspiration to him. Hayden became SDS Field Secretary in Atlanta where Sandra Cason worked with Ella Baker in the YWCA office.[18] This strategic position brought Hayden into direct and continuous contact with SNCC and exposed him to the radical decentralist ideas of "group-centered leadership" which Ella Baker had fostered in that organization.[19]

In August and September 1961, SNCC organized its first voter registration project in McComb, Mississippi, under the leadership of Robert Moses. It was a bold and dangerous move that was immediately met with white vigilantism and violent repression. Hayden traveled to McComb with Paul Potter, National Vice President of the NSA and future President of SDS. It was a baptism by fire. Arriving secretly on October 9, Hayden and Potter were forced to meet clandestinely with Moses and other SNCC organizers. Two days later, Hayden and Potter were dragged from a car and beaten by a white assailant. An Associated Press photograph of the incident went out over the wire service and made Hayden an instant symbol of the new student activism.

This experience of risk, commitment, and violence led Hayden to write his most important political articles up to that time. Reprinted as an SDS pamphlet entitled "Revolution in Mississippi," Hayden's reflections on the transformative power of the Southern civil rights struggle reveal the deep changes which it had wrought in this young man. It seems clear that Tom Hayden who would author the *Port Huron Statement* had been profoundly radicalized by this "revolution" of which he wrote and in which he had been a participant. "Revolution in Mississippi" ends with a quote from the anti-fascist Italian writer Ignazio Silone, whose novel *Bread and Wine* was a Bible of political and moral thought for many thoughtful activists of Hayden's generation. Silone wrote:

I am convinced that it would be a waste of time to show a people of intimidated slaves a different manner of speaking, a different manner of
gesticulating, but perhaps it would be worthwhile to show them a different way of living. No word and no gesture can be more persuasive than
the life, and if necessary, the death, of a man who strives to be free...a
man who shows what a man can be.[20]

The Port Huron Statement

Though there was a genuine effort to make the Port Huron Statement a collective
undertaking, in fact it is largely the work of Tom Hayden. He was delegated the task
of drafting a broad statement of principles and political direction for SDS in the win-
ter of 1962. Over the ensuing months, Hayden read widely and produced prelimi-
nary drafts of the document. These were distributed to members for comment, and
he intended to incorporate criticisms in his revisions. The process did not work well.
In reality, the most important criticism, coming generally from critics of Old Left
backgrounds, was directed at Hayden's opening section on values. It simply did not
fit well into the mind-set of people who had grown up in the various versions of the
Marxist tradition to begin a political manifesto with a statement of values.[21]

Hayden responded to this criticism by rearranging his text in such a way that
the values section was placed less prominently towards the middle of the document. This attempt to appease the "materialist" bias of Old Left traditionalists back-
fired in June at the Port Huron Convention itself. There the overwhelming sentiment
of the assembled representatives of SDS was in favor of Hayden's original plan, and
the decision was made to restore the statement of values to its original place near
the opening of the manifesto, immediately following a general introduction.[22] This
turnabout was deeply revealing and crucial to the long-range success of the *Port
Huron Statement*. It showed that the sensibilities of a representative group of
SDSers were more like Hayden's original instincts than the position of his critics.
Furthermore, it ensured that the *Port Huron Statement* would reach a wide audience and become what it was destined to be: the most popular and most influential
articulation of the political aspirations of a new generation of young American radicals. Had the section on values been displaced by a traditional Marxist-inspired "materialist" analysis, the document would have probably joined a long list of left-wing
manifestos read only by those already initiated into the esoteric language and
world-view of the Old Left. By breaking with that tradition—by placing values
first—the *Port Huron Statement* was able to stand as the foundation of a new political movement that still speaks to the hearts and minds of sensitive people in the late

20th century [and the 21st century, ed]. It ensured that Students for a Democratic Society would, for a time, be a broad-based movement of grassroots democratic radicalism instead of another troublesome but irrelevant Marxist sect.

"A first task of any social movement," the *Statement* reads, "is to convince people that the search for orienting theories and the creation of human values is complex but worthwhile."[23] It goes on to say: "we are aware that to avoid platitudes we must analyze the concrete conditions of social order." But, having recognized the need for such analysis of "concrete conditions," the author then asserts the primacy of values and their *a priori* character. The next sentences read: "But to direct such an analysis we must use the guideposts of basic principles. Our own social values involve conceptions of human beings, human relationships, and social systems" (p.6).

It seems clear that the old order of social scientific thought was being overturned. Instead of values being derived from the "materialist" analysis of society, prior values must be appealed to which are "the guideposts of basic principles." And what are these basic principles which are being appealed to? They are, I believe, a statement of the values of the kind of spiritual humanism which was beginning to flourish in America among the ranks of humanistic psychologists like Abraham Maslow and which would inform much of what came to be called the human potential movement. The succeeding paragraph spells out these spiritual humanistic values:

> We regard *men* as infinitely precious and possessed of unfulfilled capacities for reason, freedom, and love. In affirming these principles we are aware of countering perhaps the dominant conceptions of man in the twentieth century: that he is a thing to be manipulated, and that he is inherently incapable of directing his own affaires. We oppose the depersonalization that reduces human beings to the status of things—if anything the brutalities of the twentieth century teach that means and ends are intimately related, that vague appeals to "posterity" cannot justify the mutilations of the present. We oppose, too, the doctrine of human incompetence because it rests essentially on the modern fact that men have been "competently" manipulated into incompetence—we see little reason why men cannot meet with increasing skill the complexities and responsibilities of their situation, if society is organized not for minority, but for majority, participation in decision-making (p.5).

Then comes the statement of human potential and goals:

Men have unrealized potential for self-cultivation, self-direction, self-understanding, and creativity. It is this potential that we regard as crucial and to which we appeal, not to the human potentiality for violence, unreason, and submission to authority. The goal of man and society should be human independence: a concern not with image of popularity but with finding a meaning of life that is personally authentic: a quality of mind not compulsively driven by a sense of powerlessness; nor one which unthinkingly adopts status values, nor one which represses all threats to its habits, but one which has full, spontaneous access to present and past experiences, one which easily unites the fragmented parts of personal history, one which openly faces problems which are troubling and unresolved; one with an intuitive awareness of possibilities; an active sense of curiosity, and ability and willingness to learn (pp.5-6).

This powerful statement of the potential of a truly human individuality is followed by a short, but carefully worded paragraph designed to distinguish this vision from any notion of rampant individualism. "This kind of independence," it states, "does not mean egotistic individualism—the object is not to have one's way so much as it is to have a way that is one's own. Nor do we deify man—we merely have faith in his potential."

The *Statement* then goes on to present a set of ideals governing the conception of human relationships and human community.

Human relationships should involve fraternity and honesty. Human interdependence is contemporary fact; human brotherhood must be willed, however, as a condition of future survival and as the most appropriate form of social relations. Personal links between man and man are needed, especially to go beyond the partial and fragmentary bonds of function that bind men only as worker to worker, employer to employee, teacher to student, American to Russian (p.6).

But how are these "partial and fragmentary bonds of function" to be overcome? The answer lies in a spiritual as well as political transformation that transcends the socially fragmenting forces of the dominant materialism.

Loneliness, estrangement, isolation describe the vast distance between man and man today. These dominant tendencies cannot be overcome by better personnel management, nor by improved gadgets, but only when a love of man overcomes the idolatrous worship of things by man.

As the individualism we affirm is not egoism, the selflessness we affirm is not self-elimination. On the contrary, we believe in generosity of a kind that imprints one's unique individual qualities in relation to other men, and to all human activity. Further, to dislike isolation is not to favor the abolition of privacy; the latter differs from isolation in that it occurs or is abolished according to individual will (p.7).

The realization of these spiritual ideals is to be achieved through the democratic transformation of social, political, and economic life. "We would," the *Statement* affirms,

...replace power rooted in possession, privilege, or circumstance by power and uniqueness rooted in love, reflectiveness, reason, and creativity. As a social system we seek the establishment of a democracy of individual participation, governed by two central aims: that the individual share in those social decisions determining the quality and direction of his life; that society be organized to encourage independence in men and provide the media for their common participation (p.7).

This dramatic and poetic vision is followed by the basic statement of the meaning and principles of participatory democracy:

In a participatory democracy, the political life would be based in several root principles:
- that decision-making of basic social consequence be carried on by public groupings;
- that politics be seen positively, as the art of collectively creating an acceptable pattern of social relations;
- that politics has the function of bringing people out of isolation and into community, thus being a necessary, though not sufficient, means of finding meaning in personal life;
- that the political order should serve to clarify problems in a way instrumental to their solution;
- it should provide outlets for the expression of personal grievance and aspiration; opposing views should be organized so as to illuminate choices and facilitate the attainment of goals; channels should be commonly available to relate men to knowledge and to power so that private problems—from bad recreation facilities to personal alienation—are formulated as general issues (pp.7-8).

This formulation of the politics of participatory democracy is striking chiefly because it is a bold and decisive restatement of the classical view of political life as formulated in the beginning of the Western tradition by the Greeks. Politics is once again seen as the art of creating the *polis*, of building the community of a shared life which is the "necessary, though not sufficient, means of finding meaning in personal life." This notion "that politics has the function of bringing people out of isolation and into community" is dramatically modern in its formulation and yet truly classical in its inspiration. Here again politics is "seen positively, as the art of collectively creating an acceptable pattern of social relations." Gone is liberal cynicism about the political realm: gone too is Marxist economic determinism. The "political" is restored to its central, creative role in the determination of human affairs without, at the same time, overwhelming the "personal" or making utopian claims that a democratic society will answer all the questions of humanity's search for meaning.

This declaration of the political principles of participatory democracy is followed by a statement of economic principles which are clearly subordinate to and derived from the preceding political values and ideals. This reversal of the traditional materialist subordination of politics to economics is essential to the meaning of the *Port Huron Statement*. It meant that economic questions would always have as their primary criterion of judgment the prior political principle of democratic participation. In the words of the *Statement* itself:

The economic sphere would have as its basis the principles:

- that work should involve incentives worthier than money or survival. It should be educative, not stultifying; creative, not mechanical; self-directed, not manipulated, encouraging independence, a respect for others, a sense of dignity, and a willingness to accept social responsibility, since it is this experience that has crucial influence on habits, perceptions, and individual ethics;

- that the economic experience is so personally decisive that the individual must share in its full determination;

- that the economy itself is of such social importance that its major resources and means of production should be open to democratic participation and subject to democratic social regulation (p.8).

This subordination of economic principles to democratic political principles suggested that, at the level of economic restructuring, SDS was searching primarily for a vision of economic democracy rather than the traditional formulations of socialism. The guidelines for economic change for the New Left were to be "democratic participation" and "democratic social regulation." This formula is vitally important because a vision of economic democracy governed by these principles pointed in the direction of decentralization and grassroots control rather than in the traditional socialist direction of state ownership (nationalization) and centralization, and thus it reinforced the decentralist tendency of the New Left which would be its most authentic expression.

Hayden's choice of language was not based on naïveté. Though not from an Old Left background, he was well acquainted by 1962 with the rhetoric and dogmas of the Marxist socialist tradition. He regarded that language as stultified and increasingly empty of content. The vision of socialism as a state-controlled planned economy was far from the aspiration of the young democratic radicals of the New Left who had seen the limits and disasters of both state socialism and welfare state capitalism. However, as we shall see later, SDS failed in the *Port Huron Statement* to match its vision and values with a satisfactory economic and political program.

The values section of the *Port Huron Statement* ends with the assertion that just like "the political and economic ones, major social institutions—cultural, educational, rehabilitives, and others—should be generally organized with the well-being and dignity of man as the essential measure of success." Furthermore, it is unequivocal in its support of nonviolence, arguing that in

> ...social change or interchange, we find violence to be abandoned because it requires generally the transformation of the target, be it a human being or a community of people, into a depersonalized object of hate. It is imperative that the means of violence be abolished and the institutions—local, national, international—that encourage non-violence as a condition of conflict be developed (p.8).

These were "the central values" which were to move and guide the message of SDS to the growing constituency of student activists in the United States and even abroad. Many who read it were deeply moved. Its power and beauty lie in its successful presentation of democratic political ideals in a language of spiritual humanism that dared to speak of values long banished from the realm of political discourse. In so doing, it turned on its head the principles of political discourse established by Machiavelli and Hobbes, and by Lenin and Marx. It represented the covert triumph of *a philosophy of democratic idealism*.

Towards American Democracy

While insisting on the priority of values in political thought and action, the Port Huron Statement offered much more than a spiritual and moral manifesto. It contained a detailed political, social, and economic analysis of the malaise of welfare-warfare state capitalism and the failures of American democracy, and stinging indictments of the concentration of wealth and economic power; the "hard-core poverty [which] exists just beyond the neon lights of affluence" (20); the "pervasiveness of Racism in American life" (36); the paralyzing role of anti-Communism in the domestic politics and foreign policy of the United States; the madness and waste of resources of the arms race and nuclear deterrence strategy; and the anti-democratic role America's foreign and economic policies had played in the developing world.

The analysis of what was wrong with American society was followed by a detailed, specific program for economic and political change. It is in the prescriptive sections of the *Port Huron Statement* that we can see in embryo some of the fundamental ambiguities that were to plague the New Left throughout the decade of the 1960s. One way of framing these issues is to ask the question: "Was the domestic political program of the *Port Huron Statement* basically one of social democratic reform to curb the excesses of corporate capitalist society, or did it propose a truly radical democratic alternative?"

Phrased in these terms, the question elicits a fairly straightforward answer: the *Port Huron Statement* offers a basic set of social democratic reforms designed to expand government control of the economy through the enlargement of the (non-military) "public sector" and the expansion and improvement of the social programs of the welfare state. Insofar as this is true, the *Port Huron Statement* fails to develop a political program which realizes the radical democratic vision of participatory democracy and fails to make the values it espouses operational in its concrete programmatic proposals. Having said this, it is then necessary to point out that there is a second voice in the section of domestic programs which is radically democratic and decentralist but which is heard only intermittently and is much less fully developed than the dominant social democratic theme. Finally, it should be understood that there was a fundamental contradiction in the *Port Huron Statement* between these reformist proposals and the kind of radical democratic movement SDS was heralding and proposing to build. That movement, inspired by the kinds of vision and values Tom Hayden had elaborated, was the truly radical proposal of SDS at Port Huron, and, as it grew, it would be increasingly at odds with the social democratic reformism of its stated political program. But it is appropriate to pause here and explore the program briefly.

There are six points.

The first falls into the strategy called *realignment*—"America must abolish its political party stalemate" (p.46). Realignment was a political strategy strongly favored by the social democratic wing of SDS in New York. The argument was basically that Dixiecrats should be driven out of the Democratic Party to force a realignment of liberals and conservatives and to incorporate blacks into the Democratic Party. The Democratic Party would then become a left-liberal or social democratic party and the Republicans would develop into the truly conservative party. Not all of this argument was made explicit in the *Port Huron Statement*, but realignment was the basic strategy which was being proposed when it stated: "Two genuine parties, centered around issues and essential values, demanding allegiance to party principles shall supplant the current system of organized stalemate which is seriously inadequate to a world in flux." The demand is raised that the President "no longer tolerate the Southern conservatives in the Democratic Party" who are referred to as "racist scoundrels" (pp.46-47).

The second proposal is: "Mechanisms of voluntary association must be created though which political information can be imparted and political participation encouraged" (p.47). Even realignment of political parties "would not provide adequate outlets for popular involvement." Something is needed to counter the "giant lobby interest of business." This is a call for the creation of institutions "that engage people with issues and express political preference...in national decision-making enterprise." Basically this is a blueprint for citizens' lobbies designed to encourage public participation and to offset corporate power in government (p.47).

Thirdly, the domestic program argues: "Institutions and practices which stifle dissent should be abolished, and peaceful dissent should be actively promoted" (p.47). This is an appeal for the reaffirmation of the "First Amendment freedoms of speech, assembly, thought, religion and press" which are "guarantees, not threats to national security" and for the abolition of "institutions bred by fear and apathy," namely, "the House Un-American Activities Committee, the Senate Internal Security Committee, the loyalty oaths on Federal loans, the Attorney General's list of subversive organizations, the Smith and McCarran Acts." Abolition of these "blighting institutions is the process of restoring democratic institutions" (p.47).

The fourth point is strangely ambiguous in its wording: "Corporations must be made publicly responsible" (p.47). The sense of the proposal is that corporate power must be democratized, for, "It is not possible to believe that true democracy can exist where a minority utterly controls wealth and power." The interests and actions of corporation and industrial leaders "should become structurally responsible to the people." "A new reordering" is necessary which includes "changes in the rules of society by challenging the unchallenged politics of American corporations." Efforts at government "regulation," even if realized, "would be inadequate without increased worker participation in management decision-making, strengthened and independent regulating power, balances of partial and/or complete public ownership, various means of humanizing the conditions and types of work itself, sweeping welfare programs, and regional *public* development authorities." These suggestions are offered as "examples of measures to re-balance the economy toward public—and individual—control" (p.48). This hardly adds up to a program for "socialism" (a state-controlled planned economy), nor is it a clear blueprint for decentralized economic democracy. The obvious ambiguities are only partially resolved in the two succeeding points.

Point five asserts: "The allocation of resources must be based on social needs. A truly "public sector" must be established, and its nature debated and planned" (p.48). The currently existing public sector is largely the "permanent war economy" and "America must return to other mechanisms of growth besides military spending" (p.48). In addition, the "main private forces of economic expansion cannot guarantee a steady rate of growth, nor acceptable recovery from recession—especially in a demilitarizing world." However, any proposal for "major intervention into civilian production by the government" poses enormous issues:

A. "How should public vs. private domain be determined?"

B. "How should technological advances be introduced into society?"

C. "How shall the 'public sector' be made public, and not the arena of a ruling bureaucracy of 'public servants'?" (pp.49-50).

In all three areas an attempt is made to assert public need or interest over private interest or monopoly. It is a formula for a mixed economy with a social democratic direction. Only in the third area (C), do we get a glimmer of a decentralist alternative. The problems of a "ruling bureaucracy" (which are inherent in social democratic systems) are to be met by "steadfast opposition to bureaucratic coagulation...Bureaucratic pile-ups must be at least minimized by local, regional, and national economic planning...[and] by experiments in *decentralization*, based on the vision of man as master of his machine and his society (p.50).

These *important experiments in decentralization* are not spelled out in great detail after having been accorded pride of place. The most daring suggestion is that our "monster cities, based historically on the need for mass labor, might now be humanized, broken into smaller communities, powered by nuclear energy, arranged according to community decision" (p.50). The decentralist vision of "blueprints in civic paradise" is unwittingly marred by faith in nuclear power. Nonetheless, the social democratic perspective does not prevail without this strong voice of caution about the need for decentralization.

The sixth and final point outlines a set of social programs. "America should concentrate on its genuine social priorities: abolish squalor, terminate neglect, and establish an environment for people to live with dignity and creativeness." (50) The specifics of such a strategy should include anti-poverty programs, civil rights legislation, model cities programs, more and better mental health and public health facilities, educational and prison reform and federal support for farmers cooperatives. Finally, "science should be employed to constructively transform the conditions of life throughout the United States and the world," and the imbalance in favor of military over non-military research corrected (pp.50-53).

In retrospect, the contrast between the *manifesto of democratic radicalism* with which the *Port Huron Statement* begins and the program for social democratic reform which follows is indeed striking and somewhat bewildering. It reflected the division in SDS between the philosophy of democratic idealism that seemed to be at the core of Tom Hayden's thinking, and the tradition of socialist or social democratic leftism that had survived from the Old Left and which was basically informed by Marxist analysis.

If the *Port Huron Statement* had ended with the programmatic sections described above, it would have been disappointing. This was, fortunately, not the case and some of the élan of the manifesto was recaptured in the final two sections: "Alternatives to Helplessness" (pp.54-61) and "The University and Social Change" (pp.61-63).

What is to be done?

Surveying the political landscape of America for signs of hope and levers of change, the founders of SDS were less than sanguine about the prospects. Before presenting the possibilities of political organizing in the universities, the Statement examined each of the significant social forces in the country and found them wanting. First, the Southern civil rights movement was heralded "as the most heartening because of the justice it insists upon, exemplary because it indicated that there can be a passage out of apathy." This movement has instilled "a sense of self-determination…in millions of Negroes," it has "challenged a few thousand liberals to new social idealism," and it has won "a series of important concessions…such as token school desegregation, increased Administration help, new laws, desegregation of some public facilities." However, "fundamental social change…has not come." Instead, the "civil rights struggle has come to an impasse" that has led to the movement to enter "the sphere of politics, insisting on citizenship rights, specifically the right to vote." This "use of political means to solve the problems of equality in America" is particularly important because "the moral clarity of the civil rights movement has not always been accompanied by precise political vision" or even by "a real political consciousness" which makes "the new phase revolutionary in its implications." "Linked with pressure from Northern liberals to expunge Dixiecrats from the ranks of the Democratic party, massive Negro voting in the South could destroy the vise-like grip reactionary Southerners have on the Congressional legislative process" (pp.54-55).

Turning next to the "broadest movement for peace in several years," the framers were highly critical of its isolation from power. The peace movement was seen as operating "almost exclusively through peripheral institutions" and "individuals interested in peace have nonpolitical social roles." The social units of the peace movement "have not been located in spots of major social influence." "The results were political ineffectiveness and personal alienation." This has meant that the "organizing ability of the peace movement…is limited to the ability to state and polarize issues." Furthermore: "As long as the debates of the peace movement form only a protest, rather than an opposition viewpoint within the centers of decision-making, then it is neither a movement of democratic relevance, nor is it likely to have any effectiveness except in educating outsiders to the issue." This rather harsh indictment is followed by a suggestion that the peace movement might "prepare a *local base*, especially by establishing civic committees on the techniques of converting from military to peacetime production" (pp.55-57).

The appraisal of organized labor reveals a New Left impaled on the horn of an old dilemma. On the one hand,

"Labor's presence today as the most liberal of mainstream institutions" is duly noted while, on the other hand, "it would be irresponsible not to criticize labor for losing much of the idealism that once made it a driving movement." This amounts to a somewhat tangential recognition that while organized labor exists as a social force there is no labor movement as a real force for change. This situation is recognized to be "only partly due to anti-labor politicians and corporations. Blame should be laid, too, to labor itself for not mounting an adequate movement." This failure stems in part from the fact that "Labor has too often seen itself as elitist, rather than mass-oriented, and as a pressure group rather than an 18-million-member body making political demands for all America."

There are "indicators…that labor might regain some of its missing idealism." These signs stem from "workers' discontent" with collective bargaining gains and "occasional splits among union leaders" on "nuclear testing or other Cold War issues." More importantly, the "permanence of unemployment, and the threat of automation" are creating these "feelings of unrest" as are "the growth of unorganized ranks in white-collar fields." Finally, there is "the tremendous challenge of the Negro movement" for labor's support.

There is a good deal of ambivalence in this assessment of labor's political future. The situation is seen as "a profound crisis: either labor will continue to decline as a social force, or it must constitute itself as a mass political force." One voice at Port Huron argues that "A new politics must include a revitalized labor movement," and that it is "the best candidate for the synthesis of the civil rights, peace, and economic reform movements." Another voice says that "the new politics is still contained; it struggles below the surface of apathy, awaiting liberation. Few anticipate the breakthrough and fewer still exhort labor to begin. Labor continues to be the most liberal—and most frustrating institution in mainstream America" (pp.57-59).

It would have been more honest to admit the dilemma outright. The rather tortuous reworking of the "labor question" suggests real differences and real political struggles among the participants at Port Huron. If there is a lack of clarity about these differences, it is because a sincere effort was being made to contain somewhat conflicting viewpoints within a single document. By obscuring these differences, the framers produce positions lacking precision and clarity.

The survey of social forces includes a brief glance at the Democratic Party and the ill-fated "Liberal Project" of Wisconsin's Representative Kastenmeier—an attempt to create a "liberal force in Congress." The sheer brevity of the discussion of the Democrats at this juncture leads one to suspect that a lot was left unsaid. In fact, of course, there was relatively little evidence that that Democratic Party deserved to be listed among those "social forces" which stood as harbingers of change in America (p.59). The political strategy that follows the assessment of social forces is basically another statement of "realignment." "An imperative task for these disinherited groups, then, is to demand a Democratic Party responsible to their interests" (p.60).

The University and Social Change

The pessimism that seems to flow from this appraisal of the potential forces of change in America is countered in the final section of the Port Huron Statement by an assessment of the potential role of universities.

> There is perhaps little reason to be optimistic about the above analysis. True, the Dixiecrat-GOP coalition is the weakest point in the dominating complex of corporate, military, and political power. But the civil rights, peace, and student movements are too poor and socially slighted, and the labor movement too quiescent, to be counted with enthusiasm. From where else can power and vision be summoned? We believe that the universities are an overlooked seat of influence (p.61).

Central to SDS's conception of the building of a New Left was its particular view of the university as an institution and students as actors. Students were "breaking the crust of apathy and overcoming the inner alienation that remain the defining characteristics of American college life" (p.9). Furthermore, this awakening among students was taking place in an institution that had become pivotal in American society. SDS was perhaps unique in its grasp of the importance of this conjuncture of institutional and social forces. No other group seems to have realized so early that students and the university constituted in and of themselves a key focus for social ferment and political change. Those gathered at Port Huron may in fact have underestimated the power that the university constituency would have in the emerging New Left, but they certainly did grasp the centrality of its position and invested great hope in its potential. Their vision of students and the university was basically as catalytic agents that would energize other sectors of the society. They almost certainly did not share the same analysis of students and university-trained workers that was later associated with notions of "the new working class."

The *Port Huron Statement* lists four reasons for the importance of the university. First, it is "located in a permanent position of social influence" and is a "crucial institution in the formation of social attitudes." Second, "it is the central institution for organizing, evaluating, and transmitting knowledge." Third, "the extent to which academic resources presently are used to buttress immoral social practice" (revealed through "defense contracts," the use of social science as a "manipulative aspect of American politics") demonstrates "the unchangeable reliance by men of power on the men and store-houses of knowledge." All this "makes this university functionally tied to society in new ways, revealing new potentialities, new levers for change." Fourth, it is "the only mainstream institution that is open to participation by individuals of nearly every viewpoint." "Social relevance, the accessibility to knowledge, and internal openness...make the university a potential base and agency in a movement of social change" (p.61).

This brief analysis is followed by a six-point declaration that outlines the essential features that this new movement in universities must display. First, "Any new left in America must be...a left with real intellectual skills" and "the university permits the political life to be an adjunct to the academic one, and action to be informed by reason." Second, "A new left must be distributed in significant social roles" which is the case of universities. Third, "A new left must consist of younger people who matured in the post-war world" which makes universities "an obvious beginning point" for recruitment. Fourth, "A new left must include liberals and socialists, the former for their relevance, the latter for their sense of thoroughgoing reforms in the system" and universities are "a more sensible place than a political party" for dialogue between them. Fifth, "A new left must start controversy across the land" and "the ideal university is a community of controversy." Sixth, "A new left must transform complexity into issues that can be understood and felt close up be every human being." It must (in a paraphrase of C. Wright Mills), "give form to the feelings of helplessness and indifference, so that people may see the political social, and economic sources of their private troubles and organize to change society" (p.62). (This challenge to link *the personal and the political* prefigured a major theme of the women's liberation movement later in the decade.[24]) Finally there is the recognition that a new movement cannot rely solely on the old levers of economic deprivation to motivate people in the direction of change: "a new left cannot rely on only aching stomachs to be the engine force of social reforms" (p.62).

The *Statement* ends with a clear recognition that a new left movement in universities will not be sufficient in itself and must seek allies and build bridges to other constituencies "in labor, civil rights, and other liberal forces outside the campus." In long range terms, the "bridge to political power...will be built through genuine cooperation, locally, nationally, and internationally between a new left of young people and an awakening community of allies." On campuses there must be "national efforts at university reform by an alliance of students and faculty" that would "wrest control of the educational process from the administrative bureaucracy." Moreover, students and faculty "must make debate and controversy, not dull pedantic cant, the common style for educational life…and consciously build a base for their assault upon the loci of power" (pp.62-63).

The *Statement* ends with this pronouncement:

As students for a democratic society, we are committed to stimulating this kind of social movement, this kind of vision and program in campus and community across the country. If we appear to seek the unattainable, as it has been said, then let it be known that we do so to avoid the unimaginable (p.63).

An Open-ended Discourse

Not unexpectedly, the presentation of participatory democracy in the Port Huron Statement raised more questions than it answered. Its "creative ambiguity" was both a boon and a burden, for there were basically two different interpretations that could be given to that phrase and they were fundamentally irreconcilable. The ambiguity was further reinforced by the obvious disparity between the radical democratic vision of the first part of the document and its reformist program. This meant that there were many people who would be attracted to the radical potential of the ideal of participatory democracy when reading the first part of the Port Huron Statement but who would be dismayed or bored by the programmatic section. People like this would adopt the language of participatory democracy and begin to draw their own conclusions about its implications. This was how ambiguity became the basis for real political conflict in the New Left. Each side felt it represented the authentic interpretation of the vision of democratic participation.

On the one hand, there was a "liberal reformist" interpretation which could argue that that basic institutions of the liberal democratic capitalist order needed new mechanisms that would increase democratic participation in political processes and would facilitate further social and economic reforms. This position, whether its supporters like the label or not, was basically "social democratic." Its logic implied that the proper direction for American political life was to build on the achievements of the New Deal welfare state and extend reforms in the direction of a full-blown social democracy. This position was more or less compatible with both "left-liberal" ideology and with reformist (or "revisionist") Marxism of the social democratic or "democratic socialist" variety. On the other hand, there was to be a "radical decentralist" interpretation which regarded the vision of a participatory democracy as basically incompatible with the centralized, hierarchical, and dominative institutions of corporate capitalism and the modern state. This second position led in the direction of radical decentralizing change in political, social, and economic life and emphasized anti-authoritarian or libertarian values and the importance of alternative, liberatory cultural values and experimentation. This second position was highly skeptical of liberal electoral politics and was likely to seek its historical inspiration in the decentralist, libertarian, anarcho-pacifist, or anarcho-syndicalist traditions. Since, however, relatively little was known in the United States about these traditions, the decentralist position was slow to articulate its differences from the left-liberal or social democratic positions.

These two interpretations were inherent in the problematic framed by the discourse on participatory democracy. The two positions are the logical outcome of raising questions about liberal capitalist democracy from a radical democratic viewpoint. And therein lay the dilemma: even if the intent of *some* of the framers of the *Port Huron Statement* was predominantly left-liberal or social democratic, the critique of liberalism inherent in the phrase "participatory democracy" led inevitably to radical democratic conclusions. This was the case because the demand for democratic participation implies that power should function from the bottom up, and liberal capitalist "democracy" perpetuates power from the top down. It was this dynamic which led to the fundamental distinction that New Leftists came to draw between "liberal" and "radical."

Thus, however much certain of the original members and leaders of SDS wanted to maintain the liberal reformist or social democratic perspective, they had adopted a document whose language had radical implications that would be explored and elaborated whether they liked it or not. Furthermore, participatory democracy was just the kind of concept that would attract increasing numbers of young democratic radicals with decentralist values and libertarian instincts and an aversion to the ideological baggage of all left-wing debates, whether Marxist or anarchist. Participatory democracy offered a new and exciting way to talk about radical democratic ideas and in so doing it created the opportunity for the rebirth of a genuinely American radicalism. The very open-ended character of this new discourse was an invitation to creativity, but it was also the seedbed of ambivalence and honest confusion. It was possible for people with fundamentally different political perspectives to believe that participatory democracy spoke for their different viewpoints. As the New Left grew during the 1960s, these differences would become increasingly apparent and shift the direction of SDS.

Notes

1. This interpretation is disputed in its essentials by James Miller in his book, *Democracy in the Streets: From Port Huron to the Siege of Chicago,* (Simon & Schuster: New York, 1987). In particular, Miller regards the notion "that [the New Left] owed its key ideas, including 'participatory democracy' to the example of black civil rights activists in the South" as one of the major "misleading assertions about the origins of the New Left." See p. 16. I regard his narrow focus on intellectual history and biography as responsible for his failure to recognize the importance that the SNCC experience had for the development of the political ideas of the New Left. Otherwise, his book is an invaluable source of information.

2. Kirkpatrick Sale, *SDS* (Random House, Vintage Edition: New York, 1974), p. 23. Quoted in A.D. Morris, *Origins of the Civil Rights Movement: Black Communities Organizing for Change*, (Macmillan, The Free Press: New York, 1984), p. 222.

3. *Ibid.*, p. 222.

4. *Ibid.*, based on an article by Richard Flacks, "Who Protests: The Social Bases of the Student Movement," in Julian Foster and Durward Long, eds., *Protest! Student Activism in America* (New York: William Morrow, 1970), pp. 134-57.

5. *Ibid.*

6. *Ibid.*, p. 223, from an interview with Robert Alan Haber, April 24, 1982, Berkeley, Calif.

7. *Ibid.*

8. Miller, *"Democracy in the Streets,"* p. 23.

9. *Ibid.*, Chapter 2, "On the Road," pp. 41 ff.

10. *Ibid.*, Chapter 4, "The Prophet of the Powerless," pp. 78 ff.

11. *Ibid.*, p. 16.

12. Sheldon Wolin, *Politics and Vision* (Boston: Little, Brown and Company, 1960), Chapter 9, "Liberalism and the Decline of Political Philosophy," pp. 286 ff.

13. Miller, *"Democracy in the Streets,"* p. 48.

14. *Ibid.*, pp. 48-50. See also, Sara Evans, *Personal Politics: The Roots of Women's Liberation in the Civil Rights Movement and the New Left* (New York: Random House, Vintage Books edition, 1980), pp. 33-34.

15. Miller, *"Democracy in the Streets,"* pp. 50-51.

16. *Ibid.*, pp. 51-52.

17. *Ibid.*, p. 54.

18. *Ibid.*, pp. 55-56.

19. *Ibid.*, p. 56. Morris, *The Origins of the Civil Rights Movement*, p. 223.

20. Miller, *"Democracy in the Streets,"* pp. 60-61.

21. *Ibid.*, p. 104.

22. *Ibid.*, pp. 110, 119.

23. *Port Huron Statement* (Students for a Democratic Society, 1962; reprinted Chicago, 1966), p. 6. Subsequent references will appear in the text. The complete text of the Statement is also available as an "Appendix" in Miller, *"Democracy in the Streets,"* pp. 329-74.

24. See Evans, *Personal Politics*.

THE WAY WE WERE AND THE FUTURE OF THE PORT HURON STATEMENT

by Tom Hayden

Outside of Port Huron, Michigan, where a dense thicket meets the lapping shores of Lake Huron, the careful explorer will come across rusty and timeworn pipes and a few collapsed foundations, the last traces of the labor camp where sixty young people finalized the *Port Huron Statement*—the seminal "agenda for a generation"—in 1962.

Some hope that our legacy will be washed out with the refuse in those pipes. Out of sight, out of mind. For the conservative icon Robert Bork, the *Port Huron Statement (PHS)* was considered "a document of ominous mood and aspiration," because of his fixed certainty that, by misreading human nature, utopian movements turn out badly. David Horowitz, a former sixties radical who turned to the hardcore right, dismisses the *PHS* as a "self-conscious effort to rescue the communist project from its Soviet fate." Another ex-leftist, Christopher Hitchens, sees in its pages a conservative reaction to "bigness and anonymity and urbanization," even linking its vision to the Unabomber![1] More progressive writers, such as Garry Wills, E.J. Dionne, and Paul Berman, see the *PHS* as a bright moment of reformist vision that withered due to the impatience and extremism of the young. Excerpts of the *PHS* have been published in countless textbooks, and an Internet search re-

---

Tom Hayden, who drafted The Port Huron Statement *in 1962 when he was twenty-one years old, was among the founders of Students for a Democratic Society, a Freedom Rider in the segregated South, a community organizer in the slums of New Jersey, an opponent of the Vietnam War who was indicted by Richard Nixon, and eventually a legislator in both the California State Senate and Assembly for eighteen years. He lives in Los Angeles, where he teaches at Occidental College. He is the author of nine books, including a new edition of* The Port Huron Statement: The Visionary Call of the 1960s Revolution, *(Thunder's Mouth Press: New York, 2005).*

turns numerous references to "participatory democracy," its central philosophic theme. Grassroots movements in Argentina and Venezuela today use "participatory democracy" to describe their popular assemblies and factory takeovers. The historian Thomas Cahill writes that the Greek *ekklesia* was "the world's first participatory democracy" and the model for the early Catholic Church, which permitted no restrictions on participation: no citizens and non-citizens, no Greeks, and non-Greeks, no patriarchs and submissive females."[2] In modern popular culture, authorship of the *PHS*, has been claimed by the stoned hippie character played by Jeff Bridges in *The Big Lebowski*.

The story of the 1962 Port Huron convention has been told many times by participants and later researchers, and I will describe it here only briefly so as to focus more on the meaning of the statement itself.[3] The sixty or so young people who met in Port Huron were typically active in the fledgling civil rights, campus reform, and peace movements of the era. Some, like myself, were campus journalists, while others were active in student governments. Some walked picket lines in solidarity with the southern student sit-in movement. More than a few were moved by their religious traditions. My adolescent ambition was to become a foreign correspondent, which was a metaphor for breaking out of the suffocating apathy of the times. Instead, I found myself interviewing and reflecting on southern black dispossessed sharecroppers; students who were willing to go to jail, even die, for their cause; civil rights leader Dr. Martin Luther King Jr. as he marched outside my first Democratic convention; and candidate John Kennedy, giving his speech proposing the Peace Corps on a rainy night in Ann Arbor. I was thrilled by the times in which I lived, and I chose to help build a new student organization, the Students for a Democratic Society, rather than pursue journalism. My parents were stunned.

SDS was the fragile brainchild of Alan Haber, an Ann Arbor graduate student whose father had been a labor official during the last progressive American administration, that of President Franklin Delano Roosevelt. Al was a living link with the fading legacy of the radical left movements that had built the labor movement and the New Deal. He sensed a new spirit among students in 1960 and recruited me to become a "field secretary," which meant moving to Atlanta with my wife, Casey, who had been a leader of the campus sit-ins in Austin, Texas. While participating in the direct action movement and mobilizing national support by writing and speaking on campuses, I learned that passionate advocacy, arising from personal experience, could be a powerful weapon.

Haber and other student leaders across the United States became increasingly aware of a need to connect all the issues that weighed on our generation-apathy, *in loco parentis*, civil rights, the Cold War, the atomic bomb. And so, in December 1961, at twenty-two years of age and fresh from jail as a Freedom Rider in Albany, Georgia, I was asked to begin drafting a document that would express the vision underlying our action. It was to be a short manifesto, a recruiting tool, perhaps five or ten single-spaced pages. Instead it mushroomed into a fifty-page, single-spaced draft prepared for the Port Huron convention in May 1962. That version was debated and rewritten, section by section, by those who attended the five-day Port Huron meeting and was then returned to me for final polishing. Twenty thousand copies were mimeographed and sold for thirty-five cents each.

The vision grew from a concrete generational experience. Rarely, if ever, had students thought of themselves as a force in history or, as we phrased it, an "agency of social change." We were rebelling against the experience of apathy, not against a single specific oppression. We were moved by the heroic example of the black youth in the South, whose rebellion taught us the fundamental importance of race. We were treated legally as wards under our universities' paternal care and could not vote, but as young men we could be conscripted to fight in places we dimly understood, such as Vietnam and Laos. The nation's priorities were frozen by the Cold War: a permanent nuclear arms race benefiting what President Eisenhower had called "the military-industrial complex," whose appetite absorbed the resources we believed were necessary to address the crises of civil rights and poverty, or what John Kenneth Galbraith termed "squalor in the midst of affluence."

Apathy, we came to suspect, was what the administrators and power technicians actually desired. Apathy was not our fault, not an accident, but rather the result of social engineering by those who ran the institutions that taught us, employed us, entertained us, drafted us, bored us, controlled us, wanted us to accept the absolute impossibility of another way of being. It was for this reason that our rhetoric emphasized "ordinary people" developing "out of apathy" (the term was C. Wright Mill's) in order to "make history."[4] Since many of us had emerged from apathetic lives (neither of my parents were political in any sense, and I had attended conservative Catholic schools), we began with the realization that we had to relate to, not denounce, the everyday lives of students and communities around us in order to replicate the journey out of apathy on a massive scale.

We chose to put "values" forward as the first priority in challenging the conditions of apathy and forging a new politics. Embracing values meant making choices as morally autonomous human beings against a world that advertised in every possible way that there were no choices, that the present was just a warm-up for the future.

The Lasting Legacy of Participatory Democracy

The idea of participatory democracy, therefore, should be understood in its psychic, liberatory dimension, not simply as an alternative concept of government organization. Cynics such as Paul Berman acknowledge that the concept of participatory democracy "survived" the demise of the New Left because it "articulated the existential drama of moral activism." (italics added)[5] The notion (and phrase) was transmitted by a philosophy professor in Ann Arbor, Arnold Kaufman, who attended the Port Huron convention. Its roots were as deep and distant as the Native American tribal traditions of consensus.[6] It rose among the tumultuous rebels of western Massachusetts who drove out the British and established self-governing committees in the prelude to the American Revolution. It was common practice among the Society of Friends and in New England's town meetings. It appeared in Thomas Paine's Rights of Man in passages exalting "the mass of sense lying in a dormant state"in oppressed humanity, which could be awakened and "excited to action" through revolution.[7] It was extolled (if not always implemented) by Thomas Jefferson, who wrote that every person should believe himself or herself to be "a participator in the government of affairs, not merely at an election one day a year, but every day.[8] Perhaps the most compelling advocate of participatory democracy, however, was Henry David Thoreau, the nineteenth-century author of Civil Disobedience, who opposed taxation for either slavery or war, and who called on Americans to vote "not with a mere strip of paper but with your whole life." Thoreau's words were often repeated in the early days of the sixties civil rights and antiwar movements.

This heritage of participatory democracy also was transmitted to SDS through the works of the revered philosopher John Dewey, who was a leader of the League for Industrial Democracy (LID), the parent organization of SDS, from 1939 to the early 1950s. Dewey believed that "democracy is more than a form of government; it is primarily a mode of associated living, of conjoint communicated experience." It meant participation in all social institutions, not simply going through the motions of elections, and notably, "the participation of every mature human being in the formation of the values that regulate the living of men together."[9]

Then came the rebel sociologist C. Wright Mills, a descendent of Dewey and prophet of the New Left, who died of a heart attack shortly before the *Port Huron Statement* was produced. Mills had a profound effect in describing a new stratum of radical democratic intellectuals around the world, weary of the stultifying effects of bureaucracy in both the United States and the Soviet Union. His descriptions of the power elite, the mass society, the "democracy without publics," the apathy that turned so many into "cheerful robots," seemed to explain perfectly the need for democracy from the bottom up. The representative democratic system seemed of limited value as long as so many Americans were disenfranchised structurally and alienated culturally. We believed, based on our own experience, that participation in direct action was a method of psychic empowerment, a fulfillment of human potential, a means of curing alienation, as well as an effective means of mass protest. We believed that "ordinary people should have a voice in the decisions that affect their lives," because it was necessary for their dignity, not simply a blueprint for greater accountability.

Some of the Port Huron language appears to be plagiarized from the Vatican's *Pacem in Terris (Peace on Earth)*.[10] That would be not entirely accidental, because a spirit of peace and justice was flowing through the most traditional of institutions, including southern black Protestant churches, and soon would flourish as Catholic "liberation theology," a direct form of participatory democracy in Third World peasant communities. This "movement spirit" was present everywhere-not only in religion but in music and the arts as well. We studied the lyrics of Bob Dylan more than we did the texts of Marx and Lenin. Dylan even attended an SDS meeting or two. He had hitchhiked east in search of Woody Guthrie, after all. Though never an activist, he expressed our sensibility exactly when he described mainstream culture as "lame as hell and a big trick," where "there was nobody to check with," and folk music as a "guide into some altered consciousness of reality, some different republic, some liberated republic."[11]

The experience of middle-class alienation drew us to Mill's *White Collar*, Albert Camus's *The Stranger*, or Paul Goodman's *Growing Up Absurd*. Our heady sense of the student movement was validated in Mill's "Letter to the New Left" or *Listen Yankee!* The experience of confronting structural unemployment in the "other America" was illuminated by Michael Harrington and the tradition of Marxism. Liberation theology reinforced the concept of living among the poor. The reawakening of women's consciousness was hinted in Doris Lessing's *The Golden Notebook* (which some of us read back-to-back with Clancy Sigal's *Going Away*) or Simone de Beauvoir's *The Second Sex*. The participatory ethic of direct action —of ending segregation, for example, by actually integrating lunch counters— drew from traditions of anarchism as well. (At a small SDS planning meeting in 1960, Dwight Macdonald gave a keynote speech on "The Relevance of Anarchism."[12] The ethos of direct action leaped from romantic revolutionary novels like Ignazio Silone's *Bread and Wine*, whose hero, a revolutionary masked as a priest, said it "would be a waste of time to show a people of intimidated slaves a different manner of speaking...but perhaps it would be worthwhile to show them a different way of living."[13]

The idea was to challenge elite authority by direct example on the one hand, and on the other to draw "ordinary people," whether apathetic students, sharecroppers, or office workers, into a dawning belief in their own right to participate in decisions. This was the method—call it consciousness-raising—of the Student Nonviolent Coordinating Committee, which influenced SDS, the early women's liberation groups, farm workers' house meetings, and Catholic base communities, eventually spreading to Vietnam's veterans' rap groups and other organizations. Participatory democracy was a tactic of movement-building as well as an end itself. And by an insistence on *listening* to "the people" as a basic ethic of participatory democracy, the early movement was able to guarantee its roots in American culture and traditions while avoiding the imported ideologies that infected many elements of the earlier left.

Through participatory democracy we could theorize a concrete, egalitarian transformation of the workplaces of great corporations, urban neighborhoods, the classrooms of college campuses, religious congregations, and the structures of political democracy itself. We believed that representative democracy, while an advance over the divine right of kings or bureaucratic dictatorships, should be replaced or reformed by a greater emphasis on decentralized decision-making, remaking our world from the bottom up.

Some of our pronouncements were absurd or embarrassing, like the notion of "cheap" nuclear power becoming a decentralized source of community-based energy, the declaration that "the International Geophysical Year is a model for continuous further cooperation," or the unquestioned utilization of grating sexist terminology ("men" instead of "human beings") in sweeping affirmations about dignity and equality. We could not completely transcend the times, or even predict the near-term future: the rise of the women's and environmental movements, the war in Vietnam, the political assassinations. The gay community was closeted invisibly among us.[14] The beat poets, such as Jack Kerouac and Allen Ginsberg, had stirred us, but the full-blown counterculture, psychedelic drugs such as LSD and mescaline, the Beatles, and the writings of Hebert Marcuse, were two years away.

Yet through many ups and downs, participatory democracy has spread as an ethic throughout everyday life and has become a persistent challenge to top-down institutions all over the world. It has surfaced in campaigns of the global justice movement, in struggles for workplace and neighborhood empowerment, resistance to the Vietnam War draft, in Paulo Freiere's "pedagogy of the oppressed," in political platforms from Green parties to the Zapatistas, in the independent media, and in grassroots Internet campaigns including that of Howard Dean in 2004. Belief in the new participatory norm has resulted in major, if incomplete, policy triumphs mandating everything from freedom-of-information disclosures to citizen participation requirements in multiple realms of official decision-making. It remains a powerful threat to those in established bureaucracies who fear and suppress what they call "an excess of democracy."[15]

The Port Huron Strategy of Radical Reform

If the vision of participatory democracy has continuing relevance, so too does the strategic analysis of radical reform at the heart of the PHS. Our critique of the Cold War, and liberals who became anticommunist Cold Warriors, bears close resemblance to the contemporary "war on terror" and its liberal Democratic defenders. The Cold War, like today's war on terror, was the organized framework of dominance over our lives. This world was bipolar, divided into good and evil, allies and enemies. The U.S.-led Cold War alliance included any dictators, mafias, or thieving politicians in the world who declared themselves anticommunist. The Cold War alliance scorned the seventy-plus nonaligned nations as being "soft on communism." The United States and its allies engaged in violence or subversion against any governments that included communist or "pro-communist" participation, even if they were democratically elected, such as Guatemala (1945) or Chile (1970). Domestically, the American communists who had helped build the industrial unions, the Congress of Industrial Organizations, the defense of the Scottsboro Boys, the racial integration of major league baseball, who had joined the war against Hitler, suddenly found themselves purged or blacklisted as "un-American" for the very pro-Soviet sympathies that had been popular during World War II.[16] The parallels with today's war-on-terror coalition (including unstable dictatorships like Pakistan and Uzbekistan), and between the McCarthy-era witch hunts and today's Patriot Act roundups of "suspicious" Muslims, are eerie. Then it was a ubiquitous "atomic spy ring," today it is the omnipresent AlQaeda. The externalizing of the feared, ubiquitous, secretive, religiously alien, and foreign "communist" or "terrorist" enemy, the drumbeat of fear issuing from "terror alerts" and mass media sensationalism, the dominance of military spending over any other priority, and the ever-increasing growth of a National Security State—all of these themes of the Cold War have been revived in our country's newest crusade.

Of course the "threat" of violence is not imaginary. Raging militants have attacked innocent Americans and are likely to do so again. Our government's $30 billion intelligence budget failed to stop them. But those who question the current military priorities or dare to speak of root causes-addressing the abject misery and poverty of billions of people that contributed to the growth of communism in the past or Islamic militancy today-are dismissed too often as enemy sympathizers or soft-headed pacifists who cannot be trusted with questions of national security ("sentimentalists, the utopians, the wailers," historian Arthur Schlesinger called them during the Cold War).[17] Today such people are accused of "blaming America first" by critics from neoconservative Jeanne Kirkpatrick to former SDS leader Todd Gitlin.[18] In the Cold War days, the CIA routinely funded a covert class of liberal anticommunists everywhere from the American Committee for Cultural Freedom to the AFL-CIO to the U.S. National Student Association.[19] There is a direct line, even a genealogical one, from the leaders of those groupings, such as Irving Kristol and Norman Podhoretz. To their neoconservative descendants, such as William Kristol, editor of the *Weekly Standard*, and John Podhoretz, and from the forties celebration of "the American Century" to today's neoconservative project, the Project for the New American Century. As for the definition of "the enemy," during the Cold War it was a conspiracy centralized in Moscow through a myriad of puppet regimes and parties; today it is Al Qaeda, an invisible network consolidated and controlled by Osama bin Laden and a handful of conspirators.

The *Port Huron Statement* properly dissociated itself from the Soviet Union and communist ideology, just as antiwar critics today are opposed to Al Qaeda's religious fundamentalism or terror against civilians. But the *PHS* broke all taboos by identifying the Cold War itself as the framework that blocked our aspirations.[20] As a result, SDS was accused of being insufficiently "anticommunist" by some of its patrons in the older liberal left who had been deeply devoted to the liberal anticommunist crusade.[21] The truth lay in contrasting generational experiences: we were inspired by the civil rights movement, by the hope of ending poverty, with the gap between democratic promise and inequality as reality. The Cold War focused our nation's attention and its budget priorities outward on enemies abroad rather than on the enemies in our face at home. The nuclear arms race and permanent war economy drained any resources that could be devoted to ending poverty or hunger, either at home or among the wretched of the earth. Most, not all, of the liberal establishment-the people we had looked up to-left behind their idealistic roots and became allied to the military-industrial complex. Today a similar transition has occurred among many within the Democratic Party's establishment. Despite their roots in civil rights and antipoverty programs, they have become devotees of a corporate agenda, promoting the privatization of public assets from Latin America to the Middle East, creating the undemocratic World Trade Organization, whose rules taken literally would define the New Deal as a "restraint on trade."[22] With the attacks of September 11, 2001, many of the same liberals have abandoned their pasts in the anti-Vietnam movement, or the McCarthy, Kennedy, and McGovern campaigns, to pass the Patriot Act, invade Afghanistan and Iraq, justify the use of torture and detention without trial, and expand the Big Brother national security apparatus, while leaving the United States at the bottom among industrialized countries in its contributions to United Nations programs to combat hunger, illiteracy, and drinking-water pollution.[23] Consistent with the Cold War era, any politician who questions these priorities, even a decorated war veteran, will be castigated as soft on terrorism and effectively threatened with political defeat.[24]

The *Port Huron Statement* called for a coalescing of social movements: civil rights, peace, labor, liberals, and students. It was an original formulation at the time, departing from the centrality of organized labor, or the working class, that had governed the left for decades and it caused some of our elders to grind their teeth. The *PHS* reaffirmed that labor was crucial to any movement for social change, while chastising the labor "movement" for having become "stale." The Port Huron vision was far more populist, more middle-class, more quality-of-life in orientation than the customary platforms of the left. The election of an Irish Catholic president in 1960 symbolized the assumed assimilation of the white ethnics into the middle class and offered hope that people of color would follow in turn. The goal of racial integration was little questioned. Women had not begun to challenge patriarchy. Environmentalism had yet to assault the metaphysic of "growth." And so we could envision unifying nearly everyone around fulfillment of the New Deal dream. The *PHS* connected issues not like a menu, not as gestures to diverse identity movements, but more seamlessly, by declaring that the civil rights, antipoverty, and peace movements could realize their dreams by refocusing America's attention to an unfulfilled domestic agenda instead of the Cold War.

The document contained an explicit electoral strategy as well, envisioning the "realignment" of the Democratic Party into a progressive instrument. The strategy was to undermine the racist "Dixiecrat" element of the party through the southern civil rights movement and its national support network. The Dixiecrats not only dominated the segregationist political economy of the South but the crucial committees on military spending in the U.S. Congress as well. The racists also were the hawks. By undermining the southern segregationists, we could weaken the institutional supports for greater military spending and violent anti-Communism. The party would thus "realign" as white southerners defected to the Republicans, black southerners registered as Democrats, and the national party retained its New Deal liberal leanings. Through realignment, some of us dreamt, a radical-liberal governing coalition could achieve political power in America-in our lifetime, through our work.

This is the challenge that SDS took on: to argue against "unreasoning anti-Communism," to demand steps toward arms reductions and disarmament, to channel the trillions spent on weapons toward ending poverty in the world and at home. It was the kind of inspired thinking of which the young are most often capable, but it also was relevant to the times. After Port Huron, Haber and I traveled to the White House to brief Arthur Schlesinger on our work, hoping to spark a dialogue about the new movements. There were a handful of liberal White House staffers like Harris Wofford and Richard Goodwin who seemed to take an interest. We also had funds and the goodwill of Walter Reuther, president of the United Auto Workers (whose top assistant, Mildred Jeffrey, happened to be the mother of Sharon Jeffrey, an Ann Arbor SDS activist).

History has completely ignored, or forgotten, how close we came to implementing this main vision of the *Port Huron Statement*. President John Kennedy and his counterparts in Moscow were considering a historic turn away from the Cold War arms race, sentiments the president would express quite boldly just before he was killed. At a time when his generals sought a first-strike policy, Kennedy promoted a nuclear test ban treaty and offered a vision beyond the Cold War in August 1963, three months before the assassination. At the same time, Kennedy's positions on civil rights and poverty were rapidly evolving as well. At first the Kennedys had been taken aback by the Freedom Riders, with Attorney General Robert Kennedy wondering aloud if we had "the best interest of the country at heart" or were providing "good propaganda for America's enemies."[25] President Kennedy can be heard on White House tapes calling the Student Nonviolent Coordinating Committee (SNCC) and its chairman, future Congressman John Lewis[26] "sons of bitches"[27] "The problem with you people," Kennedy once snapped, (is that) you want too much too fast."[28] In this sense, the Kennedys were reflecting, not shaping, the mood of the country. Sixty-three percent of Americans opposed the Freedom Rides that preceded Port Huron. The *New York Times* opined that "nonviolence that deliberately provokes violence is a logical contradiction."[29] President Kennedy, who at first opposed the March on Washington as being too politically provocative, finally changed his mind and instead welcomed the civil rights leadership to the White House.[30] By the time of his assassination, he and his brother Bobby were almost becoming "brothers" in the eyes of the civil rights leadership. In addition to their joint destiny with the civil rights cause, Kennedy was sparking a public interest in attacking poverty, having read and recommended Mike Harrington's *The Other America.* One of the original plans for the War on Poverty, according to a biography of Sargeant Shriver, was "empowering the poor to agitate against the local political structure for institutional reform," which would have aligned the administration closely—perhaps too closely—with SNCC and SDS community organizers.[31]

For Kennedy to truly address poverty and racism in a second term would have required a turn away from the nuclear arms race and the budding U.S. counterinsurgency war in Vietnam. Robert Kennedy suggested as much in a 1964 interview: "For the first few years...(JFK) had to concentrate all his energies... on foreign affairs. He thought that a good deal more was needed domestically. The major issue was the question of civil rights... Secondly, he thought that we really had to begin to make a major effort to deal with unemployment and the poor in the United States."[32] Despite efforts by today's neoconservatives to portray Kennedy as a Cold War hawk, the preponderance of evidence is that he intended to withdraw all American troops from Vietnam by 1965. Two days before his murder, for example, the administration announced plans to withdraw 1,000-1,300 troops from South Vietnam. But two days after his death, on November 24, a covert plan was adopted in National Security Memorandum 273 that authorized secret operations, "graduated in intensity," against North Vietnam.[33]

The assassination of President John F. Kennedy was the first of several catastrophic murders that changed all our lives; and the trajectory of events imagined at Port Huron was also changed. The dates must be kept in mind: most of us who assembled there were about twenty-one years old in June 1962. An idealistic so-cial movement was exploding, winning attention from a new administration. Just as we had hoped, the March on Washington made race and poverty the central moral issues facing the country; the peace movement would hear a president pledging to end the cold war. But then a murder derailed the new national direc-tion. I was about to turn twenty-four when Kennedy was killed. The experience will forever shadow the meaning of the sixties. The very concept of a presidential as-sassination was completely outside my youthful expectations for the future. No matter what history may reveal about the murder, the feeling was chillingly ines-capable that the sequence of the president's actions on the Cold War and racism soon led to his death. The subsequent assassinations of the Reverend Martin Lu-ther King Jr. and Senator Robert Kennedy in 1968 permanently derailed what re-mained of the hopes that were born at Port Huron. Whether one believes the murders were conspiracies or isolated accidents, the effect was to destroy the pro-gressive political potential of the sixties and leave us all as "might-have-beens," in the phrase of the late Jack Newfield.

Hope died slowly and painfully. There still was hope in the year following President Kennedy's murder—for example, in the form of the Mississippi Freedom Democratic Party, the most important organized embodiment of the Port Huron hope for political realignment. Organized by SNCC in 1963-1964, the MFDP was a grassroots Democratic Party led by Mississippi's dispossessed blacks, with the goal of seeking recognition from the national Democratic Party at its 1964 conven-tion in Atlantic City. The MFDP originated in November 1963, the very month of the Kennedy assassination, when ninety thousand blacks in Mississippi risked their lives to set up a "freedom vote" to protest their exclusion from the political pro-cess. Then came Freedom Summer 1964, including the kidnapping and murders of James Cheney, Andrew Goodman, and Mickey Schwerner. FBI director J. Ed-gar Hoover at first suggested that the missing activists had staged their own disap-pearance to inflame tensions, or perhaps that "these three might have gotten rather fresh."[34]

Next, just before the Democratic convention, on August 2, the United States fabricated a provocation in the Gulf of Tonkin that expanded the Vietnam War along the lines suggested in NSM 273 ("a very delicate subject, " according to Pen-tagon chief Robert McNamara[35]). President Johnson drafted his war declaration on August 4, the same day the brutalized bodies of three civil rights workers were found in a Mississippi swamp. On August 9, at a memorial service in a burned-out church, SNCC leaders questioned why the U.S. government was declaring war on Vietnam but not on racism at home. On August 20, Johnson announced the official "War on Poverty" with an appropriation of less than one billion dollars while signing a military appropriation fifty times greater.[36] The War on Poverty—the core of the Port Huron generation's demand for new priorities-was dead on arrival. The theory, held by historian William Appleman Williams among others, that foreign policy crises were exploited to deflect America's priorities away from racial and class tensions, seemed to be vindicated before our eyes.

Johnson was plotting to use the party's leading liberals, many of them sympathetic to the fledgling SDS, to undermine the civil rights challenge from the Mississippi Freedom Democrats three weeks after the Gulf of Tonkin incident. Hubert Humphrey was assigned the task, apparently to test his loyalty to Johnson before being offered the vice presidential slot. He lectured the arriving freedom delegation that the president would "not allow that illiterate woman (the MFDP leader Fannie Lou Hamer) to speak from the floor of the convention."[37] Worse, the activists were battered by one of their foremost icons, the UAW's Walter Reuther, who was flown by private jet to quell the freedom challenge; he told Humphrey and others that "we can reduce the opposition to this to a microscopic fraction so they'll be completely unimportant."[38] White House tape transcripts show clearly that Johnson thought the Freedom Democrats would succeed if the matter was put to a convention vote.

This became a turning point between those who tried bringing their "morality to politics, not politics to their morality," said Bob Moses, then a central figure for both SNCC and SDS. It was so intense that Humphrey broke down and cried. At one point LBJ stole off to bed in the afternoon, spending the next twenty-four hours vowing to quit the presidency.[39] The Mississippi Freedom Democrats and the hopes of the early sixties were crushed once again, this time not by the clubs of southern police but by the hypocrisy of liberalism. If Johnson had incorporated the Mississippi Freedom delegation, we believed, he still could have defeated Barry Goldwater that November and hastened the political realignment we stood for. But the possibility of transformation evaporated. In the resulting vacuum the first Black Panther Party for Self-Defense was born, in Lowndes County, Alabama, in response to the rejection of the MFDP. Only days after the convention, while Johnson was mouthing the words "no wider war," his national security advisor, McGeorge Bundy was suggesting that "substantial armed forces" would be sent.[40]

That fall, the Port Huron generation of SDS met in New York to ponder the options. Just two years before, the war in Vietnam seemed so remote that it was barely noted in the *PHS*. Some of us, following the SNCC model and convinced that the realignment was under way, had moved to inner cities to begin organizing a broad coalition of the poor, under the name Economic Research and Action Project (ERAP). Others were excited about the Berkeley Free Speech Movement and prospects for campus rebellion. Still others were planning protests if the Vietnam War should escalate. Amid great apprehension, the SDS national council adopted the slogan "Part of the Way with LBJ." While the president vowed never to send America's young men to fight a land war in Southeast Asia, even on election day the White House was nevertheless drafting plans for expanding the war.[41] By springtime, 150,000 young American men were dispatched to war. In May, SDS led the largest antiwar protest in decades in Washington, D.C. But it was too late to stop the machine. Having learned that assassinations could change history, our generation now began to also learn that official lies were packaged as campaign promises.

The utopian period of Port Huron was over, less than three years after the *PHS* was issued. The vision would flicker but would never be recovered amid the time of radicalization and polarization ahead. Since the Democratic Party had failed the MFDP and launched the Vietnam War, those favoring an election strategy were frustrated and marginalized. Resistance grew in the form of urban insurrections, GI mutinies, draft card burnings, building takeovers, and bombings. Renewed efforts at reforming the system, such as the 1967-1968 Eugene McCarthy presidential campaign, helped to unseat LBJ but failed to capture the Democratic nomination. RFK was the last politician who had rekindled the hopes of realizing the vision of Port Huron, not only with interest in antipoverty programs and his gradual questioning of Vietnam, but most eloquently with his 1967 speech challenging the worth of the Gross National Product as a measure of well-being. I supported his candidacy, stood over his coffin, and finally embraced the transmutation of hope to rage. After Nixon's election, I was convicted as part of the so-called Chicago Eight of inciting a riot at the 1968 Democratic convention, a judicial process that ended in our acquittal in 1973. By then the long-awaited political realignment was partly under way, starting with Senator George McGovern's 1972 presidential campaign, then leading to the ascension of southern liberals like Jimmy Carter, Bill Clinton, Al Gore, Andrew Young, and John Lewis to national power. But by now it was too late to keep white southerners in the Democratic

Party with populist economic promises. The threat to their southern white traditions drove them into the Republican Party. It was Richard Nixon's strategy of realignment that prevailed.[42]

The importance of the mid-sixties turning points, however, are missed by
most historians of the era, who tend to blame SDS for "choosing" to become more
radical, sectarian, dogmatic, and violent, as if there was no context for the evolution of our behavior. Garry Wills, whose book *Nixon Agonistes* extolled the *Port
Huron Statement*,[43] later blamed the young radicals for having prolonged the Vietnam War.[44] In his view, the movement should have practiced constructive nonviolence, as Dr. King promoted, which aimed at gaining national acceptance. This
analysis ignores the fact that Dr. King himself was becoming radicalized by 1966,
and starting to despair of nonviolence. Liberal bastions like the *New York Times*
editorially blasted him for speaking out against the Vietnam War in 1967. His murder and that of Robert Kennedy stoked violent passions among many of the
young. Wills also writes that it was easier to unite Americans against the manifest
evil of racism than against the Vietnam War, in which, he believes, "the establishment was not so manifestly evil."[45] But for our generation, the fact that the U.S.
government dropped more bombs on Vietnam than it did everywhere during
World War II, while lying to those it was conscripting, was a manifest evil. Wills
writes that the Chicago police simply "lost their heads" in Chicago, as if the beat-
ings and gassings of more than sixty journalists was somehow "provoked." Wills
laments that "civil disobedience had degenerated into terrorism,"[46] but does not
acknowledge the causes or the fact that violent rebellions were taking place in
both the armed forces and American ghettos and barrios at an unprecedented
rate. Were the student radicals to blame for this turn toward confrontation, or was
it explainable by the failure of an older generation to complete the reforms begun
in the early sixties instead of invading Vietnam? As Wills himself wrote in his 1969
book, "the generation gap is largely caused by elders who believe they have escaped it."[47]

Similarly, some still believe that the election of Hubert Humphrey in 1968
would have ended the Vietnam War and restored liberalism as a majority coalition.
Who is to say? Humphrey remains an icon for an older generation of liberals to this
day. For the Port Huron generation of SDS and SNCC, however, he remains the
symbol of how liberalism, driven by opportunism, chose Vietnam over the Mississippi Freedom Democrats. Regardless of which view one chooses, the forgotten
fact is that Humphrey probably would have won the 1968 election if he had taken

an independent antiwar stand. In late October, Nixon led 44-36 percent. With the election one week away, the United States ordered a bombing halt and offered talks. On November 2 both the Gallup and Harris Polls showed Nixon's lead shaved to 42-40 percent. According to historian Theodore White, "had peace become quite clear, in the last three days of the election of 1968, Hubert Humphrey would have won the election."[48] The final result was Nixon 43.4 percent, Humphrey 42.7 percent-a margin of 0.7 percent. Would Humphrey have ended the war? Perhaps, perhaps not. But there is no single factor that leads to a loss by less than 1 percent. Anyone who magnifies the blame toward one group or another is indulging in self-interested scapegoating.[49]

There is no doubt that by the decade's end many of us, myself certainly included, had evolved from nonviolent direct action to acceptance of self-defense, or street fighting against the police and authorities, or hiding fugitives underground. On the day the Chicago Eight were convicted, for example, there were some several hundred riots in youth communities and college campuses across the country, including the burning of a Bank of America by university students in Isla Vista. No one could have ordered this behavior; it was the spontaneous response of hundreds of thousands of young people to the perceived lack of effectiveness of either politics or nonviolence. As Kirkpatrick Sale notes, a Gallup Poll in the late sixties showed one million university students identifying themselves as "revolutionary."[50] What many fail to ask is where it all began, where the responsibility lay for causing this massive alienation among college students, inner-city residents, and grunts in the U.S. military. It is convenient to blame the teenagers and twenty-somethings in the sixties for "losing their heads," unlike the heavily armed and professionally trained Chicago police who knew their "riot" would be approved by their mayor. "Vietnam undid the New Left," Wills writes, because it "blurred the original aims" of the SDS.[51] One wishes in this case that Wills had dwelt on how Vietnam undid America.

When the period we know as "the sixties" finally ended—from exhaustion, infighting, FBI counterintelligence programs and, most of all, from success in ending the Vietnam War and pushing open doors to the mainstream[52]—I turned my energies increasingly toward electoral politics, serving eighteen years in the California legislature, chairing policy committees on labor, higher education, and the environment. This was not so much a "zigzag" as an effort to act as an outsider on the inside.[53] It was consistent with the original vision of Port Huron, but played itself out during a time of movement decline or exhaustion.

The lessons I learned while in office were contradictory. On the one hand, there was much greater space to serve movement goals on the inside than I had imagined in 1962; one could hold press conferences, hire activist staff, call watchdog hearings with subpoena power, and occasionally pass far-reaching legislation (divestment from South Africa, antisweatshop guidelines, endangered species laws, billons for conservation, etc.). Perhaps the most potent opportunities were insurgent political campaigns themselves, raising new issues in the public arena and politicizing thousands of new activists in each cycle. On the other hand, there was something impenetrable about the system of power as a whole. The state had permanent, neo-Machiavellian interests of its own, deflecting or absorbing any democratic pressures that became too threatening. The state served and brokered a wider constellation of private corporate and professional interests that expected profitable investment opportunities and law and order, when needed, against dissidents, radicals, or the angry underclass. These undemocratic interests could reward or punish politicians through their monopoly of campaign contributions, media campaigns and, ultimately, capital flight. The absence of a multiparty system with solidly progressive electoral districts was another factor in producing compromised and centrist outcomes. I think of those two decades in elected office as an honorable interlude, carrying forward or protecting the gains of one movement while waiting for others to begin, as happened with the antisweatshop and anti-WHO campaigns in the late 1990s.

The Achievements of The Sixties

SDS could not survive the sixties as an organization. In part, the very ethos of participatory democracy conflicted with the goal, shared by some at Port Huron, of building a permanent New Left organization. Not only was there a yearly turnover of the campus population, but SDS activists were committed in principle to leave the organization in two or three years to make room for new leadership. Meanwhile, it seemed that new radical movements were exploding everywhere, straining the capacity of any single organization like SDS to define, much less coordinate, the whole. Administrators, police, and intelligence agencies alternated between strategies of co-optation, counterintelligence, and coercion. SDS disintegrated into rival Marxist sects that had been unimaginable to us in 1962, and those groups devoured the host organization by 1969. (I would argue that one of them, the Weather Underground, was an authentic descendent of the Port Huron generation, rebelling in part against the failure of our perceived reformism.)

But it would be a fundamental mistake to judge the participatory sixties through any organizational history. SDS, following SNCC, was a catalytic organization, not a bureaucratic one. The two groups catalyzed more social change in their seven-year lifespans than many respectable and well-funded nongovernmental organizations accomplish in decades.[54] If anything, the sixties were a triumph for the notions of decentralized democratic movements championed in the *Port Huron Statement*. Slogans like "let the people decide" were heartfelt. The powerful dynamics of the sixties could not have been "harnessed" by any single structure; instead, the heartbeat was expressed through countless innovative grassroots networks that rose or fell based on voluntary initiative. The result was a vast change in public attitudes as the sixties became mainstreamed.

In this perspective the movement outlived its organized forms, such as SDS. Once any organizational process became dysfunctional (national SDS meetings began drawing three thousand participants, for example), the movement energy flowed around the structural blockages, leaving the organizational shell for the squabbling factions. For example, in the very year that SDS collapsed, there were millions in the streets for the Vietnam Moratorium and the first Earth Day. In the first six months of 1969, based on information from only 232 of America's 2,000 campuses, over 200,000 students were involved in protests, 3,652 were arrested, and 956 suspended or expelled. In 1969-1970, according to the FBI, 313 building occupations took place. In Vietnam, there were 209 fraggings (slang for an attack on a superior) by soldiers in 1970 alone. Public opinion had shifted from 61 percent supporting the Vietnam War in 1965 to 61 percent declaring the war was wrong in 1971.[55] The goals of the early SDS were receiving majority support while the organization became too fragmented to benefit.

When a movement declines, no organization can resuscitate it. This is not to reject the crucial importance of organizing, or the organizer's mentality, or the construction of a "civil society" of countless networks. But it is to suggest a key difference between movements and institutions. The measure of an era is not taken in membership cards or election results alone, but in the changes in consciousness, in the changing norms of everyday life, and in the public policies that result from movement impacts on the mainstream. Much of what we take for granted—voting by renters, weekends, clean drinking water, the First Amendment, collective bargaining, interracial relationships—is the result of bitter struggles by radical movements of yester-year to legitimate what previously was considered antisocial or criminal. In this sense, the effects of movements envisioned at Port Huron, and the backlash against them, are deep, ongoing, and still contested.

First of all, American *democracy indeed became more participatory* as a result of the sixties. More constituencies gained a voice and a public role than ever before. The political process became more open. Repressive mechanisms were exposed and curbed. The culture as a whole became more tolerant.

Second, there were structural or institutional *changes that redistributed political access and power*. Jim Crow segregation was ended in the South, and 20 million black people won the vote. The eighteen-year-old vote enfranchised another 10 million young people. Affirmative action for women and people of color broadened opportunities in education, the political process, and the workplace. The opening of presidential primaries empowered millions of voters to choose their candidates. New checks and balances were imposed on an imperial presidency. Two presidents, Lyndon Johnson and Richard Nixon, were forced from office.

Third, *new issues and constituencies were recognized in public policy:* voting rights acts, the Clean Air and Water Acts, the endangered species laws, the Environmental Protection Agency, the Occupational Health and Safety Act, consumer safety laws, nondiscrimination and affirmative action initiatives, the disability rights movement, and others. A rainbow of identity movements, including the American Indian Movement (AIM), the Black Panther Party, and the Young Lords Party, staked out independent identities and broadened the public discourse.

Fourth, *the Vietnam War was ended and the Cold War model was challenged.* Under public pressure, the U.S. Congress eliminated military funding for South Vietnam and Cambodia. The Watergate scandal, which arose from Nixon's repression of antiwar voices, led to a presidential resignation. The United States ended the military draft. The Carter administration provided amnesty for Vietnam-era deserters. Beginning with Vietnam and Chile, human rights was established as an integral part of national security policy. Relations with Vietnam were normalized by President Bill Clinton, a former McCarthy and McGovern activist, Senator John Kerry, a former leader of Vietnam Veterans Against the War (VVAW), and Senator John McCain, a former POW in Hanoi.[56]

Fifth, the *sixties consciousness gave birth to new technologies,* including the personal computer, which led to participatory democracy in global communication. I remember seeing my first computer as a graduate student at the University of Michigan in 1963; it seemed as large as a room, and my faculty advisor, himself a campus radical, promised that all our communications would become radically decentralized with computers the size of my hand. "It is not a coincidence," writes an industry analyst, "that, during the 60s and early 70s, at the height of the protest against the war in Vietnam, the civil rights movement and widespread experimentation with psychedelic drugs, personal computing emerged from a handful of government-and-corporate-funded laboratories, as well as from the work of a small group...(who) were fans of LSD, draft resisters, commune sympathizers and, to put it bluntly, long-haired hippie freaks."[57] While it is fair to say the dream of technology failed, there is no doubt that the Internet has propelled communication and solidarity among global protest movements like never before, resulting in a more participatory, decentralized democratic process.

The sixties, however, are far from over. Coinciding with their progressive impacts has been a constant and rising backlash to limit, if not roll back, the social, racial, environmental, and political reforms of the era. Former President Clinton, an astute observer of our political culture, says that the sixties remain the basic fault line running through American politics to this day and provide the best measure of whether one is a Democrat or a Republican. It is important to note that the sixties revolt was a global phenomenon, producing a lasting "generation of '68" that shares power in many countries, including Germany, France, Mexico, Brazil, Argentina, Uruguay, Chile, Northern Ireland, South Africa, South Korea, to name only a few.

Social movements begin and end in memory. The fact that we called ourselves a "new" left meant that our radical roots largely had been severed, by McCarthyism and the Cold War, so that the project of building an alternative was commencing all over again. Social movements move from the mysterious margins to the mainstream, become majorities, then are subject to crucial arguments over memory. The sixties are still contested terrain in schools, the media, and politics precisely because the recovery of their meaning is important to social movements of the future and because the suppression or distortion of that memory is vital to the conservative agenda. We are nearing the fiftieth anniversary of every significant development of the sixties, including the *Port Huron Statement*. The final stage of the sixties, the stage of memory and museums, is under way.

Students, The Universities, And The Postmodern Legacy
Of all the contributions of the Port Huron Statement, perhaps the most important was the insight that university communities had a role in social change. Universities had become as indispensable to economics in what we called the automation age as factories were in the age of industrial development. Robert McNamara,

after all, was trained at the University of Michigan. In a few years, University of California president Clark Kerr would invent the label "multiversity" to explain the importance of knowledge to power.

Clearly, the CIA understood the importance of universities; as early as 1961, as the *Port Huron Statement* was being conceived, its chief of covert action wrote that books were "the most important weapon of strategic propaganda."[58]

We saw the possibilities, therefore, in challenging or disrupting the role of the universities in the knowledge economy. More important however, was the alienation that the impersonal mass universities bred among idealistic youth searching for "relevance," as described in some of the most eloquent passages of the *PHS*. We wanted participatory education in our participatory democracy, truth from the bottom up, access to the colleges and universities for those who had historically been excluded. Gradually, this led to a fundamental rejection of the narratives we had been taught, the myths of the American melting pot, the privileged superiority of (white) Western civilization, and inevitably to the quest for inclusion of "the other"—the contributions of women, people of color, and all those who had been marginalized by the march of power. The result of this subversion of traditional authority became known as mulitculturalism, deconstruction, and postmodernism. In his perceptive 1968 study, *Young Radicals: Notes on Committed Youth*, Harvard researcher Kenneth Kenniston was among the first to conclude that our "approach to the world-fluid, personalistic, anti-technological, and non-violent-suggests the emergence of what I will call the post-modern style."[59] It could also be called the Port Huron style—the endless improvising, the techniques of dialogue and participation, learning through direct action, the rejection of dogma while searching for theory. It was typical of this style that the *PHS* was offered as a "living document," not a set of marching orders.

When I first met Howard Zinn, he was a professor at a black women's college in Atlanta, where both of us were immersed in the early civil rights movement. He was one of the most deeply-engaged intellectuals I had ever met. While witnessing and participating in the civil rights movement, he was discovering a "story" far different than the conventional one he knew as a trained historian. It eventually was published as *A People's History of the United States*, selling over a million copies, even though Zinn was fired once from Spelman and almost fired from Boston University for promoting civil rights and anti-Vietnam activism.

Thanks to Zinn and numerous subsequent writers, the "disappeared" of history were suddenly appearing in new narratives and publications developed in ethnic studies, women's studies, African American studies, Chicano studies, queer studies, and environmental studies. Films like *Roots, The Color Purple*, and *Taxi Driver* expanded and deepened this discovery process. Conservatives like Lynne Cheney, wife of vice president Dick Cheney, were distressed that more young people knew of Harriett Tubman than the name of the commander of the American Revolutionary Army (George Washington).[60]

Cheney has been working since the Reagan era to undercut the sixties cultural revolution, but the effort is not simply Republican. Among the corporate Democrats, Larry Summers, former treasury secretary and now president of Harvard, is devoted to "eradicating the influence of the 1960s," according to a recent biography.[61]

The unexpected student revolt that produced the *Port Huron Statement* was the kind of moment described by the French philosopher of deconstruction, Jacques Derrida, who took the side of the French students at the barricades in 1968. In his words, Derrida tried to "distinguish between what one calls the *future* and *'l'avenir.'* There's a future that is predictable, programmed, scheduled, foreseeable. But there is a future, l'avenir (to come), which refers to someone who comes whose arrival is totally unexpected. For me, that is the real future. That which is totally unpredictable. The Other who comes without my being able to anticipate its arrival. So if there is a real future beyond this other known future, it's l'avenir in that it's the coming of the Other when I am completely unable to foresee its arrival."[62]

The *Port Huron Statement* announced such an unexpected arrival with a simple introductory sentence: "We are people of this generation, bred in at least modest comfort, housed now in universities, looking uncomfortably at the world we inherit." Now as that same Port Huron generation enters into its senior years, it is worth asking whether we are uncomfortable about the world we are passing on as inheritance, and what may still be done. For me, the experience of the sixties will always hold a bittersweet quality, and I remain haunted by another question raised by Ignazio Silone in *Bread and Wine*: "What would happen if men remained loyal to the ideals of their youth?"[63]

Now that deconstruction has succeeded, is it time for reconstruction again? The postmodern cannot be an end state, only a transition to the unexpected future. Transition to what? Not an empire, not a fundamentalist retreat from modernity, for they are not answers to the world crises. As the *Port Huron Statement* said, "The world is in transition. But America is not." New global peace and justice movements, symbolized by the 1999 Seattle protests against the World Trade Organization, declare that "another world is possible," echoing the Zapatista call for "a world in which all worlds fit." The demands of these new rebels are transitional too, toward a new, inclusive narrative in addition to the many narratives of multiculturalism.

Perhaps the work begun at Port Huron will be taken up once again around the world, for the globalization of power, capital, and empire surely will globalize the stirrings of conscience and resistance. While the powers that be debate whether the world is dominated by a single superpower (the U.S. position) or is multi-polar (the position of the French, the Chinese, and others), there is an alternative vision appearing among the millions of people who are involved in global justice, peace, human rights, and environmental movements-the vision of a future created through participatory democracy.

Notes

1.Christopher Hitchens, "Where Aquarius Went," *New York Times Book Review*, Dec. 19, 2004.

2. Thomas Cahill, "The Price of Infallibility," *New York Times*, April 5, 2005.

3. See Tom Hayden and Dick Flacks, "The Port Huron Statement at 40," *The Nation*, Aug. 5 and Aug. 12, 2002; Tom Hayden, *Rebel: A Personal History of the Sixties* (Los Angeles: Red Hen, 2002); Todd Gitlin, *The Sixties: Years of Hope, Days of Rage* (New York: Bantam,1987); Richard Flacks, *Making History: The American Left and the American Mind* (New York: Colombia University Press, 1988); James Miller, *Democracy Is in the Streets: From Port Huron to the Siege of Chicago* (New York: Simon and Schuster, 1987); and Kirkpatrick Sale, *SDS* (New York: Random House, 1973). See also the documentary film *Rebels with a Cause*, by Helen Garvy and Robert Pardon

4. These distinctions are discussed elegantly in Flacks, *Making History*

5. Paul Berman, *A Tale of Two Utopias: The Political Journey of the Generation of 1968* (New York: Norton, 1996), 54. Italics added to quote for emphasis.

6. At various times, Benjamin Franklin, Thomas Paine, and Thomas Jefferson wrote approvingly of Indian political customs. As one historian described Iroquois culture, there were "no laws or ordinances, sheriffs and constables, judges and juries, or courts or jails." These idyllic themes evolved into the later sixties communes, organic gardening and medicine, environmentalist lifestyles, and other practices. See Howard Zinn, *A People's History of the United States, 1492-Present* (1980; New York: Harper Collins, 2003), 1-23. John Adams wrote in 1787 that "to collect together the legislation of the Indians would take up much room but would be well worth pains," as cited in an excellent collection by Oren Lyons, John Mohawk, Vine Deloria, Laurence Hauptman, Howard Berman, Donald Grinde, Curtis Berkey, and Robert Venables, *Exiled in the Land of the Free: Democracy, Indian Nations, and the U.S. Constitution* (Santa Fe, N. Mex.: Clear Light, 1992), 109. The 1778 Articles of Confederation Congress actually proposed an Indian state headed by the Delaware nation (ibid.,113).

7. Thomas Paine, *Rights of Man* (1792; New York: Penguin, 1984), 70,176.

8. In a Jefferson letter dated Feb. 2, 1816, cited by Berman, *Tale of Two Utopias*, 51.

9. John Dewey, quoted in Berman, *Tale of Two Utopias*, 53.

10. Retreating both from enlightenment beliefs in "infinite perfectibility" and negative beliefs in "original sin," the statement asserted that human beings are "infinitely precious" and possessed of "unfulfilled capacities for reason, freedom and love." The wording was provided by a Mexican-American Catholic activist, Maria Varela, who quoted from the copy of a Church encyclical she happened to carry. Casey Hayden spoke of those years as a "holy time."

11. Bob Dylan, *Chronicles*, vol. 1 (New York: Simon and Schuster, 2004), 34-35.

12. Sale, *SDS*, 27.

13. Iganzio Silone, *Bread and Wine* (1936; New York: Signet 1986); see also Miller, *Democracy Is in the Streets*, 53

14. For example, the late Carl Wittman, who joined SDS shortly after Port Huron and worked with me as a community organizer in the Newark project, eventually came out of the closet to write "A Gay Manifesto," a defining document of the gay liberation movement, six years after Port Huron. See David Carter, Stonewall: *The Riots That Sparked the Gay Revolution* (New York: St. Martins, 2004), 118-19.

15. The phrase is that of Harvard professor Samuel Huntington in a speech to the elite Trilateral Commission in 1976 during the bicentennial of the Declaration of Independence. Hunnington noted, "The 1960s witnessed a dramatic upsurge of democratic fervor in America," a trend he diagnosed as a "distemper" that threatened both governability and national security. Huntington proposed there be "limits to the extension of political democracy." See account in Zinn, *People's History*, 558-60.

16. The sudden reframing of America's relationship with the Soviet Union was described by Cyrus Sulzberger in the *New York Times* as follows: "The momentum of pro-Soviet feeling worked up during the war to support the Grand Alliance had continued too heavily after the armistice. This made it difficult for the administration to carry out the stiffer diplomatic policy required now. For this reason... a campaign was worked up to obtain a better balance of public opinion to permit the government to adopt a harder line" (Mar. 21, 1946). Instead of seeking coexistence with the Soviet Union, the United States began talk of a "Cold War," an "iron curtain," and an "iron fist" instead of "babying the Soviets"; the Republican Party campaigned in 1946 on a platform of "Republicanism versus Communism," and the U.S. Chamber of Commerce collaborated with the FBI in distributing anticommunist materials, all *before* the Chinese communist revolution or Soviet testing of an atomic bomb. See Virginia Carmichael, *Framing History: The Rosenberg Story and the Cold War* (Minneapolis: University of Minnesota, 1993), 32-33.

17. See Paul Buhle, "How Sweet It Wasn't: The Scholars and the CIA," in John McMillian and Paul Buhle, *The New Left Revisited* (Philadelphia: Temple University Press, 2003), 263.

18. See Todd Gitlin, *Letters to a Young Activist* (New York: Basic Books, 2003). Gitlin has not moved to the conservative camp but has been identified himself with "progressive patriotism," including use of military means to quell terrorism and denunciations of street

demonstrators at places like the 2004 Republican convention. Oddly, his advice to the new radicals in *Letters* omits taking a position on the wars in Afghanistan and Iraq.

19. Buhle, "How Sweet It Wasn't," on the Committee on Cultural Freedom. In 1967, *Ramparts* magazine exposed the longtime CIA funding of the U.S. National Student Association. The CIA and State Department have long provided funding for international AFL-CIO projects designed to subvert radical labor movements in Latin America and elsewhere. According to U.S. Senate hearings held by Sen. Frank Church, the CIA funded several hundred academics on over two hundred campuses to "write books and other material to be used for propaganda purposes." See Zinn, *People's History*, 555-56.

20. Drafted in part by Michael Vester of the German SDS, then a student at Bowdoin College, the section on the Cold War foreshadowed the later movements to demilitarize Europe.

21. For my own account, see Hayden, *Rebel*, 79-84; or Gitlin, *The Sixties*,113-26.

22. See Lori Wallach and Patrick Woodall, *Whose Trade Organization? A Comprehensive Guide to the WTO* (New York: New Press, 2004).

23. The portion of America's gross national income given in foreign aid has declined by nearly 90 percent since the time of the *Port Huron Statement*, from 0.54 percent in 1962 to 0.16 percent in 2004, ranking the U.S. government behind twenty other nations. (Celia W. Dugger, "Discerning a New Course for World Donor Nations," *New York Times,* April 18, 2005).

24. Recent victims of the "soft on terrorism" charge were U.S. Senator Max Cleland, a paraplegic Vietnam veteran, in 2002, and of course U.S. Senator and decorated Vietnam War hero John Kerry in the 2004 presidential race.

25. Taylor Branch, *Pillar of Fire: America in the King Years,* 1963-64, (New York: Simon and Schuster, 1998), 475-76.

26. At the time, Lewis was the chairman of the Student Nonviolent Coordinating Committee, the most radical and frontline civil rights organization. Attempts were made to edit and dilute his speech given at the March on Washington, which asked a good question: "Where is our party?" Later Lewis became an elected Atlanta congressman and prime sponsor of the Smithsonian's African-American Museum, near the spot where the 1963 march took place.

27. Jonathan Rosenberg and Zachary Karabell, *Kennedy, Johnson, and the Quest for Justice: The Civil Rights Tapes* (New York: Norton, 2003), 172.

28. Ibid.,31.

29. The 63 percent disapproval of Freedom Rides is noted in Taylor Branch, *Parting the Waters: America in the King Years, 1954-63* (New York: Simon and Schuster, 1988), 478. *New York Times* editorial, Branch, 478 as well.

30. Rosenberg and Karabell, *Kennedy, Johnson, and the Quest*, 130.

31. Scott Stossel, Sarge*: The Life and Times of Sargeant Shriver* (Washington, D.C.: Smithsonian Books, 2004), 476.

32. Edwin O. Guthman and Jeffrey Schulman, *Robert Kennedy in His Own Words: The Unpublished Recollections of the Kennedy Years* (New York: Bantam, 1988), 300.

33. Richard Parker, *John Kenneth Galbraith: His Life, His Economics, His Politics* (New York: Farrar, Straus, Giroux, 2005), 405. James K. Galbraith, "Exit Strategy: In 1963, JFK or-

dered a complete withdrawal from Vietnam," *Boston Review,* October/November 1963. Robert McNamara confirmed Kennedy's plan for a complete withdrawal by 1965 in a speech at the LBJ Library on May 1, 1995, based on White House tapes. On October 4, 1963, a memorandum from General Maxwell Taylor stated that "All planning will be directed towards preparing RVN (Republic of Vietnam) forces for the withdrawal of all U.S. special assistance units and personnel by the end of calendar year 1965." In a conversation with Daniel Ellsberg, Robert Kennedy stated, " We wanted to win if we could, but my brother was determined never to send ground troops to Vietnam...I do know what he intended. All I can say is that he was absolutely determined not to send ground units... We would have fuzzed it up. We would have gotten a government that asked us out or that would have negotiated with the other side. We would have handled it like Laos." Daniel Ellsberg, *Secrets: A Memoir of Vietnam and the Pentagon Papers* (New York: Viking, 2002), 195. In an earlier, more ambiguous interview in 1964, while he was mulling his own thoughts about Vietnam, RFK gave noncommittal answers to John Barlow Martin: "Q: But at the same time, no disposition to go in? A: No. Everybody, including General MacArthur, felt that land conflict between our troops-white troops and Asian-would only end in disaster." Guthman and Schulman, *Robert Kennedy*, 395. On these issues, I disagree with Noam Chomsky and numerous others who have claimed that LBJ's escalation of the war was simply a "continuation of Kennedy's policy," to quote Stanley Karnow as cited in Galbraith, "Exit Strategy."

34. Michael R. Beschloss, *Taking Charge: The Johnson White House Tapes, 1963-1964* (New York: Simon and Schuster, 1997), 439.

35. Ibid.,508.

36. Ibid., 455.

37. This is according to SNCC participants in the meeting.

38.Beschloss, *Taking Charge*, 534.

39. Ibid., 532-33.

40. Ibid., 546.

41. According to Daniel Ellsberg, then at the Pentagon, the president set up an inter-agency task force the day before the November 3 election to make plans for escalation. "It hadn't started a week earlier because its focus might have leaked to the voters... Moreover, we didn't start the work a day or week later, after the votes were cast, because there was no time to waste... It didn't matter that much to us what the public thought." Ellsberg, *Secrets,* 50-51.

42. See Kevin Phillips, *The Emerging Republican Majority* (New Rochelle, N.Y..: Arlington House, 1969).

43. Garry Wills, *Nixon Agonistes: The Crisis of the Self-Made Man* (New York: Signet, 1969), 327-33.

44. Garry Wills, *A Necessary Evil: A History of American Distrust of Government* (New York: Simon and Schuster, 1999), 289-98.

45. Ibid.,293.

46. Ibid.

47. Wills, *Nixon Agonistes*, 301.

48. Hayden, *Rebel,* 299.

49. In 2000, by comparison, I campaigned for Al Gore over the third-party campaign of Ralph Nader.

50. Sale, *SDS*.

51. Wills, 294.

52. Many of us were targeted for "neutralization" by the FBI. See Hayden, *Rebel,* for FBI documents. For declassified FBI counterintelligence documents against dissenters over the years, see Ward Churchill, Jim Vander Wall, *The Cointelpro Papers: Documents from the FBI's Secret Wars Against Dissent in the United States* (1990; Cambridge, Mass.:South End, 2002).

53. The "zigzag" accusation is from Berman, *Tale of Two Utopias*, 109.

54. One exemption to this rule is the National Organization for Women (NOW), which has managed to balance the catalytic and bureaucratic poles since its inception in 1965. Another is the Sierra Club. In both cases, the grassroots membership plays a key role in the energy flow through the organizational machinery.

55. All figures in Zinn, *People's History*, 490-92.

56. The then-secret Pentagon papers quote administration advisors in 1968 as saying " this growing disaffection, accompanied as it certainly will be, by increased defiance of the draft and growing unrest in the cities because of the belief that we are neglecting domestic problems, runs great risks of provoking a domestic crisis of unprecedented proportions." In his memoirs, President Nixon wrote; " although publicly I continued to ignore the raging antiwar controversy… I knew, however, that after all the protests and the Moratorium, American public opinion would be seriously divided by the war." Note that these concerns were based purely on cost/benefit calculations, not on moral or public policy grounds. In Zinn, *People's History*,500, 501.

57. John Markoff, *What the Dormouse Said: How the Sixties Counterculture Shaped the Personal Computer Industry* (New York: Viking, 2005). See Andrew Leonard, "Book of the Times, California Dreaming: A True Story of Computers, Drugs and Rock 'n' Roll," *New York Times*, May 7, 2005.

58. From Senate hearings, in Zinn, *People's History*, 557. At the time, in 1961, I was writing a pamphlet on the civil rights movement for the U.S. National Student Association for international distribution. Without my knowledge, CIA funds were paying for it, presumably to show an idealistic image at international youth forums.

59. Kenneth Keniston, *Young Radicals: Notes on Committed Youth* (New York: Harcourt Brace, 1968),235.

60. Lynne V. Cheney, *Telling the Truth* (New York: Touchstone, 1996), 33.

61. Richard Bradley, *Harvard Rules* (New York: HarperCollins, 2005). Quoted in *New York Times* review, March 27, 2005.

62. Kirby Dick and Amy Ziering Kofman, *Derrida: Screenplay and Essays on the Film* (New York: Routledge, 2005), 62.

63. Silone, *Bread and Wine*, 146.

—CONTINUITY—

CONTINUITY
An Introduction

by Natasha Kapoor

It appears that there is a thirty year cycle in the resurgence of mass grassroots movements. At the beginning of the 20th century, the 1930s became historically renowned for the massive movements for social and political change. Some of the protest movements moved to the Right and many also moved to the Left.

The cycle of mass grassroots movements was repeated in the 1960s but involved a new array of movements and issues. This time the tendency was to the Left, and in most instances toward a new Left, with a primary focus on large political and social issues. From the 1970s into the 1990s a variety of single issue movement took the succession. But into the 1990s the thirty year cycle of protest and insurgency emerged again in the form of the most massive and genuinely supranational movement, around issues related to the globalization of the world economy and the deteriorating environment. The focus of the new and renewed movements returned to economic and socio-political concerns.

Legacy and Continuity—The Bridge

The greatest virtue of the New Left of the 1960s lay in its determination to build that sense of popular participation at every level of its work.[1]

In the 1990s, we live in a world transformed by the message of participatory democracy and active nonviolence based on spiritual values which was the greatest gift of the American New Left of the 1960s to our brothers and sisters around the planet.[2]

Natasha Kapoor is a movement activist, working and living in Vancouver and Seattle. She has a PhD in anthropology and travels widely linking organisations into coalitions working within the principles of the charter of the World Social Forum.

Yet through many ups and downs, participatory democracy has spread as an ethic throughout everyday life and has become a persistent challenge to top-down institutions all over the world. It has surfaced in campaigns of the global justice movement, in struggles for the workplace and neighourhood empowerment, resistance to the Vietnam War draft, in Paulo Freire's 'pedagogy of the oppressed,' in political platforms from Green parties to the Zapatistas, in the independent media, and in grassroots Internet campaigns... Belief in the new participatory norm has resulted in major, if incomplete, policy triumphs mandating everything from freedom-of-information disclosures to citizen participation requirements in multiple realms of official decision-making. It remains a powerful threat to those in established bureaucracies who fear and suppress what they call 'an excess of democracy.'[3]

There is an alternative vision appearing among the millions of people who are involved in global justice, peace, human rights, and environmental movements—the vision of a future created through participatory democracy.[4]

In the U.S. and Western Europe, the first real pressure for a more thorough-going democracy began with the restlessness of a new generation brought up on a commitment to democracy and against the background of a real war fought to defend it. They expected the reward for the sacrifices of earlier generations to mean more than an occasional choice between barely distinguished middle-aged men with overgrown egos. The challenge began with the students in the late 1960s rebelling against both the authoritarianism of higher education and the imperialism of the U.S. against the Vietnamese. A radical momentum developed through the 1970s with the feminist movement, radical grassroots trade unionism, militant community anti-racist organising, and movements around gay and disability rights, and it shook up established social democratic parties and parts of government. These diverse movements [I don't want to imply that they were all saying the same thing or that their relationships with each other were always harmonious] provided, in their different ways, a basis for reinvigorating democracy at a very timely moment.[5]

Elites across the world reacted with alarm to the lack of deference of the 1968 generation, their confident sense of the rights of the people and their pressure to open up what had become the cosy institutions of government. The Trilateral Commission through which U.S., Japanese and European political and economic leaders discussed issues of common concern declared in the early 1970s that 'expectations were becoming dangerously high for the stability of democracy.' But it was not just conservative elites who felt threatened by these challenges to established authority. In the early 1970s, when demands for greater popular participation started rearing their alarming heads, a worried member of the U.S. ruling elite, David Rockefeller of the Chase Manhattan Bank, founded the Trilateral Commission to bring together the elite of the three industrialized continents of the capitalist world. Its report on the threat the new movements posed for parliamentary democracy aimed to put ruling institutions on the alert. It organised annual gatherings of leading politicians, industrialists, financiers and academics to provide a mechanism to develop common responses. This was just a sign that potentially profound change was underway. It was also a sign that an international establishment was forming to control the impact of this unrest. Interestingly the Trilateral Commission led to the establishment of the Davos-based World Economic Forum.[6]

To be sure, the instinct of the radicals of the 1960s New Left who framed the fundamental political debate during that decade, in terms of 'value-centered democratic theory,' was articulated as participatory democracy, and laid the basis for the new political discourse that has guided radical democratic experimentation in one way or another for the generations that followed. Much of the political reflection of the 1960s was based on Aristotle's insistence that morality and politics cannot be separated. "The study of ethics may not improperly be termed a study of politics."[7] This discourse of democratizing democracy has won over all others and it now remains for us to deepen its meaning and fulfill its promises just as the framers of the Port Huron Statement insisted some four decades ago.

The Importance of Culture

The 1960s also had an important and very visible cultural dimension. The mix of culture and politics goes back a long time.

The answer lies not just in the politics but in the culture of Athens. This is the home of Pericles—and of Sophocles, Euripides, and Socrates. It was a culture of monumental aesthetes, of Sophist philosophers who hawked their lawyer-like skills in the marketplace, and wealthy producers who paid to put on plays in the 17,000 seat amphitheatres carved into the hills around the city. But it was also a democratic culture, at least for the 20 per cent or so of the population who were citizens. And this culture was visible above all in the marketplace—the agora. What transpired as high rhetoric up mountainside in the Assembly often began down in the agora as whispered gossip. Without a village square, without a town barbershop or general store or petrol station, without the local pub or workers' café or literary coffeehouse where citizens can gather informally, no democratic political business is possible. Citizens exhibit their skills and concerns in the meeting hall or the assembly, but they acquire them on the school board or the bazaar committee or in the beer hall. The final decisions are taken formally, but the opinions are developed around woodstoves or before a communal television set in a village school.[8]

We need to recall that the political culture of the Greeks, developed through education and direct democratic practises allowed a citizenry of 22,000 to 30,000 persons to regularly gather (six to eight times a year) to make decisions. The quorum of 6000 citizens.

Seattle—A Political Maternity Ward

It was singularly significant that the last major public demonstration in the U.S. in the 20th century was a protest over global economics and trade. More than forty thousand people came to Seattle to oppose the policies of the World Trade Organisation [WTO], which since 1995 has functioned like an international cabal in league with powerful corporate and financial interests. Trade unionists went to Seattle to force the WTO to enact trade sanctions against nations that use child labour, prohibit labour unions and that pay slave wages to their workers. Environmental activists came to Seattle to pressure the WTO to ensure environmental safeguards would be part of any global trade agreements.

The size, diversity of interests represented, and the militancy of the protests in Seattle in 1999 made them some of the most successful popular street actions since the spring of 1971 in Washington, D.C. That spring D.C. saw the Vietnam Veterans Against the War stage its legendary Dewey Canyon III protest, followed by various left and liberal organizations which were then followed by a massive direct action called by the Mayday Tribe and designed to shut that city down. The police reaction to that attempt was the declaration of martial law and the detention of over 12,000 citizens. They didn't succeed in shutting down the city, but did delay the opening of official Washington's bureaucracy for several hours.

What motivated both labour and the environmentalists in Seattle is the political recognition that issues like human rights, employment and healthcare cannot be addressed individually as separate issues. Nor can they be effectively discussed only in the context of a single nation-state. Capital is now global in a new manner, and any analysis of specific socio-economic problems that may exist in any one country must be viewed from an international perspective.

The WTO was set up to be the global headquarters for drafting and enforcing trading rules. When one member country challenges another's trading practices, disputes are settled secretly by panels of trade experts. The rules of the WTO are based on the desirability of privatization, free trade and few regulations on the use of the environmental. The WTO rules value corporate power and commercial interests over labour and human rights, environmental and health concerns and diversity. They increase inequality and stunt democracy. The WTO version of globalization is not a rising ride lifting all boats, as free traders insist, but a dangerous race to the bottom.

What kind of dangerous priorities are envisaged? The WTO's rules deny Third World countries the right to have automatic licensing on patented but absolutely essential medicines. So for example, even when African nations currently ravaged by diseases such as AIDS acquire the scientific and technical means to manufacture drugs to save millions of lives, the WTO's first concern is the protection of the patents and profits of the powerful drug corporations.

The WTO defines itself as a 'Trade Organisation,' which is incapable of pursuing social goals, such as extending the rights of freedom of collective trade union bargaining to Third World and poor workers. Thus when an authoritarian regime markets clothing and athletic shoes that were produced by child labour under sweatshop conditions, the WTO claims that there is nothing it can do.

The demonstrations in Seattle, however, showed that growing numbers of Americans are recognizing that all of these issues—Third World sweatshops, the destruction of unions, deteriorating living standards, the dismantling of social programmes inside the U.S.—are actually interconnected. "Globalization" is not some abstraction, but a destructive social force that has practical consequences on how we live, work and eat. There is a direct connection between the elimination of millions of jobs that can sustain families in the U.S., and the exportation of jobs into countries without unions, environmental and safety standards. As real jobs disappear for millions of workers, and as welfare programs are eliminated, the only alternative is to use the prisons as the chief means of regulating unemployment. Thus in the 1990s a period of so-called unprecedented capitalist expansion, the number of prisoners in federal, state and local prisons roughly doubled in the U.S. Between 1995 to 1997, according to the U.S.-based National Jobs for All Coalition, the average incomes of the poorest 20 percent of female-headed families fell. In 1998, 163 cities and 670 counties had unemployment rates that were more than 50 percent higher than the national average. These deep pockets of joblessness and hunger are not accidental: they represent the logical economic consequences of a nation, like the U.S., that builds one hundred new prison cells a day and sanctions the exportation of millions of jobs.

By reflecting on the slogan 'Think Globally, Act Locally' one can see an inescapable connection between Seattle and prisons, between global inequality and the brutalization of Third World labour and what's happening to black, brown and working people in the U.S. As globalized capitalism destroys democracy, unions and the environment aboard, it is carrying out a similar agenda at home. For these reasons, among others, new organizations emerged as well as a new political language that unified internationally many into large scale protest. The challenge, after Seattle, was to build new political networks and information sources across the borders of ethnic group, gender, nationality and even class. Many of these connections, in the fight for democracy in the 21st century, emerged in Seattle.

In Seattle, the anti-WTO protesters achieved something important. The actions brought the WTO out from behind closed doors and began discussions among the citizenry of the world about this capitalist enclave's true interests and intentions. The fundamental analysis and subsequent action that occurred in and around Seattle on the nature of capitalism has not occurred on a mass basis since the labour struggles in the early part of the 20th century. The single issued, and 'identity politics' type of movements of the last twenty odd years, were absorbed in one cataclysmic week, uniting indigenous people, prisoners rights activists, anti-war organizations, women's movements, labour and environmentalists and others, including anarchists, into a popular movement against those men and women who have played with the Earth as if it was theirs alone for most of the past century. Equally important is that this movement has become truly international. The WTO protests in Seattle were just one of a series of anti-capitalist actions that have occurred not only during that week but over the past several years outside of meetings of the International Monetary Fund, the G8 meetings and other summits of the capitalist world's leading shakers and movers.

Bill Clinton's tour into Seattle brought out the local army. After a day of protests marked by their size and the ferocity of the police attacks against them, the state's governor mobilized the National Guard. Anyone who was there or followed the demonstrations live on CNN or some kind of live video feed via the Internet, saw the police actually move to create disorder. The police attacks on demonstrators blocking streets and yelling at the representatives of big capital trying to enter the WTO meetings were nothing short of unprovoked. It was only after some non-violent demonstrators were attacked with tear gas and other weapons that other protesters began a counterattack on police and stores and banks in downtown Seattle.

At Seattle, the WTO meeting was disrupted. The diversity of the over 50,000 marchers and the organisation's tactical intelligence, plus the fact that the demonstrations occurred at all, especially on such a scale, surprised the Establishment. The WTO meeting ended in an embarrassing fiasco without completing its agenda.

Everywhere Clinton went during this period there were large demonstrations against his presence. In Turkey, the demonstrators were attacked by police and beaten. But in Greece, the demonstrations were so large, that the Clinton visit was cancelled.

The Anti-Globalisation Fight Was Possible and Worthwhile

For the next one and a half years, a series of protests inspired by Seattle disrupted and publicly marred the image of every major gathering of the leading international powers and institutions, including the World Economic Forum [WEF] meeting (a gathering of representatives of the world's leading corporations and countries) at Davos, Switzerland, in January 2000; the International Monetary Fund-World Bank spring meeting in Washington in April 2000; the WEF summit in Melbourne in September 2000; the IMF-World Bank annual meeting in Prague in September 2000; the European Union (EU) summit in Nice in December 2000; the Davos meeting in January 2001; the Quebec City economic summit to set up the free trade area of the Americas in April 2001; the EU summit in Gothenburg in June 2001; the WEF meet in Salzburg in July 2001; the World Economic Summit of the G8 in Genoa in July 2001.

Inevitably, the summit leaders and the corporate media accused the protesters of carrying out acts of meaningless destruction. However, the main immediate
thrust of the mass movement's actions was quite straightforward: to physically
prevent the delegates gathering thus preventing these conferences from completing their agenda.

Demonstrations alone have never blocked the plans of international capital,
but the wave of militant demonstrations were at least effective in disrupting 'business as usual.' From Seattle we can trace the events at Washington's IMF-World
Bank meeting where the U.S. government had to shut offices in a sizeable area
around the two institutions' headquarters, and demonstrators managed to block
many top officials—including the French finance minister—from reaching the conference site. At the Melbourne meeting, the Australian prime minister, John
Howard, and one of the world's richest men, Bill Gates, were trapped along with
other delegates at the conference site. Since the entrances and exists were
blocked by 30,000 demonstrators, the delegates had to be ferried back and forth
by helicopters and boats. In Prague, the conference centre was completely
blocked for hours, and many prospective delegates stayed away from the meeting. In Nice, the state authorities' attempts to keep out 100,000 protesters kept the
delegates themselves in a state of siege. A NATO conference scheduled to be held
in December 2000 at Victoria was cancelled for fear of demonstrations, as was a
World Bank meeting in Barcelona in June 2001. At Davos in January 2001 what the
Financial Times described as 'unprecedented security' (including mass arrests and
a shut down of road and rail) did not prevent hundreds of protesters making it to
the site. At the Quebec City meeting, the entire focus of attention shifted from the
official discussion on the 'Free Trade Agreement of the Americas' to the demonstrations. And in Gothenburg, the city was converted into a virtual battlefield.

Each successive meeting attempted to lace larger areas officially out of
bounds by erecting legal and physical barricades. These efforts peaked in Genoa,
where a four meter high iron fence protected a large deserted 'red zone' near the
conference venue. Inhabitants were not allowed to receive visitors for days, and
sharpshooters manned terraces and balconies. Even this level of quarantine was
insufficient for the leaders of the world's eight most powerful countries, who
stayed on the cruise ship 'European Vision,' guarded by minesweepers, specialist
divers, and units with anti-aircraft guns. Rail and air traffic to the city was stopped;
motorways were blocked; bus, underground and tram traffic were largely shut
down; and large numbers of people were turned back at the Italian border. Reveal-

ingly, the very authorities who talked of a 'united Europe' and were busy removing national restraints on capital flows aggressively used national borders to block the flow of protesters. Hence the slogan of the marchers in Prague: 'Open up the borders, smash the IMF.'

The slogans and causes of the participants in this series of demonstrations varied greatly, ranging from the reformist to the revolutionary (and even, in the U.S., a few chauvinist ones). But as the *Economist* (23/9/2000) editorialized, by and large what the marchers 'have in common is a loathing of the established economic order, and the institutions—the IMF, the World Bank and the WTO—which they regard as either running it or serving it.' The rallies indeed became schools to their heterogeneous participants: many previously non-political forces, or forces limited to single issues, were exposed to broader political perspectives and were radicalized in the course of their experience. And far from flagging, their strength appeared to be growing: at Genoa a record 150,000 protesters overcame extraordinary hurdles and managed to reach the city.

For those behind the project of a united Europe—the European corporations—the unprecedented involvement of organised labour in these protests was a particularly ominous sign.

The European corporations and their political representatives, in the course of fashioning a single superpower, are moving step by step to strip the European working class of all its security and social rights. A militant working class challenge joining hands across borders would endanger their project.

Repression

From the start the protesters had to face considerable repression. In Seatle-1999 tear gas (canisters were sometimes fired at protesters' faces), truncheons, plastic bullets and concussion grenades were used. Over 600 were arrested, often merely for handing out or even receiving leaflets within the giant 'no-protest zone'; the National Guard was called out; night-time curfew and martial law was declared. In Davos 2000 and 2001, the police used water-cannons (at below-freezing temperatures), tear gas and warning shots; in Washington April 2000 tear gas, pepper gas (some demonstrators were sprayed in the eyes) and truncheons; in Nice, stun grenades and tear gas; in Quebec City, water-cannons, tear gas and rubber bullets.

The Gothenburg EU summit of June 2001 marked a turning point. The Swedish police not only attacked the protesters with horses, truncheons and dogs, but, for the first time in the post-Seattle protests, fired live ammunition. Three protesters were wounded, one seriously. British prime minister Blair nevertheless asserted that people were 'far too apologetic' about demonstrators who disrupted gatherings of world leaders. 'These guys don't represent anyone...I just think we've got to be lot more robust about this.'

In line with Blair's sentiments, the repressions at Genoa were unprecedented stop and search of anyone in the city. There was a complete ban on distribution of leaflets. On the first day of the conference, police shot Carlo Giuliani, a 23-year-old protester who allegedly threw a fire extinguisher at a police van, in the head; the van then reversed over Giuliani where he lay on the ground, killing him. On the night of July 21-22, the police stormed the school building which served as the dormitory of many protesters. Those sleeping there were beaten with steel torches, wooden truncheons and fists so badly that 72 were injured; more than a dozen had to be carried out on stretchers, some unconscious; and many had to be hospitalized. All were eventually released without charge. According to Amnesty International, detainees were 'slapped, kicked, punched and spat on and subjected to verbal abuse, sometimes of an obscene sexual nature...deprived of food, water and sleep for lengthy periods, made to line up with their faces against the wall and remain for hours spread-eagled, and beaten if they failed to maintain this position.' In addition,' some were apparently threatened with death and, in the case of female detainees, rape.'[9]

Eighteen months later, the Italian police confessed to a parliamentary inquiry that they had fabricated evidence against the protesters: one senior officer admitted planting two Molotov cocktails in the school, and another admitted faking the stabbing of a police officer. A *Guardian* investigation at the time of the protests has found that certain 'demonstrators' who committed acts of looting and attacks on reporters were in fact provocateurs from European security forces. Not surprisingly, 'few, if any' of these persons were arrested. This was, then, a pre-planned assault by the leaders of Europe on the burgeoning anti-capitalist movement.

After the Repression

While 'robust' repression remained an essential tool of dealing with the new movement, it was not sufficient to stop it. For, contrary to Blair's assertion that 'Those guys don't represent anyone,' it was clear that indeed they represented vast and growing numbers, even within the developed countries themselves where the current politics were affected. Early on, the Canadian Security Intelligence Service warned that 'Seattle and Washington reflect how large the antagonistic audience has become and the lengths to which participants will go in their desire to shut down or impede the spread of globalisation.'[10]

The aggressively pro-'globalisation' *Economist* (23/9/2000) in an editorial titled 'Angry and effective'; lamented that 'The threat of renewed demonstrations against global capitalism hangs over next week's annual meetings of the IMF and World Bank. This new kind of protest is more than a mere nuisance: it is getting its way.' It warned that 'it would be a big mistake to dismiss this global militant tendency as nothing more than a public nuisance, with little potential to change things. It already has changed things,' counting the Multilateral Agreement on Investment as its first victim.

The *Economist* traced the effectiveness of the protests not to the methods employed but to the fact that they 'enjoy the sympathy of many people in the West... Many of the issues they raise reflect popular concern about the hard edges of globalisation—fears, genuine if muddled; about leaving the poor behind, harming the environment, caring about profits more than people, unleashing dubious genetically modified foods, and the rest. The radicals on the streets are voicing an organised and extremist expression of these widely shared anxieties.... The protesters are prevailing over forums, international institutions and governments partly because, for now, they do reflect that broader mood. If their continuing success stimulates rather than satisfies their appetite for power, global economic integration may be at greater risk than many suppose.'

A sophisticated response was required. In Melbourne, at a conference site besieged by demonstrators, World Economic Forum founder Klaus Schwab commented revealingly that 'If I learned one thing from here, I will try in future to install a dialogue corner where some business people here and some people in the street could meet in a safe corner and just exchange ideas.' The *Economist* noted that the Czech president tried unsuccessfully 'to broker a meeting between the protesters [at Prague] and the boss of the World Bank.... Mr.Havel has since managed to set up a forum on September 23rd that will be attended by Bank and Fund officials and by assorted opponents of globalisation.'

Such efforts are not new: The Bank, IMF, the UN, and other such institutions have for some years been sponsoring parallel NGO meets at each major international gathering. Indeed, at Seattle, in December 1999, the WTO itself hosted a parallel social summit the day before the opening of the WTO conference, where the new International Labour Office Director-General Juan Somavia spelled out the programme: 'What we need today is a more fruitful collaboration between the ILO, the WTO, the IMF and the World Bank with the objective of creating a Social Chapter within the incipient structures of world governance... We need to create structures where the fears and anxieties of civil society can be fully aired and addressed."[11]

At the gathering, former WTO Director-General Renatto Ruggiero warned that 'if all actors in today's global economy are not included to address the widening range of public concerns within this global system... they may turn to alternative solutions that could possibly destabilize the entire architecture of the global economy.... Certainly we must continue to advance trade liberation within the multilateral system. But unless we achieve a consensus and cooperation with all the political actors, we cannot build the necessary support for trade liberalization and global economy.'

The efforts of the 1999 Seattle social summit to engage the protesters in consensus-building for trade liberalization were, to put it mildly, unsuccessful. And through all the militant protests that followed, it was clear that those sponsored efforts at consensus-building with the protesters, organised as they were under the auspices of the same international bodies that were the targets of the protests, carried no credibility with the marchers.

The Roots of a New International—The World Social Forum

It was during the following turbulent year, 2000, that the 'alternative' to the Seattle-type confrontations took shape—with remarkable speed, starting within three months of the Seattle events.

According to a member of the International Council of the World Social Forum [WSF], in February 2000, Bernard Cassen, the head of the French NGO ATTAC (French acronym for Association for Taxation of Financial Transactions for the Aid of Citizens), Oden Grajew, head of a Brazilian employers' organisation, and Francisco Whitaker, head of an association of Brazilian NGOs, met to discuss a proposal for a 'world civil society event'; by March 2000, they formally secured the support of the municipal government of Porto Alegre, controlled by the Brazilian Workers' Party [PT]. In June 2000, the proposal for such an event was presented by the vice-governor of the state of Rio Grande do Sul (where the city of Porto Alegre is situated) at an alternative UN meeting in Geneva.[12] The World Bank website dates the WSF to this meeting, referring to it as 'a new organizational perspective launched in June 2000 in Geneva by the major organisations of civil society.'

This political trend, which was already present within the protest movement, stepped up its efforts to influence it. A group of French NGOs, including ATTAC, Friends of *L'Humanite*, and Friends of *Le Monde Diplomatique*, sponsored an Alternative Social Forum in Paris titled 'One Year after Seattle,' in order to prepare an agenda for the protests to be staged at the upcoming European Union summit at Nice. The speakers, called for 'reorienting certain international institutions such as the IMF, World Bank, WTO...so as to create a globalization from below' and 'building an international citizens' movement, not to destroy the IMF but to reorient its missions.' While strongly endorsing the project of the European Union, the organizers called for Social Europe, 'on the basis of a Third Way (i.e. neither capitalism nor socialism), that could implement policies against unemployment, insecurity, and the undermining of workers' rights.'

World Social Forum Charter

The charter of the WSF describes the Forum as 'a permanent process of seeking and building alternatives,' 'an open meeting place for...groups and movements of civil society that are opposed to neoliberalism and to domination of the world by capital and any form of imperialism,' a 'plural, diversified, non-confessional, non-governmental and non-party context,' and so on. The charter bars the WSF from making decisions at its world meetings that are then imposed on the many organisations of civil society that are associated with it. 'The meetings of the WSF do not deliberate on behalf of the WSF as a body.... The participants in the Forum shall not be called on to take decisions as a body, whether by vote or acclamation, on declarations or proposals for action that would commit all, or the majority, of them.... It thus does not constitute a locus of power...' Thus the WSF as such has not taken a position on the U.S. invasion of Iraq, but the various organisations meeting at the social forum have discussed, debated, networked and then embarked on protest action around the world.

The WSF's diversity is very evident, but this is not all inclusive. 'Neither party representations nor military organisations shall participate in the Forum.' Thus organisations that advance or use armed struggle are not welcome. 'Government leaders and members of legislatures who accept the commitments of this Charter may be invited to participate in a personal capacity.'

While barring the participation of armed organisations, the WSF Charter mentions that it will 'increase the capacity for non-violent social resistance to the process of dehumanization the world is undergoing and the violence used by the State.'

WSF 2001, 2002, 2003

The actual gatherings of the World Social Forum in 2001, 2002, and 2003 were marked by a sharp upward growth. Over 5000 registered participants and thousands of other Brazilian participants at the first event; 12,000 official delegates and tens of thousands of other participants at the second; and 20,000 delegates at the third, which had a total attendance of 100,000.

WSF in Mumbai 2004, and After

Held from January 16th until January 21st, attendance was many thousands over 75,000. Cultural diversity was notable. The fifth WSF in 2005 returned to Porto Alegre with 155,000 registered participants. The sixth WSF was held jointly in Caracas, Bamako, and Karachi. The seventh was in Nairobi, with 66,000 registered attendees: 1400 participating organizations from 110 countries.

Community in the Global Picture

Moral choices, solidarity, personal commitment, and community: these were the basic elements that went into the new youth movement of the 1960s and awoke a society in slumber complacency, and in the case of the U.S. of dreams of power. The Port Huron Statement was very much a reflection of the classical tradition of political philosophy, which beginning with Aristotle, had seen politics as a branch of ethics and made the issues of civic virtue and a virtuous citizenry central concerns of political thought and action. Values and an ethical basis to politics is at the heart of participatory democracy.

The politics of participatory democracy is a bold and decisive restatement of the view as formulated by a number of Greek philosophers. Politics, which the Greeks invented, is once again seen as the art of creating the city or the society of proximity, of building community, of a shared social life reflecting the 'necessary, though not sufficient, means of finding meaning in personal life.' This idea 'that politics has the function of bringing people out of isolation and into community' is dramatically modern in its formulation and yet ancient in its inspiration. Here again politics is 'seen positively, as the art of collectively creating an acceptable pattern of social relations.' Gone is liberal cynicism about the political realm, a terrain dominated by politicians and political parties disconnected from a public forum; gone too is Marxist determinism and its focus on stages of development determined by iron laws of history. The 'political' is restored to its central, creative role in the determination of human affairs without, at the same time, overwhelming the 'personal' or making utopians claims that a democratic society will answer all the questions of humanity's search for meaning.

The connection of community and the politics of participatory democracy is evident in an opening section of the Port Huron Statement. From the chapter on "Values":

> As a *social system* we seek the establishment of a democracy of individual participation, governed by two central aims: that the individual share in those social decisions determining the quality and direction of his life; that society be organized to encourage independence in men and provide the media for their common participation.
>
> In a participatory democracy, the political life would be based in several root principles:
>
> - that decision-making of basic social consequence be carried on by public groupings;
> - that politics be seen positively, as the art of collectively creating an acceptable pattern of social relations;
> - that politics has the function of bringing people out of isolation and into community, thus being a necessary, though not sufficient, means of finding meaning in personal life;
> - that the political order should serve to clarify problems in a way instrumental to their solutions; it should provide outlets for the expression of personal grievance and aspiration; opposing views should be organized so as to illuminate choices and facilitate the attainment of goals; channels should be commonly available, to relate men to knowledge and to power so that private problems—from bad recreation facilities to personal alienation—are formulated as general issues.[13]

The Port Huron Statement goes on to extend these values to the economic sphere.

The new global movement of the 21st century, the most massive in the history of humankind, is again fusing ethics and politics, as one.

Notes

1. *Democracy from the Heart* by Gregory Nevala Calvert, page 264-5, Communitas Press, 1991, Eugene.

2. Ibid., p.271.

3. The phrase is that of Harvard professor Samuel Huntington in a speech to the elite Trilateral Commission in 1976 during the bicentennial of the Declaration of Independence. Huntington noted, 'The 1960s witnessed a dramatic upsurge of democratic fervor in America,' a trend he diagnosed as a 'distemper' that threatened both governability and national security. Huntington proposed there be 'limits to the extension of political democracy.' See account in Zinn, *People's History*, Harperperennia, New York, 1989, p.558-60.

4. *The Port Huron Statement—The Vision Call of the 1960s Revolution* by Tom Hayden, Thunder's Mouth Press, 2005, New York, p.35.

5. *Reclaim the State: Experiments in Popular Democracy* by Hilary Wainwright, Verso 2003, London, p.4.

6. Ibid., p.8 and p.206.

7. *Rhetoric*, Book 1, c.11, #7 by Aristotle.

8. *The Struggle for Democracy* by Patrick Watson and Benjamin Barber, Lester & Orpen Dennys, Totornto, 1998, p.21.

9. "FAIR—Fairness & Accuracy in Reporting—'Media Advisory: Media Missing New Evidence about Genoa Violence," January 10, 2003.

10. 'USA: Seattle WTO Protests Mark New Activist Age,' AP, November 25, 2000.

11. "How Not to Fight Globalization," Alan Benjamin, *The Organizer*, www.theorganizer.org /to/to nd-3.htm.

12. Teivo Teivainen, "World Social Forum: What should it be when I grows up?" www.opendemocracy.net.net /debates/article-3-31-1342.jsp.

13. *The Port Huron Statement*, op. cit., p.53–54.

ORIGINS, LEGACY AND CONTINUITY

by Dimitrios Roussopoulos

As the capitalist globalization of the world economy unfolds, it exposes its bankruptcy in every respect—politically, economically, ecologically and ethically. The ethical bankruptcy of this world economy is rooted in the reduction of every aspect of daily life to consumption for the sake of consumption, production for the sake of production, driving us into being spectators of our own demise. Enmeshed in gross materialism and wholesale violence, our will to survive has been weakened. Our every humanity is daily undermined by the most powerful hegemonic reactionary forces.

Nevertheless, a new life cycle has begun—typically in unexpected forms, times and places. Our entire bodies cry out for peace, freedom and for the democratization of democracy. The largest worldwide oppositional movement in human history has burst forth. The odds of reversing the current dominant course are clearly very uneven. For those of us who try to reflect deeply on what has happened and what needs to happen, we must, as always, ask why, what and how. Why are we in this critical situation? What does it really mean? How do we get out of it?

Origins

As a child I was most wounded by Second World War film footage and stories of the wholesale murder of civilian women, children and men and the death of young soldiers. As a young person, the struggle to understand the causes and consequences of war became my singular focus.

At the same time, I was brought up to appreciate, understand and love the beautiful through the arts. I developed a growing desire to preserve and protect the beautiful, which rapidly evolved into a pre-occupation with aesthetics. Early on, I came to believe that all human beings had the potential to appreciate and deeply enjoy the beautiful, and to contribute to its creation whether on a major or minor scale. This democratically shared human potential, in a constant state of gestation and facing the vagaries of circumstance, was the social and political challenge which had to transform into politics.

I wondered about both the obstacles and the conditions conducive to the emergence of a global society living in peace and freedom surrounded by beauty, enjoyed in an egalitarian and democratic environment? Thus began my life-long pursuit of that vision, which I did not consider a static utopia but a requisite to human survival. Such a society would be in flux, constantly developing, and would have to posses sophisticated means of conflict resolution. It would not be a society without contradictions, disagreements, and even a dark side. I entered a period of intense learning, attempting to grasp and grapple with millennia of human history and to explore successive movements of radical ideas.

Out of an ocean bed of material experiences and expectations, I was determined to live and act with a purpose in this very troubled world. At the age of 15, I began a long lonely road of self and social realization. I was absolutely determined to remain unfettered by any institutional constraints. I regarded my personal freedom as a necessity for my radicalism. It allowed me the latitude to devote myself to social revolution. My family education was crucial as it grounded me in the philosophical and cultural heritage of the Greeks. Most of the fundamental philosophical questions, I discovered very early on, had already been asked. I saw it as my task to contribute to creating the contemporary conditions for peace and freedom to emerge and flourish. I sought out a community of like-minded people and found it first in the massive nuclear disarmament movement of the late 1950s in Europe. I had many great teachers and friends who could be grouped into two broad categories: the philosophers, who imparted some meaning to particular cycles and stages of daily life and history, and the critical thinkers whose brilliance and insights would influence my understanding of the today and the tomorrow. My main intellectual mentors—Aristotle, the anarchist philosophers Bakunin and Kropotkin, Marx and the libertarian Marxist tradition up to the Frankfurt School and including Henri Lefebvre, Cornelius Castoriadis, Bertrand Russell, Jane Jacobs and above all the contemporary anarchist theorist Murray Bookchin. I was also nourished by giants in the arts, particularly in music. Most influential for me were and are the pubic intellectuals who actively test theory in practice, return to refine theory, and return again to the field of human experience. Politics thus meant praxis. I felt that to live a meaningful, creative life I needed to refuse all contracted ties to corporate organisations like universities. Turning my energies to help build social movements, I made my contributions and my living by speaking, organising, teaching, writing, editing and publishing.

By the sixties, my anti-militarism found expression in the new left's broader vision of participatory democracy, which represented a renewal of the ideals of the libertarian left. Excited by this renaissance, I collaborated with C.George Benello, a leading anarchist specialist in organizational theory, to publish the first book on participatory democracy in 1969-70. In addition, since my academic background was in political economy, I pursued my inquiry into the nature and evolution of the economy and how the system as a whole has been shaped.

Capital and State

It is my basic case that the separate social movements and campaigns in which we have all been active, and the separate questions with which we have all been concerned, run back, in their essence, to a single political system and its alternatives. The system we now oppose can only survive by the willed separation of these important questions, and the resulting fragmentation of consciousness. Our first position should be that all these questions—gender, ethno-cultural, industrial and political, international and domestic, economic and cultural, humanitarian and radical—are deeply connected; that what we oppose is a political, economic and social system; that what we work for is a different whole society. The problems of whole women and men are now habitually relegated to specialized and disparate fields, where the society offers to manage or adjust them by this or that consideration or technique. Against this, we define socialism again as ecological humanism: recognition of the social reality of people in all our activities in balance with Nature, and of the consequent struggle for the direction of this reality and this for ordinary women and men, young and older.

We live in the face of a new capitalism which brings with it problems of a fundamentally new kind. Both in this country and elsewhere capitalism has to adapt and change, in order to survive. In Canada, the attempt to manage such an adaptation had been the main task of post-war governments—undertaken in a piece-meal manner. Their purpose has been to reshape an economy, structurally imbalanced in relation to the outside world economy, backward in many sectors, paralysed by modest growth, inflation, recession and balance of payments crisis over a number of past decades: and to create in its place a 'new model' capitalism, based on organized, rapid expansion. An essential part of this strategy has been the containment and ultimate incorporation of the trade union movement. An essential pre-requisite is the redefinition of 'progressive reform politics' and social democracy itself, and the internal adaptation of the agencies for change—including the NDP or similar provincial parties—within some broad consensus. The current orientation is, then, a phase in the transition from one stage of capitalism to another on a global level. It is this re-focusing that occurs when a system, already beset by its own contradictions and suffering from entropy, nevertheless seeks to stabilize itself at a 'higher' level.

The new capitalism, though a development from liberal or 'free-market' capitalism, is—in terms of its essential drives and its modes of operation and control—a distinct variant. It is an economic order dominated by private accumulation, where decisive economic power is wielded by a few hundred very large corporations in each economic sector. The scales of operation, the complex organisation, the advanced techniques required to managed and control such units and their pervasive impact upon society at large, are so great that the allocation of resources and the pattern of demand can no longer be left to the play of the 'free-market.' Technological innovation, the need for long-term, self-financed investment and growth, the desire to predict and pre-structure investment and growth, the desire to predict and pre-structure consumer demand—these factors have already substantially modified the mechanism of capitalism in practice. What is needed now, according to the controlling ideology, is a further process of global rationalization into an integrated world economy, such as would enable societies to go over consciously to an administered price system, wage negotiation within the framework of agreed norms, managed demand, and the efficient, effective transmission of orders from the top. This would represent, in effect, a major stabilization of the system. The market, once the central image of capitalism is being by-passed for the sake of greater management and control at an international level, and the rewards are to be economic growth. This shift makes some kind of planning imperative: enter the World Economic Forum in Davos which is followed by a multitude of regional forums feeding networks of commercial relationships throughout the year in various locations, the World Trade Organisation, the World Bank, the G8 and many such organisations.

But planning in this sense does not mean what socialists or anarchists have understood—the subordination of private profit (and the directions which profit-maximization imposes on the whole of society) to social priorities. The fact that the same word is now used to mean different things is important, for it is by

way of this linguistic sleight-of-hand that the social democratic left and its sympathizers mystify and confuse its supporters, taking up the allegiance of the labour
movement to one concept of planning while attaching another meaning, another
kind of content, to the word in practice. Planning economic development mean
planning economic growth which in turn means better forecasting, better coordination of investment and expansion decisions, and a more purposeful control over
demand. This enables the more technologically equipped and organized units in
the private sector to pursue their goals more efficiently, more 'rationally.' It also
means more control over unions and labour's power to bargain freely over wages
and working conditions. This involves another important transition. For in the
course of this rationalization of capitalism, the gap between corporations and the
State has been narrowed. The State makes itself responsible for the overall regional management of an economy by fiscal means. It must tailor the production
of trained labour to the needs of the economic system. In the political field, the
State must hold the ring within which the necessary bargains are struck between
competing interests. It must manipulate the public consensus in favour of these
bargains, and take on the task directly of intervening to whip labour into line. In relation to labour, and the unions, it is the State which draws the unions into the consensus, identifies them with the planning decisions and the setting of standards,
and wins their collusion with the system.

　　Trade unions and their memberships, of course, can only be expected to co-
operate with the system if they regularly gain a share of the goods being produced. The first promise held out is that the State will be in a better position to
manage the inflation-recession cycles which have beset the post-war economy.
The second promise is that a stable system will be more efficient and productive,
and that, so long as it works, labour will win its share in return for cooperation.
When productivity rises, labour is supposed to share in the benefits. On the other
hand, when the economy slows down labour cannot contract our since it has become a party to the bargain. This looks on the surface like a more rational way of
guaranteeing rising standards of living: it is in fact a profound restructuring of the
relationship between labour and capital. We have noted how the word 'planning'
has been maintained, but how its contents have been redefined. The same can be
said of the word 'welfare.' Market capitalism was for a long time the enemy of the
welfare State. The welfare State was introduced as a modification of capitalism.
Like wage increases, it represented a measures of redistribution and egalitarianism, cutting into profits, imposing human needs and social priorities on the sys-

tem. But a welfare State was eventually seen by its enemies as a necessary element of organized capitalism.

There is however one vital difference which has been pioneered by the new capitalism and now forms part of the consensus. Rising prosperity—whether in the form of higher wages, increased welfare or public spending—is not funded out of the redistribution of wealth from the rich to the poor. Redistribution would eat into the necessary mechanisms of private accumulation, internal reinvestment and the high rewards to management on which the whole system rests. Rising prosperity must, therefore, come out of the margin of increased growth and productivity. The existing distribution of wealth and power is taken as given. New wage claims can only be met by negotiation, out of the surplus growth, and controlled by a framework of accepted standards. These standards are not the norms of social justice, human needs or claims to equality: they are arrived at by calculating the percentage rise in productivity over a given period, and by bargaining the 'necessary' return to capital and the share left over goes to wage increases and welfare costs. In effect, within this system of bargaining, wage increases must be tied to productivity agreements (not to the claims of equality), and welfare becomes a supporting structure of modern capitalism rather than a limit on or transmutation of the system). This is one of the crucial markers between the new capitalism and the old. It means that the rising prosperity of the working class is indissolubly linked with the growth and fortunes of corporations, since only by means of the productivity of the economy will there be any wage or welfare surplus at all to bargain for. A successful modern capitalist system is therefore one in which people may enjoy a measure of increased abundance and prosperity provided there is growing productivity: but it is by definition not an egalitarian system in terms of income, wealth, opportunity, authority or power. There may be a leveling of social status; nevertheless, 'open' capitalist societies, where stratification is not always obvious, are very much closed systems of elite power. Capitalism created hostile relations of a class-society: the new capitalism, where successful, seeks to end these conflicts, not by supporting all the human considerations of community and equality, in favour of the planned contentment and containment of organized producers and consumers.

Neo-liberal globalization is all about universalizing this 'successful' new capitalism into every key part of the world. A whole and well thought out economic system is being both exported and imported. It is a package deal that is offered.

This economic system is accompanied by managed 'politics.' The political aim of the new capitalism, and the State which sustains it, should be clearer but it remains murky in many important details. It is to muffle real conflict, to dissolve it into a false political consensus; to build not a genuine community of life and interest but a bogus conviviality between every social group. Consensus politics, integral to the success of the new capitalism, is in its essence manipulative, the politics of political management, and as such deeply undemocratic. Governments are still elected, M.P.'s assert the supremacy of their legislatures. But the real business of government is the management of consensus between the most powerful and organized elites.

In a consensual society, the ruling elites can no longer impose their will by coercion, but neither will they see progress as a people organising themselves for effective participation in power and responsibility. Democracy, indeed, becomes a structure to be negotiated and manoeuvred. The task of the leading politicians is to build around each issue by means of bargain and compromise a coalition of interests, and especially to associate the large units of power with its legislative programme. Consensus politics thus becomes the politics of incremental action: it is not programmed for any large-scale structural change. It is the politics of pragmatism, of the successful manoeuvre within existing limits. Every administrative act is a kind of clever performance, an exercise of political public relations. The particular politicians and party colours hardly matter, since everyone accepts the constraints of the status quo as a framework. The circle of politics has been closed.

Of course, in capitalist society, there have always been separate sources of power, based on property and control, with which governments must negotiate. But the whole essence of the new capitalism is an increasing rationalization and coordination of just this structure and on a global level through determined world bodies. Power centers within States, the high commands in each sector—the banks and insurance corporations, the federation of industrialists, the multi-national major corporations, the trade union federations—are given a new and more formal place in the political structure and this, increasingly, is the actual machinery of decision-making: in their own fields, as always, but now also in a coordinated field. This political structure, is to a decisive extent mirrored in the ownership and control of public communications.

Naturally, within the quarrels of the machine politics and the system, there are always local opportunities for effective action and particular campaigns, and sometimes these arise from the very fact that adjustments are incomplete, so that margins for movement remain. Accordingly, we are witnessing the emergence of a new cycle of mass movement in the face of a disheartening reality. A new left is arising.

Defining The Limits Of A Politics Of The Future

What must be built is a new movement in opposition to a new political system, such that it cannot be defeated by electoral action at national or regional levels, and cannot be defeated at the urban level by electoral action alone. In doing so we stop subordinating every question, every strategy, to electoral calculations and organisations.

Instead we must say:

1. The system cannot solve the major problems of society.

2. The system cannot identify or solve the new problems of society.

3. The system cannot operate with genuinely conflicting political parties and movements, and so it must try to drain these of meaning, which in practice involves disenfranchising many thousands of ordinary people in one way or another.

Sustaining the new world anti-capitalist movement will be difficult because we confront a whole system which is foreclosing upon democracy in all its forms, and which is expropriating people of their political identity as citizens. Without invoking the dangers of a rebirth of fascism, it is sufficient to note that current forms of authoritarianism hide behind the centralization of elite decision-making. It does not come with bare knuckles and revolvers in a society like ours but with political sedatives and processing. It does not segregate dissenters in concentration camps but allows them to segregate themselves in marginal publications and sectarian associations. It does not even require of its supporters that they should march through the streets to show the level of tolerance of liberal democracy, but simply that the people should be entertained as spectators.

Corporate capitalism which is now highly managed, in our own time has repented its youth. The old kind of political conflict introduces uncertainty into planning and continually reactivates centres of resistance to its dispositions. Just as the new capitalism finds it increasingly necessary to forecast and to create demand, so in its political expression it finds it necessary not to adjust but to manufacture what it calls public opinion. And unprecedented means of persuasion lie to hand.

In the struggle for democracy in the nineteenth century, dissenting minorities and the new popular movements had, if not equality, at least some comparative opportunity of access to the places where opinion was formed: the cheap printing-press, the author tours, the soapbox in a public square or street corner, the public hall. Many of these means are of course still open, but now the main channels of persuasion are difficult if not impossible to access—television, the national press, the mass political party. Opposition groups may get an occasional hearing, but on the system's terms. Consider the war in Iraq, for example. The anti-war movement has to buy space in order to communicate a coherent position, otherwise its activities and views are reported as a spectacle. On television, the occasional dissenter will be interviewed, but as part of the passing show. Balance, for example, as a principle of public service broadcasting, is balance between representatives of the parties, or at most sections of the parties. All the widely distributed newspapers are in major capitalist hands, and conduct their own continual campaigns and pressures. To be outside this system, and against its values, may allow, at times, a brief invitation to join it, or to have dissenting views processed by the established commentators. More commonly, it allows what is said to be ignored, with the confidence that the small circulation pamphlet, the serious books, the meeting in a hired hall, will not touch the majority of people. When we go out into the streets, a hundred thousand people, to campaign against war-making, we make news, but we are cast as a group outside the mainstream and therefore eccentric. This is the point, in the mode of opinion-formation under the new capitalism, the system is offered as absolute. Beyond it lies oblivion. There is no alternative. The working partnership of public and private bureaucracy in defence of established political and economic interests has the major communications system safely in its own hands, at a level of organisation and cost which makes any challenge to it appear marginal, even petty.

We are slipping into a new technocratic politics, fitted into the modern world State system. It is a politics which would replace, even at the formal level, all older theories of the sovereignty of the people through their elected representatives. It offers, instead, a congress of representatives of the new capitalist State and its consequent political relations. These will, of course, often quarrel among themselves, and the rest of us may be asked to take sides. But all actual choice will be directed towards the resolution of conflicts within that specific machinery.

The political parties remain, ironically, an element which cannot be finally assimilated; and yet whose imperfect assimilation is necessary—at least in the transitional stage—to legitmize the machine. The parties' real fights, and even their sham fights, can disturb the machine; but on the other hand, without them, it would be apparent to everybody that all the major decisions are taken, not by the people, but by the machine and the system.

The system is so refined, that no left-wing politician can resist the sirens of power, and they inevitably compromise accepting the rules becoming co-opted. Few are those who have such an understanding of the corrupting power of institutional parliamentary politics that they can resist being sucked into a moral vortex.

At this point in my case I go back to the legacy of the sixties. It is, I think, of some significance that the SDS (Students for a Democratic Society) has been re-born in the USA. And it is noteworthy that many of the seasoned veterans of that decade have attended its 2006 conferences. A new edition of The Port Huron Statement of 1962 has been reissued with a thoughtful introduction by Tom Hayden.

When I attended my first World Social Forum [WSF] in Porto Alegre, I was immediately impressed by the scope of its programme. I have attended many international conferences. But this was the first which programmatically blended the local with the regional and international questions. There was a kind of dialectical flow between these dimensions of reality. The Forum was preceded by an international conference of 'local authorities' what we can municipally elected people and activists. Significantly, the new left of the WSF emphasizes issues that echo the new left of the sixties: community, neighbourhood, the city. The world movement held its first large-scale meeting in Porto Alegre, with the organizational and financial support of the city which had itself undertaken the most radical democratization of public life through citizen participation to date. Since then the participatory budget which involves thousands of ordinary people, has not only inspired many more thousands of people elsewhere but it is now being replicated in one form or another in other cities which have formed an international support network.

The new politics is a grounded politics in urban localities as well. The new left always emphasized community organisation of the powerless and the need for citizens to participate in making all the decisions that affect their daily lives. So thirty years later we are at it again, with all that has happened since, laying in a fertile field for the future.

The Fulcrum: Geopolitics of Location and Space

Archimedes (c.287-212 B.C.E) was a pioneer in mechanics. He said "give me a place to stand and I (will) move the earth." He was asked to give an illustration of his contention that a great weight could be moved by a small force. So he found a location on which a lever was placed and got the support to move a much larger object.

We are faced with the same challenge, where can we place ourselves in relationship to the very powerful world organisations that are pressing forward with the globalization of the planet's economy, and the 400-500 major corporations that are party to this drive to create a 'free-market.'

We need not only sail by the seat of our pants. As long as we take all the usual precautions it is possible to pick up on a few broad trends affecting our society that are already setting the stage for our future. Let us consider the following.

The world continues to undergo an urban revolution in parallel with capitalist globalization. A few statistics illustrate the point. In 1800, 2% of people of the world lived in cities, 30% by 1950, over 50% by 2007 and 65% by 2050. The 21st century will be overwhelmingly urban. Every day, the world's population rises by 180,000 people, which means 1.25 million every week. This urban growth is at its strongest in the southern hemisphere: it doubles every 30 years. A billion people live in slums and by 2020 they will be two billion. A billion city dwellers have no access to drinking water and no sanitation. Almost half of the inhabitants of the cities of the South work in the informal sector. An African city dweller consumes 50 litres of water per day, whereas his western counterpart goes through 215 litres. City dwellers in the North throw away up to six times more waste than those in the South. London's ecological footprint covers 120 times its surface area. These statistics and many more highlight the way that economic, social and ecological factors are connected and interdependent but that they also rest geopolitically in concentrated locations.

In the last fifteen years, there have emerged a critical number of metropolises or 'global cities' which increasingly dominate the world economy. Although many of these urban spaces are large, the power of these global cities stems from far more than population. The global cities share a very specific set of characteristics and play crucial geopolitical roles in the globalized economy. One analyst characterizes them as follows: "They regularly host international conferences and provide a base for international institutions. They are serviced by highly sophisticated transportation and transit networks, high-tech communications systems, and major hub airports. Such cities attract head offices, foreign firms, and networks of leading business service providers. They are media centers and cultural destinations, and their academic institutions attract pre-eminent researchers. Most of all, global cities are ethnically diverse and resolutely cosmopolitan in outlook… Forget the G-8. The global city network has become the most powerful of all international clubs" (John Lorinc, The New City: Penguin 2006, pp.191-192).

There is a growing body of literature supporting this view, but much of the Left in Canada and the USA has been slow to recognize it and its implications for radical social and political change. Not so those around the World Social Forum. For them, as for me, this urban location is a possible fulcrum.

The vision of the movement of the sixties encompassed the goal of helping the powerless to organize themselves. The community organizing that took place and which was extended into subsequent decades has taken forms as diverse as housing cooperatives, land trusts, community development corporations, and workplace collectives, among others. All these efforts were attempts to move toward some form of participatory democracy. We know that this idea endured since we are witnessing a large-scale renewal of interest in participatory democracy.

How can we succeed in democratizing democracy? In my view we have to turn out attention to Murray Bookchin's neo-anarchism as an important source for some answers, in addition to a number of other thinkers who are working in a similar direction such as Chaia Heller, Janet Biehl, and Dan Chordokoff.

We know that anarchists oppose the centralization of political and economic power. Therefore they oppose the Nation-State and have sought to find libertarian alternative to this structure. Unlike some anarchists, Bookchin looks to politics as the logical realm for the creation of libertarian alternatives. But for him, politics is not the professional activity of those who hold public office in national or regional capitals. Rather, politics is direct democracy, the popular self-management of the community by free citizens—a politics he calls "the democratic dimension of anarchism." It seeks to create or recreate a vital public sphere based on debate, cooperation and community. Politics in this sense has flourished in earlier historical periods—especially in ancient Greek cities—Athens in particular—the medieval communes, the town meetings of colonial New England, revolutionary Paris in 1892, and later during the Commune, in the creation of the revolutionary soviets, and during the Spanish social revolution of 1936-39. But in more recent times it has been eroded or even crushed by the Nation-State in the service of the ruling elites.

Bookchin names this politics libertarian municipalism. Arguing that the most immediate sphere for community self-management is the urban neighbourhood, he advocates that those who would create new institutions, namely citizen assemblies, should do so in municipalities. To address large-scale problems that affect an entire region, and as an antidote to the problem of local parochialism, the democratized citizen assemblies of neighbouring municipalities would confederate themselves into large networks. Imperfect as the example is, Montreal took a small step in this direction when significant powers were decentralized from the city center to the various borough councils, which not only have decision-making powers but also budgets with which to implement innovative ideas. These borough councils, which cover the whole city, must nevertheless go along with decisions made by Montreal's city council concerning certain public policies and services. The borough councillors also sit on this city council. Bookchin goes beyond these limited measures and calls for the creation of a counterpower.

The need for an emancipatory Left that can combat a globalizing capitalism and looming ecological destruction has become ever more urgent. Libertarian municipalism may well represent the sought-after alternative: a concrete radical path to an ecological,rational society.

As Bookchin argues:

> A new political agenda can be a municipal agenda only if we are to take our commitments to democracy seriously… The living cell that forms the basic unit of political life is the municipality, from which everything—such as citizenship, interdependence, confederation, and freedom—emerges. There is no way to piece together any politics unless we begin with its most elementary forms…It is on this level that they can begin to gain a familiarity with the political process, a process that involves a good deal more than voting and information.

Continuity, the New Left and Politics

Lending weight to Bookchin's conclusions is an essay published by Serge Latouche at the beginning of 2006 in Le Monde Diplomatique which covers a range of proposals for how our species can avoid an ecological and social crisis and prevent our planet from being destroyed by our greed. In it Latouche observes that consumer societies are dependent on growth and the distribution of erstwhile scarce goods to wider swaths of the population. The addiction to growth impedes the ability of democratic societies to take the requisite measures to protect our environment. Latouche endorses a strategy of degrowth economics that balances regulations designed to force change with the ideal of a convivial utopia. He sees the revitalization of the local as paving a smoother and surer road to economic contraction than the problematic notion of a universal democracy.

Democracy can probably only function where the polis is small and firmly anchored to a set of values. For the economist Takis Fotopulos, the aim of universal democracy presupposes a 'confederation of demoi' made up of small, homogenous units of around 30,000 people, a size at which most basic needs could be provided for locally. In Fotopoulos' view, 'Given their huge size, many modern cities would probably have to be divided into a whole set of demoi.'

With our cities and towns restructured around little neighbourhood republics, we could turn our attention to a more thorough reorganization of human land use recommended by the town-planner Albert Magnaghi. He suggests 'a long and complex period [50 to 100 years] of purification. During this period people will no longer be engaged in turning more and more fens and fallow land over to farming, or in pushing transport links through such areas. Instead, we will set about cleaning up and rebuilding the environment and territorial systems that have been destroyed and contaminated by human presence. In so doing, we shall create a new geography.

> The relationships between the politics within the global village could be regulated by a democracy of cultures, in what might be called a pluriuniversal vision. This would not be a world government, but merely an instance of minimal arbitration between sovereign politics with highly divergent systems.... Or again there can be a set of bio-regions consisting of natural regions where live-stock, plants, animals, water and people form a unique and harmonious whole. We need to divorce the myth of the universal republic from the notion of a world government or system of control, or a world police force. The way to do this is by developing a different kind of relationship between bioregions.

Whatever one makes of such visions, one thing is certain, the creation of democratic local initiatives is more realistic than that of a democratic world government. Once we have ruled out the idea of tackling the power of capital head-on, what remains is the possibility of dissidence. This is the strategy of Marcos and the Zapatistas in Mexico. They have reinvented the notion of communal goods and spaces—the commons—and regained real popular control over them. Their autonomous

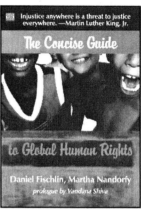